LANGUAGE
BEHAVIOR
AND
PSYCHOPATHOLOGY

HAROLD J. VETTER

Department of Psychology
University of Maryland

RAND McNALLY & COMPANY · *Chicago*

PREFACE

The subject matter of this book falls within those precincts of language behavior where the interests of the psychologist, the psychiatrist, the linguist, and the speech pathologist show tendencies toward convergence. Attention is focused upon aspects of language and paralanguage—variously, and on the whole, indifferently referred to as "deviations," "anomalies," "aberrations," or "disturbances"—which occur with sufficient frequency in relation to certain categories of personality disorder that they have occupied a prominent (and controversial) place in the psychodiagnostic process.

I should like to make it very clear at the outset that the book does not deal with such primary patterns of language disturbance as aphasia and stuttering. This is not to deny the relevance of psychopathological considerations in such disorders. The importance of emotional conflict in the pathogenesis of stuttering is amply documented; and there is abundant clinical evidence that the aphasic patient may react adversely to his lowered or altered capacities in communicating and symbolizing. However, regardless of whatever psychopathological factors may be present in aphasia or stuttering, both are essentially *linguistic* disorders. Their principal symptoms are manifested in vocal speech and their treatment requires some or a great deal of speech therapy and retraining.

On the other hand, the linguistic and paralinguistic phenomena with which the present volume is concerned occur as concomitants to conventional psychiatric syndromes. From this standpoint, such phenomena might be characterized more accurately as language symptoms than as language disturbances. This approach or interpretation also has its drawbacks, one of which is to tie language behavior too closely to a "mental-illness" model in psychopathology at a time when the medical model is under heavy attack from several quarters.

Clinical descriptions of personality disorders are predominantly descriptions of language and paralinguistic behavior. Anyone who questions this statement can satisfy his doubts simply by trying to imagine the difficulties presented by the psychodiagnostic assessment of a patient bereft of speech. Most diagnostic test behavior is language behavior; and among the chief criteria for gauging therapeutic progress is change in verbal behavior. Most therapists assume that improvement in other areas of adjustment will register in the patient's language behavior.

It seems almost superfluous to add that language behavior has an even more crucial function as the medium for therapeutic change. Apart from behavior modification techniques, which are applied directly to the behavior in question, most of the more orthodox or traditional approaches in psychotherapy rely heavily upon some variant or other of the "talking cure." Although substantial quantities of research have been conducted with a view to identifying and examining the relevant variables in therapeutic communication, investigative efforts in the specification and assessment of language behavior in the psychodiagnostic context have been far less extensive, systematic, or satisfactory.

The first stage in most research projects is a review of the literature. It is my opinion that such a review is long overdue in the area of language and psychopathology. Evaluating past research may be less stimulating and interesting than formulating new investigations, but the effort may well prove to be justified if it leads to clarification of some basic trends and issues.

I have organized the material covered by this volume into three sections. The first part (BASIC ISSUES) begins with a brief survey of psychopathological language studies from both systematic and historical vantage points. In the following chapter there is some discussion of the organic/functional distinction as it applies to language disturbances and problems and approaches in the classification of linguistic and paralinguistic phenomena. The third chapter presents a brief review of the salient features of normal language development; and the section concludes with a brief consideration of the adaptative and defensive functions of language.

The second part (LANGUAGE BEHAVIOR IN SPECIFIC SYNDROMES) reviews language behavior in relation to conventional psychopathological categories. The treatment here is selective: Some of the chapters (e.g., "Language Behavior and Verbal Conditioning in the Psychopath") are scarcely more than sketches of some of the problems awaiting investigation. Others (such as "Language Behavior in Mental Retardation") summarize a lengthy series of painstaking descriptive studies. In any event, my purpose was not to blanket the pertinent references, but rather to concentrate on meaningful issues and developments.

The selection of contents for the third section (OTHER TOPICS IN LANGUAGE AND PSYCHOPATHOLOGY) reflects an arbitrary decision on my part as to what is both interesting and significant enough to merit inclusion. Admittedly, the discussion of neologisms is narrowly focused, but I believe that the treatment of new-word coinage in the psychopathological context epitomizes much that stands in need of revision and renovation. Similarly, the special problems posed by the polyglot patient invite attention to a fascinating topic on which, thus far, very little evidence has been gathered. This is in contrast to the professional interest generated by the "double bind" concept and its background in interactional theory. I conclude this volume with a brief sketch of language behavior among the blind. This is an area that has been almost totally ignored by language specialists of all types.

I should like to thank my editor, Charles E. Fitz-Gerald, for his continued support, interest, and encouragement. And I owe a special debt of thanks to Betty Webber for her patience and expertise in preparing this manuscript. Finally, I should like to acknowledge my indebtedness to Larry Gaines, Fred Karls, Michael Leibowitz, Noel MacDonald, and Whiton Paine for their contributions of material and ideas. It has been both a pleasure and a privilege to share with them the evolution of the final manuscript.

Harold J. Vetter
University of Maryland

ACKNOWLEDGMENTS

I wish to express my appreciation to the following publishers for extending me permission to quote from copyrighted material: Appleton-Century-Crofts; Atherton Press; Basic Books; Harcourt, Brace, and World; Holt, Rinehart, and Winston; Houghton Mifflin; MacMillan; McGraw-Hill; C. V. Mosby Company; Pergamon Press; Pitman Medical Publishing Company; Scott Foresman and Company; Charles C Thomas; University of Chicago Press; and Williams and Wilkins Company.

Thanks are also due to the editors and professional organizations named below for granting me the right to reproduce copyrighted material: *A.M.A. Archives of Neurology and Psychiatry; American Journal of Psychiatry;* American Orthopsychiatric Association; American Psychological Association; *Behavioral Science;* The Journal Press; *Journal of Child Pyschology and Psychiatry; Journal of Chronic Disease; Journal of Pediatrics; Language and Speech;* Linguistic Society of America; *Psychiatria et Neurologia* (Basel, Switzerland); *Psychiatric Quarterly;* and *Psychiatry.*

H.J.V.

CONTENTS

PART 1

BASIC
ISSUES

CHAPTER 1

HISTORICAL AND SYSTEMATIC PERSPECTIVES

Prior to 1900 psychologists had taken relatively little direct interest in language phenomena per se. Although they had acknowledged the importance of such phenomena, language was for a long time regarded as a vehicle for the "expression of ideas." One of the forerunners of what we could identify as a modern viewpoint toward language behavior was Southard who suggested, in a pair of interesting papers (1916a, 1916b), that standard grammatical categories might be applied to the description of psychopathological conditions with greater accuracy and reliability than were afforded by conventional psychiatric terminology. Such elements as verb tense and mood, Southard proposed, could be used to depict aspects of the patient's subjective relationship with his environment. Southard confined himself to speculation on these possibilities; he did not attempt to explore his hypotheses with reference to the actual speech of his patients. Nevertheless, his observations on the potential meaningfulness of grammatical categories clearly foreshadows the thesis that the language behavior of an individual reflects his general adjustment.

About a decade later, Busemann (1925) provided the empirical complement to Southard's speculative essays. In what became the first in a series of *psychogrammatical* studies, he presented data which purported to demonstrate a relationship between emotional stability and the relative frequency of verbs and adjectives in carefully gathered samples of speech. Using shorthand transcriptions of narratives related by children of various ages on a variety of subjects, Busemann counted the number of "active" and "qualitative" constructions. The former category contained all verbs except auxiliaries; the latter category included adjectives, adjectival nouns, and all participles used as adjectives. He then divided the number of active constructions by the number of qualitative expressions to obtain an Action Quotient (Aq). The Aq, according to Busemann, showed variation from year to year for a given child. Moreover, he found that a relative increase in the number of verbs paralleled an increase in emotional instability, as rated by teachers. Among the twenty-six children who exhibited changed Aq's, those with a higher quotient received ratings of more unstable, while those with a lower quotient were rated as more stable than at the time of the last test. For the four children whose Aq's showed no change, the ratings by the teachers were also unchanged.

In 1926 William Alanson White published a critical review of language research in schizophrenia which set forth the essential conditions for a program of systematic inquiry into schizophrenic language phenomena. According to White (1926):

> A complete understanding of the language of schizophrenia would imply an understanding of language in general, of which schizophrenic language is only a part. This would further imply an understanding of thought in general, of which language is largely an expression. Because of its extent this program is quite impossible, but certain principles need to be clearly in mind in order to avoid the taking over, in any attempt to understand the language of schizophrenia, of certain misconceptions in both of those territories which are still rife, not having been as yet fully replaced by the newer ways of thinking about the matters involved. (pp. 411–12)

This statement was a remarkably clear and prophetic description of the task awaiting research in the field of language behavior in schizophrenia; and it is not without merit as an assessment of the situation that still confronts us today. And White cannot be fairly accused of undue pessimism in viewing the aims of the program he announced as impossible of attainment. The developments which were to raise linguistics to the status of a rigorous behavioral science still lay ahead in the thirties and forties, and the interests of academic psychologists in fashioning an attack on problems of language and cognition had to be deferred until even later, when American psychology had recovered from its overdose of crudely reductionist behaviorism.

Apart from his insistence on the importance of understanding language itself in the study of schizophrenic speech, White's principal contribution to subsequent research was his interpretation of schizophrenia as a regression psychosis. Drawing mainly upon the contributions of Storch (1923) and Von Domarus (1925), White formulated the concept of genetic levels in the development or evolution of language and thought. According to this "law," thought and language in their development "change from *feeling, concreteness* and *perception* in the direction of *reasoning, differentiation* and *abstraction.*" (p. 339)

If schizophrenia is a regression psychosis, it therefore follows as a consequence of this "law" of development that the language and thought of the schizophrenic are of a lower order of abstraction than the language and thought of a normal adult. As we shall have occasion to observe in a later chapter ("Language Behavior in Schizophrenia"), this formulation generated a good deal of research—and controversy as well. As a matter of fact, the issues raised by this conception of schizophrenia have by no means been resolved, even at this writing.[1]

By 1932 enough observations of the gross characteristics of language behavior in manic-depressive and schizophrenic patients had accumulated to permit Eisenson (1932) to sketch "linguistic profiles" for these syndromes. The manic patient is described by Eisenson as talking rapidly and incessantly. He tends to be telegraphic in his style and the rapidity of his speech frequently produces mispronunciations. He flits from topic to topic, with little concern for his listener; many connective constructions are omitted in his speech. The depressed patient, on the other hand, speaks in a manner consistent with his feelings of dejection and dysphoria. Talk of almost any kind seems as if it were a crushing burden to bear. Where the speech of the manic is variegated and telegraphic, the speech of the depressive is stereotyped and discursive. The patient speaks slowly, with monotony, and exhibits little variety of voice, tempo, or subject matter. The schizophrenic shows contempt for the listener in his frequent use of neologisms, whose meanings are impossible to discern from the context. Speech forms are distorted, content is often purely idiosyncratic, and the overall effect may be one of strangeness verging upon unintelligibility. Despite his frequent use of polysyllabic words and overly pedantic expressions, the schizophrenic's language demonstrates a low order of abstraction. He may exhibit the ultimate in scorn for the listener by choosing to remain mute.

Such descriptions convey the impression that psychotic speech presents a rough analogy with other forms of psychotic behavior. In Eisenson's (1932) terms, "A disorder in the use of speech of any type or degree reveals a disorder in personality." (p. 166) In addition, says Eisenson, "we should realize . . . that any personality change and any appreciable deviation from the norm in the mentality of an individual will be revealed in his speech." (p. 190)

---

[1] As Maher (1966) has noted, the mere demonstration of a resemblance between some feature of schizophrenic behavior and that of child behavior does not bring us appreciably nearer an understanding of the psychotic behavior. Maher concludes that the concept of schizophrenia as a psychosis of regression has not been demonstrated with respect to language, and expresses doubt as to the potential usefulness of such demonstrations in psychopathological investigation.

The manifold inadequacies of such vague and generalized descriptions led Newman and Mather (1938) to attempt a more precise and systematic analysis of psychotic language behavior. In a study which is remarkable for the sophistication of its methods,[2] the speech of a group of patients with affective disorders was recorded phonographically as they read aloud from certain selections and as they spoke spontaneously. These speech samples were then analyzed according to such variables as pitch, emphasis, articulatory movements, pauses, tempo, resonance, etc. Results presented in Table 1 show clear differences among the three syndromes described by the authors as *classical depression, states of dissatisfaction, self-pity and gloom,* and *manic syndromes.*

In their conclusion Newman and Mather state that "except in a purely formal sense, speech is not a self-contained category of behavior. Together with other behavioral forms it provides external symbols of human functioning, and one can therefore expect and find relations between speech and other modes of behavior." (p. 939)

In retrospect, it seems rather unusual that the Newman and Mather study failed to produce a host of emulators. This carefully executed piece of research marked a major advance in conception and methodology over practically all of the studies that preceded it. However, it remained a solitary achievement until nearly two decades later, when technological advances in phonometry and sound spectrography encouraged a renewal of interest in problems of acoustic measurement. In the meantime, further psychogrammatical studies proceeded in several directions (Brengelmann, 1960).

1. *Active/Qualitative Constructions*—In addition to the Busemann (1925, 1926) findings of a positive correlation between high verb index and "emotional instability" in the language of children, the VAQ (Verb/Adjective Quotient) was employed in a number of studies with patient groups: neurotics, including conversion hysterics, obsessive-compulsives, and anxiety states (Balken and Masserman, 1940); "normal" individuals with elevated scores on the Manifest Anxiety Scale (Benton, Hartman, and Sarason, 1955); manic and hysteric patients (Lorenz and Cobb, 1953); schizophrenics (Fairbanks, 1944; Mann, 1944). Research generally supported a relationship between "activity" level, as measured by a high VAQ, and various clinical manifestations of abnormality. These findings are summarized in Table 2.

2. *Pronouns*—Studies of pronoun usage involved both counts of general pronomial usage and the incidence of first person pronouns and self-reference statements. Fairbanks confirmed an hypothesized higher frequency of first person pronouns *(I, me, myself)* and self-referrals in the

---

[2] This study is reported in greater detail in Chapter 9, "Language Behavior in Affective Disorders."

TABLE 1

ANALYSIS OF SPEECH CHARACTERISTICS OF FORTY PATIENTS WITH
AFFECTIVE DISORDERS

(After Newman and Mather, 1938)

	Classical Depressions	States of Dissatisfaction, Self-pity, and Gloom	Manic Syndromes
Articulatory movements	Lax	Fairly crisp	Vigorous
Pitch range	Narrow	Wide	Wide
Pitch changes	Step-wise; infrequent	Gliding; frequent	Gliding; frequent
Emphatic accents	Absent or rare	Infrequent	Frequent
Speech tempo	Slow	Average	. . . .
Pauses	Hesitating; frequent	Frequent	Prosodic; frequent
Resonance	Pharyngeal, nasal	Pharyngeal, nasal	Oral, pharyngeal
Glottal rasping	Present	Present	Absent
Level of style	Colloquial	Colloquial	Elevated
Degree concepts	Neutral; infrequent	Neutral; infrequent	Extreme; frequent
Syntactic elaboration	Meagre	. . . .	Rich
Syntactic techniques	Limited	. . . .	Diversified
Initiation of response	Slow	Quick	Quick
Length of response	Short	Varied in length	Long
Statements in response	Developing single theme	Developing single theme	Passing from one topic to another
Rapport with question	Throughout response	Throughout response	At beginning of response

Reprinted from *American Journal of Psychiatry*, 1938, *94*, 913-42.

speech of schizophrenics. Mann, however, failed to obtain comparable results with written language in a sample group of schizophrenics. It seems premature to conclude whether the inconsistencies that have been reported in research on pronominal usage (Conrad and Conrad, 1956) are due primarily to differences in the types of patients studied or in the mode of response employed in the research, i.e., written or vocal language. In addition, Goldman-Eisler (1954) has cautioned that pronoun scores may vary according to examiner.

3. *Vocabulary Inflexibility*—Johnson (1944) introduced a research technique called the Type/Token Ratio (TTR), the ratio of different words (types) to the total number of words (tokens) in a particular pas-

TABLE 2

"ACTIVE" AND "QUALITATIVE" LANGUAGE CONSTRUCTION IN NORMALS AND ABNORMALS

(After Brengelmann, 1960)

Score	Verb-Adjective Quotient		Adjectives‡	
	High	Low	High	Low
Busemann* (1925) (normals)	unstable	stable	stable	unstable
Balken and Masserman* (1940)	anxiety states (3·11) (medium: obs.-comp. 2·17)	conversion hysterics (1·35)	hysterics (medium: obs.-comp.)	anxiety states
Lorenz and Cobb (1953)	hysterics (1·70) manics (1·68)	normals (1·07)	normals (12·2)	hysterics (10·6) manics (9·6)
Benton, Hartman and Sarason (1955)† (normals)	high anxiety (5·13)	low anxiety (4·97)	low anxiety (3·55)	high anxiety (3·38)
Fairbanks (1944)	schizophrenics (4·90)§	normals (3·43)§	normals (6·69)	schizophrenics (5·37)
Mann† (1944)	schizophrenics (2·38)§	normals (1·98)§	normals (9·45)	schizophrenics (8·33)

*Significance unknown.
†Not significant.
‡V.A.Q. of Fairbanks and Mann computed from mean scores.
§Percentage of total word sample.
Reprinted by permission of Pitman Medical Publishing Company Limited, London and Basic Books, New York.

sage. Fairbanks reported significantly lower TTR's for schizophrenics than for normals in spoken language samples. Similar findings by Mann for written language among schizophrenics are shown in Figure 1.

Fairbanks and Mann considered their results to be independent of intelligence. According to Brengelmann (1960), results of TTR studies have shown rather consistently that vocabulary usage is less flexible in schizophrenics than in normals.

In 1942, Fillmore H. Sanford published an article in *Psychological Bulletin,* entitled "Speech and Personality," which surveyed a wide range

FIGURE 1

CUMULATIVE FREQUENCY CURVES OF T.T.R.S FOR TWENTY-FOUR SCHIZOPHRENICS
AND TWENTY-FOUR NORMALS

(After Mann, 1944)

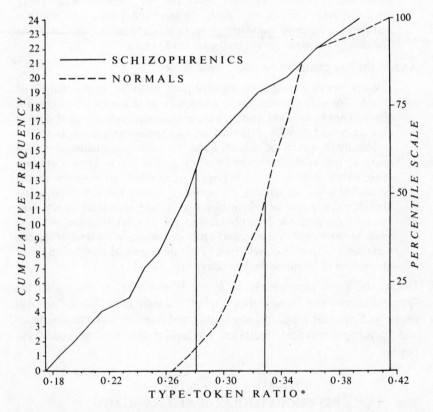

*Means are shown by vertical lines.
High T.T.R. means great "flexibility."

Reprinted with permission, from
Psychological Monographs, 1944, *56*, 41-74.

of problems in research and theory in areas which, today, would be characterized as part of psycholinguistics. Although research in language behavior and psychopathology only formed part of his broader concern with the interrelations of speech and personality, Sanford provided an incisive analysis of the problems awaiting attention:

> If the investigation of the linguistic side of personality is going to amount to a great deal, the problem of choosing and defining significant variables must be met and solved. Grammatical categories are available, but they are not psychologically conceived and may not be of maximal use in the psychological study of language. For one thing, there is great difficulty in fitting everyday speech into grammatical rubrics which were tailored to fit formal prose. For another, the grammatical category, as is possibly the case with adjectives and verbs, may include constructions which, psychologically conceived, are of a different and maybe an incompatible nature. Researchers have shown that the grammatical categories are useful in the study of individuality in speech. But there is no evidence that they are the most useful categories or that a better way of classifying linguistic phenomena cannot be found. (p. 831)

Among the key questions he asked were these:

> What sort of variables can be used most profitably in the analysis of speech? The grammarians give us a multitude of analytical categories, but this may not be much of a gift, for the grammatical rubrics are of untried objectivity and may be of limited psychological significance. Is the individuality of speech too delicate a thing to submit to quantification and analysis? Will statistics blur and obscure personality, or bring it out into the open where we can come to grips with it? What sort of speech should be studied if we are hunting for personality; does the individual reveal himself more in oral or written language? In any sample of speech, how much of the response is attributable to the stimulus situation and how much to "personal" determinants? Must we remain on the level of specific variables and specific correlations, or are there general factors and broad dimensions of linguistic individuality? (pp. 840–41)

During the years immediately following World War II, the search for "general factors and broad dimensions of linguistic individuality" in psychotic and neurotic language was transferred from formal characteristics and "psychogrammatical" factors to contextual and thematic considerations.

THEME AND CONTENT IN PSYCHOPATHOLOGICAL LANGUAGE

To the unskilled observer gross deviations of mental life that betray themselves in unorthodox language are most apt to be identified with unusual or bizarre semantic content. As professional concern with psychopathological language behavior increased in the postwar years, it was inevitable that attention would be directed toward vocabulary and word usage among psychotics and neurotics. It was also inevitable that schizophrenic language behavior would receive the lion's share of this research.

White (1949) conducted one of the earliest thematic investigations of schizophrenic language. Using an experimental procedure that included a 15-item sentence completion test, she obtained results which indicated that schizophrenics tended toward a frequent use of "universal" themes, i.e., those dealing with religion, humanity, science, etc. In contrast, normal control subjects used twice as many "personal" themes.

Arieti's (1955) contention that schizophrenics emphasize words at the expense of their referents stimulated a number of studies on semantic properties of schizophrenic language. Johnson, Weiss, and Zelhart (1964) reported the finding that words are affectively more positive for schizophrenics than for normals. Schizophrenics appear infatuated by the sound of speech rather than by its communicative possibilities. Under the heading "Disturbances in Symbol-Referent Relationships," Richman (1957) commented on the excessive separation of word and referent, implying that speech for the schizophrenic does not serve its normal communicative function.

Several word association studies have been conducted with schizophrenics. Wynne (1964), employing 54 Kent-Rosanoff terms, found that the pattern of popular word association responses is similar for both normals and patients under a variety of instructions. When the results of studies by Downing, Ebert, and Shubrooks (1963), Johnson, Weiss, and Zelhart (1964), Faibish (1961), Chapman (1958), and others are digested, we find that schizophrenics produce fewer associations, more idiosyncratic associations, and are more distracted by associatively linked words.

Word association studies were the source of Laffal's (1963, 1965) method of analysis of contextual associates in free speech. According to Maher (1966), three assumptions derived from the study of word association underlie Laffal's approach:

1. When a particular stimulus word is presented to a subject, there are very high probabilities that some, and not other, words will occur to the subject as associates of the stimulus.
2. In the absence of pathology, unusual motivation, or unusual sets, the response most likely to be produced is the one given by a large random population to the same stimulus word.
3. Where there are unique sets or motivations, an unusual response will occur, the character of this response being determined by the set or motivation. (p. 406)

Spontaneous spoken or written language does not, of course, occur in response to discrete verbal cues such as those presented in a word association task. However, the two situations are not without parallels. Says Laffal (1965):

> Two types of fault in free speech are of special interest in providing illustrations of the application of word-association models to free speech. The first is the facilitation of an unusual response by some immediately precedent response, and the second is the tongue slip. The notable feature of the response in these situations is that, despite an intention generated by the speaker, stimuli irrelevant to that intention influence the response in question. The response then, although appropriate to the generating intention, is also the product of another, incidental stimulus. (p. 79)[3]

As an example, Laffal provides an analysis of the intrusory associational processes which resulted in the inadvertent witticism "he worked in a bakery but quit because he was not rising":

FIGURE 2

SCHEMATIC REPRESENTATION OF THE REMARK,
"HE WORKED IN A BAKERY BUT QUIT BECAUSE HE WAS NOT RISING"
(AFTER LAFFAL, 1965)

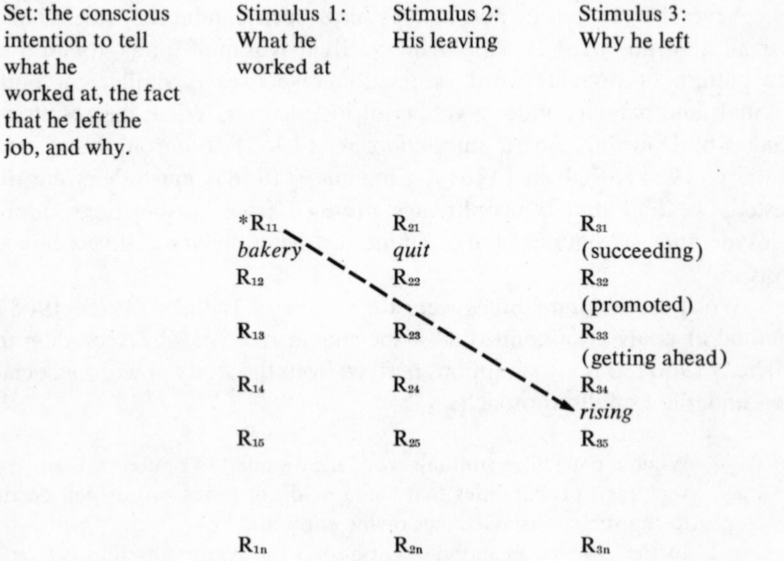

Set: the conscious intention to tell what he worked at, the fact that he left the job, and why.	Stimulus 1: What he worked at	Stimulus 2: His leaving	Stimulus 3: Why he left
	$*R_{11}$ *bakery*	R_{21} *quit*	R_{31} (succeeding)
	R_{12}	R_{22}	R_{32} (promoted)
	R_{13}	R_{23}	R_{33} (getting ahead)
	R_{14}	R_{24}	R_{34} *rising*
	R_{15}	R_{25}	R_{35}
	R_{1n}	R_{2n}	R_{3n}

$*R_a \rightarrow R_b$ indicates that response R_a influences response R_b. Words in parentheses are hypothetical, possible responses. Italicized words are those actually uttered.

The appendix to Laffal's (1965) book on pathological and normal language contains a lexicon of approximately 5,000 words listed under 114 vocabulary entries which permits an analysis of contextual associates in free speech. According to Maher (1966):

> Given this method of categorizing speech, it is possible to select a topic word—such as "female"—and tabulate all other associates that occur in conjunction with it. Laffal has applied this method to the autobiography of Daniel Schreber (Schreber, 1955), using it to identify the contextual significance of certain key concepts in the account (Laffal, 1960, 1965).
>
> So far, this technique has been used to study internal significance of individual speech or writing and has not been applied to the characteristics of schizophrenic language pathology in general. However, the rationale behind it gives promise for application to that problem. (p. 407)

Raven (1958) attempted to develop empirically based categories of "verbal dysfunction" in psychotic patients, based on vocabulary responses to 17 words selected from the Mill Hill Vocabulary Scale. The composition of his patient sample is shown in Table 3.

Although some types of response characterized all of the clinical groups, for the most part the "verbal dysfunctions" tended to be more

TABLE 3

INCIDENCE OF VERBAL DYSFUNCTION IN
DIFFERENT CLINICAL CONDITIONS*

(After Raven, 1958)

Clinical Class	No. of Patients	Mean Score	Incidence of Verbal Dysfunction
Hebephrenic Schizophrenia	12	7.0	.92
Organic Psychoses	10	9.9	.90
Dementia—Senile	15	5.9	.80
Dementia—Arteriosclerotic	12	4.8	.75
Chronic Leucotomized Patients	25	5.0	.72
Manic Depressives	10	8.1	.60
Schizophrenia Simplex	13	10.0	.46
Acute Schizophrenics before Insulin	18	7.4	.44
Paranoid Schizophrenia	11	9.5	.36
Acute Schizophrenics after Insulin	16	9.1	.19

*Analysis of the responses of 126 psychotic patients given the short form of the Mill Hill Vocabulary Scale. The experimental groups studied are arranged in order according to the frequency of verbal dysfunction.

Reprinted by permission of *Language and Speech*, London.

individual and more characteristic of specific patients. Deviant tendencies and the categories of patient in which they occurred are given by Raven as follows:

> *Disordered syntax* occurred most frequently in organic psychosis and senile dementia. For example, a patient suffering from the after-effects of a head injury said the word "View" meant: "What you can see on your own eyes as you look and regard everything you can see in the space of your own eyes."
>
> *Perseveration* occurred most frequently in senile dementia, but it also occurred frequently in hebephrenia, chronic leucotomized schizophrenics, and was found to be common to, but less frequent in, all classes of mental illness. It can in fact occur under any conditions of fatigue or exhaustion. Patients often elaborated some recurrent idea in successive responses. Thus one patient said for:——
>
> > "Cruel"—"To try and believe what you really are. It's cruel sometimes to be kind."
> >
> > "Near"—"To cure kindness you've got to be keen on kindness. Sometimes it's cruel."
> >
> > "Shrivel"—"You shrivel up if you don't believe in what you say."
> >
> > "Chivalry"—"It's sometimes more cruel to act age instead of beauty."
>
> *Bizarre content* was typical of hebephrenia, but occurred in other groups also. A good example of this is a patient who, for the word "Mingle" said: "You could say 'mingle your eyebrows with mine.' "
>
> *Rigidity of expression* was noted if the same construction was used throughout successive responses. It was frequent among manic depressive patients, and occurred in manic as well as depressed phases. To a lesser extent it occurred among chronic leucotomized schizophrenics.
>
> *Poverty of expression,* in which a patient's response amounted to little more than a monosyllable, was found chiefly in depressive psychosis.
>
> *Circumstantial talk* occurred most frequently in seniles, and, to a lesser extent, in arteriosclerotic dementia. These were talkative, superficial, often long, unstructured responses, which never got around to the meaning of the word the patient was asked to explain or use, and sometimes digressed into childhood anecdotes.
>
> *Structurally vague* responses were general to all the clinical classes. They differentiated them from healthy people, but did not differentiate one clinical class from another. These were ambiguous explanations of a word which could not be said to be grammatically incorrect, although they were comprehensible, if at all, only in an attenuated, metaphorical or esoteric sense, as for example when a patient said "Liberty" meant "Having no difficulty about doing a thing. You can do what you like on a thing. Liberty is the thing I find very easy to do. It's very easy to manage."
>
> *Distractions due to intrusions of psychological or geographical origin* were general to all classes of patient. They formed a large and interesting

group of responses in which either the patient's thoughts or his surroundings appeared to *distract* him from giving a satisfactory explanation of a word's meaning, or made it difficult for him to use it as other people do. It was as if excessive introversion or extraversion interfered with a person's normal explanation and use of a word. A woman, for example, said that "Virile" meant: "Manly, a person that's virile can frighten the thoughts, but they can't obey them always." Another patient said that "Perpetrate" meant: "To mess about, to waste. At times everybody perpetrates because their mind is disturbed and they can't concentrate on what they are doing"; also that "Verify" meant: "Thinking of turning round which was in his mind." As an example of an intrusion of geographical origin, one patient said "Mingle" meant: "A thing you could take—that's easy—the thing on the table," and another patient said that "Construe" meant: "You try out holding that form on a sensible rest!"

  Chain Associations, Telescoped Ideas, Nonsense Words, Dissipated and *Echo* responses occurred in several groups, but with low frequency.

  Stylized Language and *Negativistic* responses occurred more than once in some groups. (pp. 223–25)

Gottschalk and his associates (Gottschalk, Gleser, Daniels, and Block, 1958; Gottschalk, Gleser, Magliocco, and D'Zmura, 1961; Gottschalk and Gleser, 1964) have constructed a painstakingly detailed and finely calibrated system for analyzing the content of schizophrenic utterances. Maher (1966) has described their approach:

  Their method involved eliciting five minutes of speech, which was then tape recorded. Each subject was invited to speak on a matter of personal interest to him. Analysis of the recorded sample was made with reference to a number of variables. The majority of these were content categories, and the investigations led to the development of a scoring system for language entries in these categories that distinguished between a variety of psychopathological groups. Two kinds of data were obtained for this purpose: one was the frequency of given content themes for each group, and the other was a derived total score on a schizophrenia scale that was based upon the occurrence of typical schizophrenic themes. (p. 404)

The rating scale used in these studies is given in Table 4. It is worth noting that chronic brain syndrome patients and chronic schizophrenics produced very similar distributions on these weighted items.

NONLEXICAL ASPECTS OF
PSYCHOPATHOLOGICAL LANGUAGE

Human speech consists of two simultaneous sets of cues. The first is the articulated sound patterns which form words, phrases, and sentences. These are characterized as a rapidly changing succession of stimuli present-

TABLE 4

VERBAL ANALYSIS SYSTEM FOR RATING SEVERITY OF SCHIZOPHRENIC
DISORGANIZATION AND SOCIAL ALIENATION
(AFTER GOTTSCHALK, GLESER, ET AL. 1961)

Scores (weights)	Categories and Scoring Symbols
	I. Interpersonal references (including fauna and flora)
	A. To thoughts, feelings or reported actions of avoidance, leaving, deserting, spurning, not understanding of others
0	1. Self avoiding others
+1	2. Others avoiding self
	B. To unfriendly, hostile, destructive thoughts, feelings, or actions
+1	1. Self unfriendly to others
+⅓	2. Others unfriendly to self
	C. To congenial and constructive thoughts, feelings, or actions
−2	1. Others helping, being friendly toward others
−2	2. Self helping, being friendly toward others
−2	3. Others helping, being friendly toward self
	D. To others (including fauna, flora, things, and places)
0	1. Bad, dangerous, low value or worth, strange, ill, malfunctioning
−1	2. Intact, satisfied, healthy, well
	II. Intrapersonal references
	A. To disorientation—orientation, past, present, or future. (Do not include all references to time, place, or person, but only those in which it is reasonably clear the subject is trying to orient himself or is expressing disorientation with respect to these. Also, do not score more than one item per clause under this category.)
+2	1. Indicating disorientation for time, place, person, or other distortion of reality
0	2. Indicating orientation in time, place, person
0	3. Indicating attempts to identify time, place or person without clearly revealing orientation or disorientation
	B. To self
0	1. a. Physical illness, malfunctioning (references to illness or symptoms due primarily to cellular or tissue damage)
+1	b. Psychological malfunctioning (references to illness or symptoms due primarily to emotions or psychological reactions *not secondary* to cellular or tissue damage)
0	c. Malfunctioning of indeterminate origin (references to illness or symptoms not definitely attributable either to emotions or cellular damage)
−2	2. Getting better
−1	3. Intact, satisfied, healthy, well
+½	4. Not being prepared or able to produce, perform, act, not knowing, not sure

TABLE 4—Cont.

Scores (weights)	Categories and Scoring Symbols
+½	5. To being controlled, feeling controlled, wanting control, asking for control or permission, being obliged or having to do, think, or experience something
+3	C. Denial of feelings, attitudes, or mental state of the self
	D. To food
0	1. Bad, dangerous, unpleasant, or otherwise negative; interferences or delays in eating; too much and wish to have less; too little and wish to have more
0	2. Good or neutral
	E. To weather
−1	1. Bad, dangerous, unpleasant, or otherwise negative (not sunny, not clear, uncomfortable, etc.)
−1	2. Good, pleasant, or neutral
	F. To sleep
0	1. Bad, dangerous, unpleasant, or otherwise negative; too much; too little
0	2. Good, pleasant, or neutral
	III. Miscellaneous
	A. Signs of disorganization
+1	1. Remarks or words that are not understandable or audible
0	2. Incomplete sentences, clauses, phrases; blocking
+2	3. Obviously erroneous or fallacious remarks or conclusions; illogical or bizarre statements
	B. Repetition of ideas in sequence
0	1. Words separated only by a word (excluding instances due to grammatical and syntactical convention, where words are repeated, e.g., "as far as," "by and by," and so forth. Also, excluding instances where such words as "I" and "the" are separated by a word)
+1	2. Phrases, clauses (separated only by a phrase or clause)
+1	IV. A. Questions directed to the interviewer
+½	B. Other references to the interviewer
+1	V. Religious and Biblical references

ing semantically meaningful material. The second set of cues includes the discriminable qualitative features of the voice itself. The studies and approaches we have dealt with thus far have been addressed primarily to the first set of cues. We must now discuss some of the developments which have taken place with regard to the analysis and measurement of non-lexical aspects of language.

Soskin and Kaufman (1961) describe the second set of cues mentioned as a *carrier* on which articulated sounds are superimposed. Within this carrier may be the major cues to the individual's emotional predis-

position. Ostwald (1963) gives a graphic illustration of the distinction between carrier and semantic content. A psychiatrist asked a woman patient
undergoing psychotherapy how she felt. With a tremulous voice and an
anguished expression, she replied that she felt fine. There is a glaring
discrepancy here between the denotative meaning of "feeling fine" and the
emotive meaning inferred from the nonverbal acoustic sign (tremulous
voice) or the cues conveyed by the anguished expression. We must assume
that the emotional import of the patient's utterance which is transmitted
nonverbally alters dramatically the meaning of the words themselves.

Terminological and conceptual differences have plagued this particular field of inquiry, and as recently as 1960, Brengelmann complained
that we are still dependent upon descriptive classifications such as those
provided by Newman and Mather (1938), "despite the fact that adequate
equipment for phonometry (Murray and Tiffin, 1933; Zwirner, Maack,
and Bethge, 1955; Grunewald, 1957), and sound spectrography (Potter,
Kopp, and Green, 1947), etc., has been available for a long time."
(p. 66) There is little doubt that, until recently, the thematic content and
formal characteristics of language behavior received a disproportionate
share of professional attention. However, as Mahl (1964) points out, this
emphasis has been reversed in current research. He provides a brief summary of some of the studies which incorporate a New Look in language
behavior analysis:

> Friedhoff *et al.*, Ostwald and Starkweather all demonstrate the poten-
> tial contributions from studies using physical measurements of the fre-
> quency-intensity relations. In addition, they demonstrate the application
> of quite specific tools with which to work: the sound spectrograph, the
> ratio of chord frequency intensity to total band intensity of Friedhoff
> *et al.*, and the "time averaging technique" of Starkweather. The potential
> value of these methods is clearly shown by the demonstrations that the
> spectrographic records and derived data can reflect: (a) clinically per-
> ceptible vocal peculiarities of different individuals (Ostwald), (b) speaker
> identity (Starkweather), (c) clinically perceptible variations in a per-
> son's general voice-impression (Starkweather), (d) daily changes in
> conscious mood as indicated by self-report data (Starkweather), (e) var-
> iations in a pilot's voice over a period of time and a series of events in
> which an eventual crash of a fellow flyer in another plane becomes in-
> creasingly imminent (Starkweather), (f) the effects of "lying" by the
> speaker (Friedhoff, Alpert and Kurtzberg).
>
> Other methodological tools developed by the authors in this series are:
> the utterance duration tabulator (Hargreaves and Starkweather), the
> speech rate meter (Starkweather), the Automatic Vocal Transaction
> Analyzer (AVTA) (Cassotta, Feldstein and Jaffe) and the development
> of computer programs and ancillary procedures for processing and an-
> alyzing formal-stylistic aspects of speech during interviews (Jaffe). Much

of this growth is in the tradition started by Chapple . . . over 20 years ago and since elaborated by himself and various co-workers. These procedures do not deal with a neglected area of phenomena as is true of the acoustic methods, but they do greatly facilitate the quantitative analysis and description of phenomena and relationships which previously had been very laboriously done "by hand." (pp. 468–69)

Ostwald (1963) has reported some success in dealing with nonlexical aspects of schizophrenic speech. Using a combination of acoustic analysis and sound spectrography, he has described the speech of various types of psychotic patients in curves which are functions of sound energy, frequency, and time. He demonstrates that the "flat" voice of the depressed patient, for example, is represented by a curve with an equal distribution of sound energy across the frequencies of the spectrum. When Ostwald's three parameters (sound energy, frequency, and time) for describing depressive speech are compared with the sixteen parameters that Newman and Mather (1938) found necessary for their characterization of depressive speech, we can easily see how much the addition of electronic devices like the sound spectrograph have simplified the descriptive task.

Before concluding this brief review of historical and systematic perspectives in language behavior and psychopathology, we must take note, along with Mahl (1964) that the "relatively recent impact of linguists on psychiatry has emphasized the linguist's method of analyzing voice, which focuses on the ear's discriminatory power and the determination of discrete 'emic' variations in acoustical dimensions, not the continuous, physical measures of laboratory instruments." (p. 468) McQuown (1957), Pittenger and Smith (1957) and Pittenger, Hockett, and Danehy (1960) have already made significant methodological contributions toward the analysis of linguistic and communicative interactions in the interview situation.

SOME CRITICAL OBSERVATIONS

There is much to criticize in the work that has been done thus far on language behavior in psychopathology. Research has been almost exclusively descriptive in nature; and there is very little that qualifies as experimentation. Weak quantitative analyses have often been applied, with questionable justification, to qualitative data that do not readily lend themselves to such analyses. In many of these cases, the analyses have served to obscure rather than clarify the issues presented by the findings.

Entirely too much deductive generalization has been spent on research designs. The typical approach imposes a set of categories arrived at on the basis of a priori considerations upon the samples of language behavior elicited in the study, and one cannot help but be prey to suspicions that some significant material was accordingly pruned off in the process. A more satisfactory empirical approach would seek to derive meaningful analytic categories from within the matrix of observations, but this procedure has rarely been used in most studies.

For entirely too long a period of time, the search for functional units of language behavior in psychopathology neglected the potential contributions of linguistic science—or perhaps it would be more accurate to say that most psychiatrists and psychologists were *unaware* of such potential contributions. As we pointed out at the beginning of this chapter, language was viewed as a vehicle for the expression of ideas in the early part of the century. While such designations proved unable to withstand the vigorous onslaught of behaviorism during the twenties and thirties, it was the nomenclature and not the conception that fell as a casualty. Under the more respectable guise of "verbal behavior," language phenomena were readmitted as suitable objects for psychological research. And the cognitive, affective, and motivational components, having been placed under an interdict on the grounds of "mentalism," reappear as intervening variables or hypothetical constructs. Such an approach is as much an oversimplification of the complexity of language phenomena as the older approach; but at least it has the merit of directing attention toward the vehicle rather than the ideas.

The objectives sought in research on psychotic and neurotic language have been numerous and varied, but most of the studies reported in the literature have reflected a common orientation toward the nature of language behavior in relation to psychopathology. According to this orientation, linguistic phenomena are of concern to the psychopathologist primarily as *symptoms* of an underlying pathological condition. Viewed in this light, language behavior presents a number of undeniably attractive possibilities. Since speech and language behavior are among the more ubiquitous aspects of human functioning, the task of the psychopathologist in gathering appropriate samples of behavior is greatly facilitated in comparison with other types of behavior that are less accessible to observation. Another beckoning prospect is the possibility that a detailed analysis of the formal and contextual properties of language will eventually result in an instrument of diagnostic value for distinguishing the language behavior of patients in various nosological categories. Still further possibilities with regard to prognosis and treatment have not been ignored: it is felt that a closer understanding of language behavior will afford a sound basis for valid and reliable clinical prediction as well as contribute to furthering the aims of psychotherapy by clarifying the communication process which takes place between the patient and therapist. These various objectives have been expressed most succinctly perhaps by Forrest (1965) in regard to schizophrenia:

> Little description is needed with which to recognize the utterances of schizophrenics as such; and were its recognition the only interest in such speech, much of the extensive description that has been attempted would be useless. But psychiatry, having as its concern a system of response whose circuits are beyond tracing and probably beyond chemistry in their ordering, has had little from these circuits by way of data, and is consequently based on the study of communication. If the study of schizophrenic communication is the principal means by which the disease may be understood, its course known, and perhaps also its causes discovered, then precise description of schizophrenic language is valuable. (p. 1)

Clinicians who are in daily contact with patients, and who are obliged to cope with psychotic language behavior as part of their ordinary round of activities, can scarcely be criticized for holding such views. But even by the most pragmatic criteria, the results of forty years of research on psychopathological language—during most of which time investigations were dominated by the symptom-oriented, functional approach to linguistic phenomena—have proven to be quite disappointing. Although we have amassed a wealth of information about some aspects of psychotic and neurotic performance on tasks requiring "verbal responses," and a large body of observations on the gross characteristics of language usage among certain categories of patient, preoccupation with the "semantics of psychopathology" has mainly served to demonstrate the rather obvious fact that neurotic and psychotic patients often differ from normal persons in what they choose to talk about and how they choose to talk about it. Much less obvious, however, is the fact that neither the *what* nor the *how* of psychotic and neurotic language are related in any simple or straightforward manner to the underlying pathology of such conditions.

It is the present writer's conviction that future research in psychopathological language must be increasingly informed of, and responsive to, the revolutionary developments that have taken place within the past decade in linguistics and psycholinguistics with the advent of generative grammar. We shall have more to say about these developments in a later chapter.[4] For the present, however, we may note that relatively few studies of psychopathological language have been undertaken within the framework and perspectives of formal linguistic theory. A fresh appraisal of language and psychopathology might begin with thorough acceptance of the basic complexity of linguistic phenomena; with the premise that lan-

---

[4] See Chapter 3, "The Ontogenesis of Language."

guage behavior can never be narrowly interpreted as either a "symptom" or a "verbal response"; and with the readiness to seek the participatory contributions of specialists in linguistics, psycholinguistics, speech pathology, speech therapy, and other fields of inquiry that bear importantly upon psychopathology.

REFERENCES

Arieti, S. *Interpretation of schizophrenia.* New York: Brunner, 1955.

Benton, A. L., Hartman, C. H., and Sarason, I. G. Some relations between speech behavior and anxiety level. *Journal of Abnormal and Social Psychology,* 1955, *51,* 295–97.

Brengelmann, J. C. Expressive movements and abnormal behavior. In H. J. Eysenck (Ed.), *Handbook of abnormal psychology.* London: Pitman Medical Publishing Company, Limited, 1960; and New York: Basic Books, 1960.

Busemann, A. *Die Sprache der Jugend als Ausdruck der Entwicklungsrhythmik.* Jena: Fisher, 1925.

Busemann, A. Über typische und phasische Unterschiede der kategorialen Sprach form. *Zeitschrift der pädagogischen Psychologie,* 1926, *27,* 415–20.

Chapman, L. J. Intrusion of associative responses into schizophrenic conceptual performance. *Journal of Abnormal and Social Psychology,* 1958, *56,* 373–79.

Chamsky, N. Review of B. F. Skinner, *"Verbal behavior." Language,* 1959, *35,* 26–58.

Conrad, D. C. and Conrad, R. The use of personal pronouns as categories for studying small group interaction. *Journal of Abnormal and Social Psychology,* 1956, *52,* 277–79.

Downing, R. W., Ebert, J. N., and Shubrooks, S. J. Effects of three types of verbal distractors on thinking in acute schizophrenia. *Perceptual and Motor Skills,* 1963, *17,* 881–82.

Eisenson, J. *The psychology of speech.* New York: Crofts, 1932.

Eysenck, H. J. *Dimensions of personality.* London: Routledge and Kegan Paul, 1950.

Faibish, G. M. Schizophrenic response to words of multiple meaning. *Journal of Personality,* 1961, *29,* 414–27.

Fairbanks, H. Studies in language behavior: II. The quantitative differentiation of samples of spoken language. *Psychological Monographs,* 1944, *56,* 41–74.

Forrest, D. V. Poiesis and the language of schizophrenia. *Psychiatry,* 1965, *28,* 1–18.

Franks, C. M. L'echelle de Taylor l'analyse dimensionelle de l'anxieté. *Revue de Psychologie Applique,* 1956, *6,* 35–44.

Goldman-Eisler, F. A study of individual differences and of interaction in the behaviour of some aspects of language in interviews. *Journal of Mental Science,* 1954, *100,* 117–97.

Gottschalk, L. A., and Gleser, G. C. Distinguishing characteristics of the verbal communications of schizophrenic patients. *Disorders of Communication,* 1964, *42,* 400–13.

Gottschalk, L. A., Gleser, G. C., Daniels, R., and Block, J. The speech patterns of schizophrenic patients: A method of assessing relative degree of personal disorganization and social "alienation." *Journal of Nervous and Mental Disease,* 1958, *127,* 152–66.

Gottschalk, L. A., Gleser, G. C., Magliocco, E. B., and D'Zmura, T. L. Further studies on the speech patterns of schizophrenic patients: Measuring inter-individual differences in relative degree of personal disorganization and social alienation. *Journal of Nervous and Mental Disease,* 1961, *132,* 101–13.

Grünewald, G. Zur Schreib- und Sprechmotorik der Konstitutionstypen. *Zeitschrift für Psychotherapie und Medizinische Psychologie,* 1957, *7,* 165–76.

Johnson, R. C., Weiss, R. L., and Zelhart, P. F. Similarities and differences between normal and psychotic subjects in responses to verbal stimuli. *Journal of Abnormal and Social Psychology,* 1964, *68,* 221–26.

Johnson, W. Studies in language behavior: I. A program of research. *Psychological Monographs,* 1944, *56,* 1–15.

Laffal, J. Changes in the language of a schizophrenic patient during psychotherapy. *Journal of Abnormal and Social Psychology,* 1961, *63,* 422–27.

Laffal, J. The use of contextual associates in the analysis of free speech. *Journal of General Psychology,* 1963, *69,* 51–64.

Laffal, J. *Pathological and normal language.* New York: Atherton Press, 1965.

Lorenz, M. and Cobb, S. Language behavior in psychoneurotic patients. *A.M.A. Archives of Neurology and Psychiatry,* 1953, *69,* 684–94.

McQuown, N. A. Linguistic transcription and specification of psychiatric interview materials. *Psychiatry,* 1957, *20,* 79–86.

Maher, B. A. *Principles of psychopathology.* New York: McGraw-Hill, 1966.

Mahl, G. F. Some observations about research on vocal behavior. In D. McK. Rioch and E. A. Weinstein (Eds.), *Disorders of communication.* Baltimore: The Williams and Wilkins Company, 1964.

Mann, M. B. Studies in language behavior: III. The quantitative differentiation of samples of written language. *Psychological Monographs,* 1944, *56,* 41–74.

Miller, G. A. Some preliminaries to psycholinguistics. *American Psychologist,* 1965, *20,* 15–20.

Mittenecker, E. Eine neue quantitative Methode in der Sprachanalyse und ihre Anwendung bie Schizophrenen. *Monatschrift für Psychiatrie,* 1951, *121,* 364–75.

Murray, E. and Tiffin, J. An analysis of some basic aspects of effective speech. *Archives of Speech,* 1933, *1,* 61–83.

Newman, S. and Mather, V. G. Analysis of spoken language of patients with affective disorders. *American Journal of Psychiatry*, 1938, *94*, 913–42.

Ostwald, P. F. *Soundmaking*. Springfield, Ill.: Charles C Thomas, 1963.

Pittenger, R. E., Hockett, C. F., and Danehy, J. J. *The first five minutes: A sample of microscopic interview analysis*. Ithaca, N. Y.: Cornell University Press, 1960.

Pittenger, R. E. and Smith, H. L. A basis for some contributions of linguistics to psychiatry. *Psychiatry*, 1957, *20*, 61–78.

Potter, R. K., Kopp, G. A., and Green, H. C. *Visible speech*. New York: Van Nostrand, 1947.

Raven, C. J. Verbal dysfunctions in mental illness. *Language and Speech*, 1958, *1*, 218–25.

Richman, J. The effect of the emotional tone of words upon the vocabulary responses of schizophrenics. *Journal of General Psychology*, 1957, *56*, 95–119.

Richman, J. Symbolic distortion in the vocabulary definitions of schizophrenics. *Journal of General Psychology*, 1964, *71*, 1–8.

Sanford, F. H. Speech and personality. *Psychological Bulletin*, 1942, *39*, 811–45.

Soskin, W. F. and Kauffman, P. E. Judgment of emotion in word-free voice samples. *Journal of Communication*, 1961, *11*, 73–81.

Southard, E. On the application of grammatical categories to the analysis of delusions. *Philosophical Review*, 1916, *25*, 424–55. (b)

Southard, E. On descriptive analysis of manifest delusions from the subject's point of view. *Journal of Abnormal Psychology*, 1916, *2*, 189–202. (a)

Storch, A. *Das Archaisch-Primitive Erleben und Denken der Schizophrenen*. Berlin: Springer, 1923.

Von Domarus, E. Ueber die Beziehung des normalen und schizophrenen Denken. *Archiv für Psychiatrie*, 1925, *74*, 641.

Von Domarus, E. The specific laws of logic in schizophrenia. In J. Kasanin (Ed.), *Language and thought in schizophrenia*. Berkeley: University of California Press, 1944.

White, M. A. A study of schizophrenic language. *Journal of Abnormal and Social Psychology*, 1949, *44*, 61–74.

White, W. A. The language of schizophrenia. *Archives of Neurology and Psychiatry*, 1926, *16*, 395–413.

Wynne, R. D. The influence of hospitalization on the verbal behaviour of chronic schizophrenics. *British Journal of Psychiatry*, 1963, *109*, 380–89.

Wynne, R. D. Are normal word association norms suitable for schizophrenics? *Psychological Reports*, 1964, *61*, 121–22.

Zwirner, E., Maack, A., and Bethge, W. Vergleichende Untersuchungen über konstitutive Faktoren deutscher Mundarten. *Zeitschrift für Phonetik*, 1955, *9*, 14–30.

CHAPTER 2

LANGUAGE, SPEECH,
AND PARALANGUAGE

In their article in the *Annual Review of Psychology* for 1960, Rubenstein and Aborn state that "research in the area of language disturbances has been quite unsatisfying from a psycholinguistic point of view. . . . The fact remains that we have little by way of systematic knowledge of disturbed language and that very little more has accrued during the past five years." (p. 308) Diebold (1965) has questioned the validity of this assertion. He takes exception to the catholicity of the reviewers' criteria, "treating within this one category those aspects of stylistic variation which have been discussed elsewhere as 'paralanguage' as well as physiologically-based disorders such as aphasia." (p. 255)

Regarding the "catholic criteria" of Rubenstein and Aborn, Diebold indicates that one of the difficulties involved in dealing with the topic of language disturbance is its lack of specific demarcation. In the Rubenstein and Aborn review, for example, a well-known organically oriented study by Luria (1958), which was concerned with the correlations between various types of aphasic disorders and the site of lesions in the cortex, is discussed within the same frame of reference as a functionally oriented study by Lorenz and Cobb (1954) which sought to describe "linguistic profiles" for several categories of neurotic patient on the basis of gross characteristics of language content.

According to current terminological and classificatory practices in either psychiatry or speech pathology, there are no reliable and valid bases for distinguishing effectively between language disturbances and disturbed language—meaning by the latter those aspects of language behavior that have interested the psychopathologist. A glance at the following list of what the speech pathologist (Robbins, 1963) has classified as "language disturbances" reveals a substantial number of symptoms of what the psychopathologist would wish to designate "disturbed language."

VII. DYSPHEMIA
DISORDERS OF ARTICULATION MANIFEST IN NEUROSES AND PSYCHONEUROSES

A. Aphemia—Hysterical mutism
B. Atelophemia—Undeveloped speech
C. Idiophemia—Invented language
D. Leipophemia—Ekision
E. Paraphemia—Substitution of plosives for fricatives and sibilants
F. Pedophemia—Infantile speech
G. Polyphemia—Speech pressure
H. Spasmophemia—Stammering, stuttering
I. Stereophemia—Compulsive ideas
J. Tachyphemia—Nervous, rapid speech

VIII. DYSPHRASIA
DISORDERS IN THE EXPRESSION OF IDEAS DUE TO PSYCHOSES

A. Acataphasia—Jargon, word-salad speech
B. Aphrasia—Refusal to speak or to utter any kind of sound
C. Apatelophrasia—Delusional speech of paranoia
D. Dramatophrasia—Dramatic, grandiose speech
E. Embolophrasia—Interpolative speech, as in:
    1. Cataphrasia—Verbigeration
    2. Echophrasia—Echo speech
F. Hypophrasia—Taciturnity
G. Paraphrasia—Confusion in words
H. Planophrasia—Flight of Ideas
I. Polyphrasia—Loquacity
J. Schizophrasia—Fantastic, incoherent, disconnected speech of dementia praecox   (p. 9)

It seems just a bit unfair, therefore, to take Rubenstein and Aborn to task for failing to accomplish in their review article what the authorities in speech pathology and psychiatry have thus far failed to accomplish in their systems of classification.

THE ORGANIC/FUNCTIONAL DISTINCTION

Among the professional specialties which deal with language disturbances, the habitual dichotomizing of disturbances under the mutually exclusive headings of "organic" and "functional" has led to confounding and unreliable theories of causal phenomena, and as a result, much of the specificity required for accurate diagnosis and successful treatment has been lost. Academicians and clinicians continually complain that this dichotomy is inadequate, unreliable, and that fundamental concepts become lost in the oversimplification forced upon them by the dichotomy. Yet the classification of language disturbances as either organic or functional persists despite the most vigorous criticism.

Murphy (1964a & b) characterizes the dichotomy of organic and functional in the traditional manner, describing as organic language disturbances any voice disorder in which a structural alteration appears to be an important contributory cause, and describing as functional language disturbances those disorders in which no structural anomalies are present. He acknowledges the problems imposed by a two-valued system and admits that such a dichotomy is inadequate for describing any but the most primitive of human behaviors. He further maintains that the causal factors involved in vocal disturbances are distributed along a continuum. An essential defect of the organic/functional dichotomy lies in the fact that, like most typologies, it overgeneralizes with respect to a single property, attribute, or variable. In point of fact, the causes of language disturbance are both numerous and complex.

Even when it is clear to the diagnostician that a disturbance is due to a structural impairment, as in the case of a child with a cleft palate, the original language impairment may become more severe or take different courses as the individual reacts to the "organic" disturbance. Thus, an originally organic vocal disorder may later be diagnosed as a functional impairment.

The preceding example is only one point at which reliability can be lost in the organic/functional classification of language disturbances. It is also possible for the faulty use of a healthy organ to lead to language disturbance. This would be considered an instance of "functional" pathology. The point to be made here is that merely labeling a disturbance does not aid in identifying the original source of the problem, with regard to psychogenic or somatogenic factors. To the contrary, such labeling may impede the search for causal factors.

Murphy states that clinicians adhere to the organic/functional dichotomy for the sake of convenience and ignore the problems created by the imprecision that accompanies its usage. He emphasizes that neither condition can be viewed a priori as dominating or determining the other. At every moment the behavior of the entire organism, not merely the separate systems of mind and vocal apparatus, is essential to the study and treatment of language disturbances.

Johnson, Darley, and Spriestersbach (1963) also stress the undesirable consequences of two-valued systems. When language disturbances are dichotomized, clinician subjectivity enters into diagnosis to a greater extent; as observations are extended, it becomes obvious that language behavior can practically never be satisfactorily locked into categories. With the increasing need for accurate empirical data, precision is lost when clinicians attempt to identify all disturbances in terms of mutually exclusive organic or functional categories. To oversimplify, as Johnson, Darley, and Spriestersbach observe, is to lose something that is vital and necessary. They issue the following warning to students of language disturbances:

> In diagnostic work, beware of falling into certain careless practices. It is easy to group certain disorders under the general heading "organic" and . . . "functional." You will do well to remind yourself periodically that although this dichotomy has a certain usefulness, there is a no-man's land . . . a range rather than a line . . . between the two. Of course you will encounter certain speech problems that stem primarily from anatomical or physiological conditions, and other speech problems which clearly result mainly from faulty learning, perseveration of infantile habits, or possibly lack of adequate stimulation or motivation. But you will also find essentially normal speech where substantial organic deviations would seem to militate against it. Occasionally you may see a person who has learned to talk without a tongue, or an individual with an open cleft of the palate speaking with a high degree of intelligibility. You will see speakers with significant anatomical and physiological deviations who compensate for them and produce good speech, whereas others with similar or lesser deviations are apparently unable to compensate for them and as a result produce faulty speech. You will find cerebral palsied children with involvement of certain speech muscles displaying speech errors unrelated to their neuromuscural involvement, and you will see aphasic patients with demonstrated neurological deficits varying in the adequacy of their performance as different kinds of motivating instructions are given to them—undeniable evidence of functional components in clearly organic disorders.
>
> In short, a so-called functional problem may have a heretofore unrecognized organic component whereas an allegedly organic disorder may have a large functional component. The fact that we can use the words "organic" and "functional" separately does not mean that the processes of speech production and the various speech disorders can be effectively fragmented and classified in terms of these two words. Structure and function interact—so far, that is, as we can determine which is which. (p. 16)

Luchsinger and Arnold (1965) feel that difficulties in classification arise from the divergence in dynamic functional orientation toward pathology among voice and speech therapists and the anatomical orientation toward pathological classification of those medical specialists. The two orientations come into opposition within the clinical context when such disorders as aphasia, for example, are under consideration. They note that anatomically oriented localization theories have tended, within recent years, to give way to conceptualizations that are more receptive to psychological, linguistic, and psycholinguistic considerations.

Bay (1964) describes recent concepts of aphasia as emerging from the errors of the elaborate classification scheme of one hundred years ago, including: (1) the implication that different aphasias corresponded to respective partial functions of language, and (2) that fact that in aphasia, other factors independent of language are not involved. Performance depends upon many different factors and a disturbance of speech may actually be due to any of these factors. Furthermore, for a correct interpretation of disordered speech, nonverbal disturbances must be considered as well. These include impairment of primary articulatory muscles, changes in articulatory qualities of rhythm, pitch, lack of ideas present in aphasic speech, and repetition.

Bay takes the position that aphasia encompasses a single dimension of language deficit in contrast to possibly coordinated motor or perceptual deficits. The claim is made that there is only one kind of aphasia, amnestic aphasia, in which symptomatology and degree of deterioration of the language process vary with the individual case. Amnestic aphasia is characterized by disability in "word-finding," disorder of linguistic management of concepts, impairment of actualization, inferior quality of concepts.

LANGUAGE, SPEECH, AND COMMUNICATION

Van Riper (1963) classifies speech disorders in terms of speech behavior itself. Four major categories of speech behavior are considered to include all disorders: articulation, time (rhythm), voice, and symbolization (language) disorders. Van Riper specifies that this fourfold classification refers to the outstanding features of the behavior shown. It is also apparent that some individuals having speech disorders may demonstrate speech behavior in all four categories of disturbance.

Under disorders of articulation are included all those disorders characterized by the substitution, omission, addition, and distortion of the speech sounds, such as lalling, lisping, baby talk, delayed speech, and "oral inaccuracy," a wastebasket term for any articulatory defect. These terms are not mutually exclusive, for all could be considered examples of oral inaccuracy and may exist in any combination with one another.

Disorders of timing or rhythm involve timing of sounds and syllables which make speech conspicuous, unpleasant, or unintelligible. In stuttering, for example, the usual flow of communication is interrupted, characterized by conspicuous oscillations, fixations, repetitions, and prolongation of sounds and syllables. Stuttering also has a distinctly emotional component and often varies with the listener as a function of the amount of stress in a situation. Van Riper distinguishes between primary and secondary stuttering; the former characterized by excessive repetition, prolongation, and unawareness of difficulty; the latter stage by extreme reaction to the initial speech problem, characterized by self-perpetuating stuttering, intense fear, and possible extreme facial contortions. Cluttering is also a disorder of time and occurs in speech that is excessively rapid and disorganized. The speaker is usually unaware of the inconvenience to the listener.

Voice disorders are characterized by abnormalities of any of the sub-dimensions of voice—loudness, pitch, and quality. Examples of disorders of voice are aphonia, falsetto, and harshness.

Disorders of symbolization involve a break in the normal symbolic formulation and expressive mechanism. Aphasic disorders account for the majority of symbolization disorders.

Newman (1962) has written on the necessity for distinguishing speech disorders from language disorders and communication disorders, indicating that users of such terms are obligated to recognize speech, language, and communication as separate entities, however abstract they may be. Says Newman:

> Clarification is overdue in the differentiation of speech disorders from language disorders and communicative disorders. Language and communicative disorders presently seem to be distinguished primarily on the basis of aberration in the formulation and use of symbols. Reference to these faculties does not seem to be requisite, however, in the identification and analysis of disorders of speech. It would follow from this fact that the formulation and use of symbols are not involved in speech disorders. Certainly such a conception should not be allowed to persist: for were this the case, the correction of speech disorders would be limited strictly to drills designed for the improvement of articulatory errors, and the theory of speech pathology would comprise little more than articulatory phonetics. (p. 287)

If the term speech were restricted to "the noises we make with our faces," as Newman puts it, the task of the speech therapist would be an essentially mechanical one, i.e., restricted to soundmaking activities of the articulatory apparatus. Numerous cases are encountered, however, in which the disorder is manifested in the semantic dimension of the patient's speech. Thus, a separate designation as a language disturbance or a communicative disturbance is required.

Newman refers to the writings of De Saussure (1959) for a systematization of the relationships among speech, language, and communication:

> His identification of *le language, la langue,* and *la parole* is roughly equivalent to communication, language, and speech, respectively. Ac-

cording to the Saussurian schema, *le language,* like any social process, is subject to perpetual change. It may, therefore, be analyzed at any one time into an inherited or institutional element, or *la langue* (language), and an individual or innovational element, or *la parole* (speech). (p. 288)

Newman favors Cherry's (1957) conception of communication as "essentially the relationship set up by the transmission of stimuli and the evocation of responses." According to Newman:

> Thus, communication is a social manifestation which includes the entire complex of phenomena and activities associated wth the overall process of interaction. Though it subsumes language and speech in their entirety, communication is a much broader concept than the sum of the two, for it includes every sort of interactive phenomenon and activity, whether linguistic or nonlinguistic. (p. 288)

It also includes those aspects of the speech process which are not directly involved in the mediation of semantic content, but which play a definite communicative role to the extent they help convey other types of meaning to the listener.

PARALANGUAGE

Trager (1965) identifies the acoustic phenomena which accompany speech by the term *paralanguage.* Paralanguage is divided into *voice set* as background for, and *voice qualities* and *vocalizations* as accompaniments of, language proper.

Voice set involves the physiological and physical peculiarities that result in the patterned identification of individuals as members of a societal group, persons of a certain age, sex, state of health, body build, etc.

Voice qualities are speech events such as pitch range, vocal lip control, glottis control, pitch control, articulation control, rhythm control, resonance, and tempo.

In contrast with voice set and voice qualities, which are overall or background characteristics of the voice, the vocalizations are actual specifically identifiable sounds or aspects of sounds. Trager divided vocalizations into three types: *vocal characteristics, vocal qualifiers,* and *vocal segregates.*

Vocal characteristics include such items as laughing, crying, yelling, whispering, moaning, groaning, etc. Vocal qualifiers are divided into three kinds: those of *intensity, pitch height,* and *extent.* Each of these displays a continuum based on gradations of intensity.

Vocal segregates are those sounds that do not seem to fit into ordinary phonological frames in a language. They appear to be identical with the actual linguistic sounds in the language being studied, but do not appear in the kinds of sequences that can be called words. These include such items as the "uh-uh" for negation (in English), "uh-huh" for affirmation, and "u-uh" of hesitation.

Another investigator (Ostwald, 1963) distinguishes between *qualitative attributes, visualization of sound,* and *acoustic measurement.*

Qualitative attributes may be defined with respect to a system of complex interactions between the auditor and the sound inputs, i.e., they represent a combination of sensory and interpretative reactions on the part of the listener toward the particular sound in question. Qualitative attributes are subdivided into seven categories, each of which constitutes a gradient. The categories are: *rhythmicity, intensity, pitch, tone, speed, shape,* and *orderliness.*

Rhythmicity designates properties of sound that are defined in terms of the continuum: rhythmic _____ irregular. This is one of the most fundamental characteristics of the sounds produced by living creatures. An example would be the human heartbeat.

Intensity designates properties of sound that are identified with reference to the continuum: loud _____ soft. The upper extreme of this continuum (circa 120 decibels) is marked by the appearance of pain as an accompaniment to auditory sensation. The lower end of the continuum (approaching 0 decibels) marks the physiological threshold of hearing.

Pitch identifies the characteristics of sound defined along the gradient: high-pitched _____ low-pitched. Pitch is basically a function of the frequency of sound vibrations that reach the ear. However, it is rather difficult to specify the extremities of the pitch continuum, for judgments of pitch are influenced by the operation of other aspects of the acoustic stimulus. For purposes of general discussion, we may consider the audible frequency range as lying between 20 cycles per second (for the low end) and 20,000 cycles per second (for the high end). It should be noted that age is a significant variable; the hearing range is greater in children than in adults.

Tone is defined with respect to the continuum: tonal _____ noisy. Tonal sounds are composed of single vibratory frequencies or contain a number of vibratory frequencies which are multiples of one another. At the opposite end of the continuum is noise, which is composed of many vibratory frequencies that overlap and mingle with one another, producing extremely complex wave-forms (Beranek, 1954).

Speed is defined along the continuum: fast _____ slow. As in the case of pitch, intensity, and tone, physiological limitations of the hearing apparatus determine the capability to perceive the speed of an acoustic stimulus. At the slow end of the continuum, attention lapses after approximately .8 second. Consequently, when the impulse rate drops below one sound per second, the attention of the auditor must be sustained by additional cues. At the fast end of the spectrum, there is a merging of successive impulses to produce the impression of a steady sound.

Shape refers to the attributes of sound as defined with respect to the continuum: impulsive _____ reverberant. Shape is a property that is related to the onset, growth, steady-state, duration, decay, and termination of an individual sound. A pistol shot, for example, has a sudden beginning, rapid rise to peak intensity, and quick decay to silence. The subjective experience is that of an abrupt, crashing sound. At the reverberant end of the spectrum, there is a gradual beginning of the sound, a slow growth into a steady pattern, the maintenance of a semitonal quality (depending on the characteristics of the noisemaker and its environment), and a slow decay to silence.

Orderliness is defined along the gradient: compact _____ expanded. A sound is said to be compact when its single constituents form a recognizable and orderly configuration. At the expanded end of the continuum, sounds are lacking in tone, organized intensity, and rhythm; they are experienced as monotonous and dissonant. Unlike rhythmicity, an auditory experience that seems to be biologically determined, orderliness varies as a function of individual differences in learning. For instance, a foreign language sounds unintelligible and chaotic before one has learned to recognize its intrinsic patterns or order.

Visualization, as represented by a system such as the International Phonetic Alphabet, represents another way of dealing with sound. The phonetic alphabet consists of a series of diagrammatic sketches, as it were, of individual speech sounds. It does a more accurate job of depicting speech sounds than does our conventional alphabet, but it is much less precise than acoustic measurement.

Acoustic measurement, as Ostwald (1963) points out, is one of the most scientific methods available for dealing with sounds. Through the use of acoustic filters, analogous in their function to chemical filters, it is possible to separate sounds into their frequency components. Filters of varying fineness permit the study of different-sized spectrum bands in terms of their energy levels (Scott, 1957). Band-pass filters are of two kinds—fixed and adjustable. Fixed band-pass filters divide the sound spectrum into equal-sized bands (e.g., octaves, half-octaves) from 20 cycles per second to 20,000 cycles per second. Adjustable band-pass filters permit the measurement of sound energy levels at points anywhere across the frequency spectrum. The amount of energy passed by each filter can be measured by a meter or depicted visually by means of the sound spectrograph.

The value of acoustic measurement for psychopathology is readily apparent. It is perfectly clear from this discussion that many of the speech disorders traditionally listed under the heading of *dysphonia* (functional defects of voice quality) involve features we have identified as part of paralanguage, as this series of categories in speech pathology (Robbins, 1963) demonstrates:

XI. DYSPHONIA
FUNCTIONAL DEFECTS OF VOICE QUALITY

A. Aphonia—Voicelessness
B. Gutturophonia—Guttural voice
C. Hypophonia—Whispered voice
D. Hyporhinophonia—Denasalization
E. Idiophonia—Individual characteristics of voice
F. Megaphonia—Abnormally loud voice
G. Microphonia—Weak voice
H. Oxyphonia—Shrill voice
I. Paraphonia—Alterations in voice
J. Pneumaphonia—Breathy voice
K. Rhinophonia—Nasal voice
L. Trachyphonia—Hoarseness
M. Tromophonia—Tremulous voice   (p. 10)

Paralinguistic elements are also involved in *dysrhythmia* (functional defects of rhythm).

CONCLUDING OBSERVATIONS

Kenneth Burke, the literary critic, once remarked that a way of seeing was always, at the same time, a way of *not* seeing. Classifications, too, can be ways of not seeing, to the extent they exclude everything which does not make a perfect fit. It seems clear to the student of language disturbances that the diagnosis of language disorder implies a multitude of causal patterns, symptoms, and dynamics. Therefore, it is a gross oversimplification to place all types of language disturbance under the convenient but unreliable headings of *organic* and *functional* and then attempt to deal with them as one or the other. The accurate diagnosis and successful treatment ultimately rest upon the accuracy of the clinician's analysis, not upon the inclusiveness of his nomenclature. Some combination of behavioral description of symptoms, holistic terminology, and phonemic transcription and examination of speech would appear to offer the best possibilities for the future.

As we have already seen, attempts to carve up language disturbances and disturbed language (i.e., the linguistic and paralinguistic phenomena observed in specific psychopathological syndromes) according to the organic/functional dichotomy are essentially fruitless and tend to perpetuate a distinction which many specialists in language have criticized bitterly and would prefer to see discarded altogether. One wonders what real value would be served at the present stage of our ignorance about language behavior in psychopathology if it were possible to construct a classification schema according to which the various phenomena of language disturbance and disturbed language could be neatly and precisely ordered. It is difficult to visualize the kind of classificatory system that would accommodate, for example, the case of a schizophrenic with a cleft palate, or an aphasic with manic-depressive symptoms. As we try to advance our study of psychopathological language behavior, the uncertain bounds of the term "language disturbance" may turn out to be more an advantage than a detriment if it manages to increase productive contact between the language specialist and the psychopathologist.

REFERENCES

Bay, E. Present concepts of aphasia. *Geriatrics,* 1964, *19,* 319–31.

Bekesy, G. Von. *Experiments in hearing.* New York: McGraw-Hill, 1960.

Beranek, L. *Acoustics.* New York: McGraw-Hill, 1954.

Cherry, C. *On human communication.* Cambridge, Mass.: The M.I.T. Press, 1957.

De Saussure, F. *Course in general linguistics.* W. Baskin (Trans.). New York: Philosophical Library, 1959.

Diebold, A. R. *A survey of psycholinguistic research, 1954–1964.* Bloomington: Indiana University Press, 1965.

Eisenson, J., Auer, J. J., and Irwin, J. V. *The psychology of communication.* New York: Appleton-Century-Crofts, 1963.

Johnson, W., Darley, F., and Spriestersbach, D. C. *Diagnostic methods in speech pathology.* New York: Harper and Row, 1963.

Licklider, J. C. R. Basic correlates of the auditory stimulus. In S. S. Stevens (Ed.), *Handbook of experimental psychology.* New York: Wiley, 1951.

Lorenz, M. and Cobb, S. Language patterns in psychotic and psychoneurotic subjects. *A.M.A. Archives of Neurology and Psychiatry,* 1954, *72,* 665–73.

Luchsinger, R. and Arnold, G. E. *Voice-speech-language-clinical communicology: Its physiology and pathology.* Belmont, Calif.: Wadsworth, 1965.

Luria, A. R. Brain disorders and language analysis. *Language and Speech,* 1958, *1,* 14–34.

Murphy, A. T. *Functional voice disorders.* Englewood Cliffs, N. J.: Prentice-Hall, 1964. (a)

Murphy, A. T. *Organic voice disorders.* Englewood Cliffs, N. J.: Prentice-Hall, 1964. (b)

Newman, J. B. The categorization of disorders of speech, language, and communication. *Journal of Speech and Hearing Disorders,* 1962, *27,* 287–89.

Ostwald, P. F. *Soundmaking.* Springfield, Ill.: Charles C Thomas, 1963.

Robbins, S. D. *A dictionary of speech pathology and therapy*. Cambridge, Mass.: Sci-Art Publishers, 1963.

Rubenstein, H. and Aborn, M. Psycholinguistics. *Annual Review of Psychology,* 1960, *11,* 291–322.

Scott, H. H. Noise measuring techniques. In C. Harris (Ed.), *Handbook of noise control*. New York: McGraw-Hill, 1957.

Trager, G. L. Paralanguage: A first approximation. In D. Hymes (Ed.), *Language in culture and society*. New York: Harper and Row, 1965.

Van Riper, C. *Speech correction: Principles and methods*. Englewood Cliffs, N. J.: Prentice-Hall, 1963.

CHAPTER 3

THE ONTOGENESIS
OF LANGUAGE

Advances during the past several years in the systematic study of language have stirred controversy, not only with respect to a number of complex issues in linguistic theory, but also in regard to the presumed bases for the entire process of language development. One group of parties to the controversy comprises those who endorse the viewpoint we identified earlier as a *generative* approach toward language. The most articulate spokesman for this group, as well as one of its principal founders, is the brilliant and original linguistic theorist, Noam Chomsky.

The opposition, on the other hand, includes those whose approach to the acquisition of language derives essentially from *learning theory*. Among this group we find a predilection for models which conceptualize language as a hierarchical structure of complex elements built up out of more simple constituents, and a reliance upon reinforcement, stimulus control, and mediated generalization as explanatory principles accounting for the salient features of linguistic acquisition.[1]

The above distinction does not neatly divide linguists from psychologists. Although most linguists today in the United States appear to have accepted generative grammar, at least those aspects of the theory which involve *transformational* analysis, the approach is not without its critics. Thus, in a recent review article, Hockett (1967) refers to Chomsky as a "neo-medieval philosopher."

Nor do psychologists exhibit anything approaching unanimity of agreement on the adequacy of contemporary psychological theories, spe-

---

[1] Perhaps it should be emphasized that one can readily accept the validity and explanatory power of such concepts as reinforcement and generalization as they apply to various aspects of language *behavior* without endorsing them as a basis for language *acquisition*.

37

cifically learning theory, in accounting for language acquisition. Miller (1965) possesses impeccable credentials as a psychologist, yet he yields to no one in the vigor of his criticism of reductionist conceptualizations of language. Perhaps it would be more accurate to say that the distinction between the adherents of generative grammar and those who endorse a view based on learning theory involves some pervasive and deep-seated differences in philosophy of science, the dimensions of which are outside the limits of the present discussion. Some of the issues, however, cannot be postponed so easily, especially those that relate to the developmental features of language. To avoid the learning of some lab connotations that seem to attach to a term like language acquisition, we shall emphasize the emergence of language as part of the life cycle of the individual by referring to the process as *linguistic ontogeny*.

The question which divides the groups distinguished above is much more complex than whether or not one "learns" a language. Obviously, everyone who speaks a language—English or Urdu—had to learn it at some time or another. But learning in this sense is a trivial aspect of linguistic ontogeny. Assuming structural integrity on the part of the "learner," it is just as easy to learn one language code as it is to learn another. What is of true significance, therefore, are the fundamentals of a process which seems to operate identically to turn out an accomplished language user, given the most unpromising and sketchy types of "inputs" from the environment. Smith and Miller (1966) remark that:

> Language would be a rare achievement, indeed, if parents were required to instruct children in phonology, morphology, or syntax, for it is obvious that few parents have the slightest notion what these skills consist of. That children can acquire language so readily can mean only that they have some innate predisposition for this kind of learning, and this in turn can mean only that evolution has prepared mankind in some very special way for this unique human accomplishment. (p. 3)

A contrasting version of language acquisition set forth by Jenkins and Palermo (1964) is described below:

> ... children's language begins with a form of imitation followed by the acquisition of a number of simple S-R connections between verbal labels and salient features of the environment to which they become attached. With a core of labels available, the child attaches words with other words in sequences, and the ordering or structuring begins. (p. 164)

As Weksel (1965) tartly observes, "In these few sentences Jenkins and Palermo succeed in glossing over some of the crucial problems facing not only the formulation of a theory of language acquisition, but any attempt to establish a theory of language." (p. 696)

If all that a theory of language had to account for was "simple S-R connections between verbal labels and salient features of the environment," such connections might easily be dealt with on the basis of some "form of imitation." The deficiencies of the Jenkins-Palermo type formulation become manifest when it is called upon to deal with the fact that children, in the natural course of language development, are required to produce various types of linguistic structures in the absence of appropriate and explicit examples of such structures in their linguistic habitats. Says Weksel:

> Our knowledge of the way imitation works in the learning of syntactic structure is at best fragmentary. What knowledge we have tends to serve us negatively, in that it points up deficiencies and inadequacies in present-day approaches. For instance, that in acquiring language a child has to learn syntactic structures which are not evident in the physical signal implies that the process of imitation requires a fairly complicated integration of the structural and acoustic properties of language. How this integration comes about is relatively unknown; clearly it is beyond the ken of present-day psychological theory. (p. 696)[2]

In the above statement Weksel removes from consideration as potential candidates for a theory of language ontogeny any and all extensions and modifications of current learning theory, including sophisticated mediation models. What he suggests, that the exigencies of the situation demand, is nothing less than a revolution in psychological theory to match the one that has already taken place in linguistics with the advent of generative grammar.

Before we can even begin to discern the outlines of such revolutionary modifications in psychological theory, it seems quite apparent that we shall need a massive supplementation to our current inventory of empirical facts on linguistic ontogeny. At the present time, we are woefully deficient in hard data, particularly those relating to the earliest period of language development. Nevertheless, there are several observations that one can make about the kinds of problems a psychological theory of linguistic ontogeny will have to attempt to resolve.

As Carroll (1964) reminds us, at least three interrelated sequences in the process of language acquisition can be identified: (1) *cognitive development,* "a child's capacity to recognize, discriminate: and manipulate the features and processes of the world around him;" (2) *psychoacoustic discrimination,* "development of the capacity to discriminate and comprehend the speech he hears from others in his environment"; (3) *productive ability,* "development of ability to produce speech sounds and sequences of speech sounds that conform more and more closely to the

---

[2] Reprinted by permission of the Linguistic Society of America, Austin, Tex.

patterns of adult speech." (p. 31) An adequate psychological theory of language development will be required to make provision for the understanding of these three sequences in both their independent and integrated functioning.

A second fundamental issue in language acquisition concerns the distinction between competence and performance. Something akin to this distinction is implicit in many of the dichotomous classifications that language specialists have used in the past: *la langue* vs. *la parole,* language code vs. speech signal, etc. It is suggested by Miller's (1965) analogy of the relation between population (language) and sample (utterance), and recalls the observation attributed to the nineteenth-century philosopher Von Humboldt that language uses finite means to achieve infinite ends. According to McNeill (1966a):

> Our concern in the study of language acquisition is with the development of competence; only after we have understood this to some degree can we hope to understand performance. First, consider the general distinction. Competence is an abstraction away from performance; it represents the knowledge a native speaker of a language must have in order to understand any of the infinitely many grammatical sentences of his language; it represents a native speaker's linguistic intuitions—his realization that *the man hit the ball is* grammatical but *the man virtued the ball* is not. Performance is the expression of competence in talking or listening to speech. One is competent to deal with an infinite number of grammatical sentences; but one's performance may be distracted in various ways. Performance operates under constraints of memory, which is finite, and time, which must be kept up with. Such limitations are irrelevant to competence. (pp. 16–17)

With regard to child language, the same distinction between competence and performance must be preserved. If our goal is to account for the emergence of linguistic competence, we defeat our purpose by confusing performance with competence. In addition, McNeill states,

> . . . we are interested in eventually accounting for a child's linguistic performance, and this, too, requires that we rigorously maintain the performance-competence distinction. It is possible to describe performance, we must show how it derives from competence; that is, how the regularities in a child's grammatical knowledge produce regularities in his overt linguistic behavior. Nothing short of this will suffice. (p. 17)

A generation of psychologists reared in the rigorous empiricist and operationist tradition of post-Watsonian behaviorism can be counted on to respond to the invitation to deal with "a native speaker's linguistic intuitions" as their principal source of data with a spectrum of emotions ranging from dismay to out-and-out disbelief. But if McNeil is correct, such a reaction is Thermopylaean. A grammatical description of child language is not the same as an account of linguistic ontogeny; and some-one—the psychologist or the psycholinguist—must forge the necessary links between the two.

Finally, one of the incontrovertible facts of linguistic ontogeny is its rapidity. Says McNeill (1966b):

> At the age of eighteen months or so, children begin to form simple two- and three-word sentences. At four they are able to produce sentences of almost every conceivable syntactic type. In approximately thirty months, therefore, language is acquired, at least that part of it having to do with syntax. (p. 99)

The process of acquisition, McNeill suggests, is consequently one of *invention*: "On the basis of a fundamental capacity for language, each generation creates language anew, and does so with astonishing speed." (p. 99) In short, linguistic ontogeny recapitulates linguistic phylogeny. Concerning the question, then, of what is acquired in the acquisition of linguistic competence, one seems compelled to conclude on the basis of evidence to date that *a system of rules and exceptions to the rules* (a necessity in any language) *is acquired for generating structured linguistic utterances.* Preceding this process is a sequence of stages of prelinguistic vocalization, in which practicing and listening to a variety of human vocalizations seems to facilitate the later development of normal speech. We turn to this prelinguistic developmental phase, therefore, as the first stage in our descriptive outline of linguistic ontogeny.

PRELINGUISTIC DEVELOPMENT

Eisenson (1963) has differentiated five stages of prelinguistic vocalization ("speech"). The first stage suggested is that of *"undifferentiated crying."* This is the first reaction to the environment and is the result of reflexive, total bodily responses. These reflexive oral responses to discomfort lack specificity and direction, according to Eisenson, and are produced by the expiration of breath.

The second stage in this prelinguistic developmental sequence is *differentiated crying.* Differentiaion in the sounds of crying may become discernible after the first month of the infant's life. Crying continues to be a total bodily response to a situation, but the stimulating conditions are capable of eliciting characteristic qualities of the sound response. States Eisenson (1963), "the sensation of hunger—caused, among other things, by a contraction of the muscles of the stomach—results in changes of *all the muscles* of the body, including those involved in the production of speech sounds. These changes, when accompanied by vocalization, give rise to the type of cry which we come to recognize as a hunger cry, characterized and distinguished from others by its rhythms." (p. 191)[3]

By the third or fourth month of life, the normal infant enters the third state of prelinguistic vocalization, *babbling*. This is the stage of vocal play in which sounds are produced randomly. Differentiated crying also still occurs during this stage. Repetition of various sounds also occurs with increasing frequency in the babbling stage. According to Eisenson (1963), in this stage, the infant begins to "show responsiveness to the sounds of others around him." The child both listens to and produces sounds during the babbling stage. "The trained listener may begin to distinguish" specific sounds and combinations in the infant's vocal play. The vowel [ae] as in bat should be heard as well as "some back of the mouth consonants such as [k] and [g], and possibly some front consonants such as [p], [b], and [m]." (Eisenson, 1963, p. 192)[3]

The alleged importance of the babbling stage for later linguistic development has been argued on the basis of scanty evidence from a few cases of isolated of *feral* children (Davis, 1940; Itard, 1932; Singh and Zingg, 1942). Of the thousands of reports written on language acquisition, only these very unusual cases deal with the effects of delay in language learning opportunities beyond the normal period of linguistic acquisition. Obviously, no responsible parent or experimenter would conceive of subjecting a child deliberately to a type of deprivation which could produce an alingual child.

In addition, the available literature has failed to generate much recent interest for several reasons: (1) in the few reported cases of isolated children, expert care was administered in only one case; (2) in none of the cases reported was it possible to accurately assess the native intelligence of the child; thus, it would be impossible to say whether the socially deprived child was congenitally defective in relation to the norm to which we wish to compare him; (3) in the reported cases there is no way even to estimate either the degree of isolation present or the amount of training instituted subsequently. Notwithstanding the limitations of the literature, it is instructive to examine it in search of evidence concerning maturation and language development.

The few well-reported examples of isolated children are limited to Itard's description of the "wild boy of Aveyron," Singh's account of Amala and Kamala, two children found in the company of wolves, and Anna and Isabelle, subjects of Davis' work.

Itard's "wild boy," whom he called "Victor," was found at the age

---

[3] Reprinted by permission of Appleton–Century–Crofts, New York; © 1963 Meredith Publishing Company.

of twelve living in the forest. Victor was apparently not raised by animals, but rather was abandoned at an age where he could find food enough to keep himself alive. Victor learned to recognize the meanings of several hundred words, but was almost totally unsuccessful at producing speech. As Brown (1958) pointed out:

> It is conceivable that Victor's mentality was adequate to the full use of language and that he was simply held back by inability to master the business of articulation and phonation. Perhaps the impulse to babble which is so evident in infants operates on a maturational timetable such that it must receive social support when the readiness is there or the impulse will die. (p. 189)[4]

Amala and Kamala were believed to be feral from birth or near-birth. Amala was one and one-half years old when discovered, and showed great promise at learning to speak. However, she died one year after her discovery and so her case tells us little. Kamala was about eight years old when discovered and lived ten years in human society. During this time she learned to utter a few words and to understand many, though her training apparently was less than expert.

Anna, the first subject of Davis' article (1940) was an isolated child who was discovered and taken to a welfare home at the age of six years. Anna was taught to speak several sentences but never gained a normal fluency in recognition or production of language.

The foregoing examples illustrate isolated children who were unable to acquire normal language usage after experiencing a varying amount of social isolation. Does this mean that social isolation completely prohibits language acquisition?

The case of Isabelle, cited by Davis, contradicts this hypothesis. Isabelle was raised to the age of six and one-half years in nearly complete isolation from everyone but her deaf-mute mother. Isabelle's behavior was animal-like when she was taken from her home, but with expert care and training she was able to achieve a normal I.Q. by the time she was eight and one-half years old. In two years she learned what normally takes six years. Had Isabelle benefitted from a normal environment what sort of development would she have displayed? It is possible that she might have been very superior in intelligence. Or perhaps she progressed better than the others because her environment included more necessary social factors, and thus she was more predisposed to further socialization.

It is possible, even probable, that the other children were congenitally doomed to inferior performance. Also, the others did not receive the expert training given Isabelle.

---

[4]Reprinted by permission of the Macmillan Company, New York.

We are working here on an unscientific basis. There are no controls on either the inherited or environmentally-induced characteristics of these children. Yet the evidence points to the conclusion that at least six years and probably more (Davis suggests as many as fifteen years) of isolation from society can be overcome with proper training.

The case of Isabelle clearly illustrates that language can be learned at an accelerated rate after the maturation stage has been passed. Language learning thus conforms to the pattern of walking and other forms of behavior which have been demonstrated to take place at an accelerated rate when training begins at an advanced stage of maturation.

There are many gross behavior patterns besides the linguistic which are affected by isolation. As Brown (1958) notes, sexual depression is one of the definitive characteristics of feral man; sexuality, like speech, seems to be a function that society must develop. Presumably sexual behavior would return with socialization, although no record was found to substantiate this.

If there is a limit to the length of time a child can endure isolation from society and still attain normal fruition of his linguistic talents, what is that period? More important, what are the underlying neurophysiological factors involved in socialization which are affected by isolation? Was Victor physically different from the person he would have been under more normal circumstances? Considering the case of Isabelle again, it is difficult to put aside the possibility that isolation is not causally related to neurophysiological change.

Neurophysiological differences between individuals cause behavioral differences, but do behavioral differences, in this case, cause neurophysiological differences? We do not have enough evidence to say that isolation causes neurophysiological changes affecting language acquisition. If an irreversible change does take place, when does it begin? For how long after the onset of change does the possibility of reversal exist? Once the change has advanced to a critical stage how can it be bypassed?

As important as such questions are to an understanding of rather basic issues in language development, there seems little likelihood that answers will be found in the near future.

There are certain trends in the pattern of sounds produced by the babbling infant (Irwin, 1946), but their importance for the further development of speech has been questioned recently by linguistic investigators. For example, Lenneberg (1946) has reported that sound spectrographic analysis has revealed objective differences between the babbling sounds of children and the speech sounds of adults. Observations of this kind tend to challenge the assumption that an infant's earliest incentive for the development of speech is supplied by the discovery of similarities between the sounds he makes himself and those made by his mother while ministering to his needs. In addition, noting that mothers have been shown to be unable to imitate the babbling sounds of their children with any degree of success, Lenneberg concludes that: ". . . either sound imitation is a mere fiction or, if the infant should indeed strive for imitation . . . he is innately equipped to hear similarities between his and his mother's vocalizations where, objectively, there are definite differences." (p. 119)

Some children stop babbling about the time they begin to learn their first words. The first sounds apparent to an adult in an infant's babbling are vowels, the first of which is apt to be some variety of [a] repeated at length. The consonantal sounds begin with the labials and are followed in order by gutturals, dentals, and finally nasals (Irwin, 1946).

Lallation is the fourth stage identified by Eisenson, and it occurs during the second six months of life. Lallation is defined as the "repetition of heard sound complexes and syllables." The infant in this stage of prelinguistic vocalization learns to imitate his own accidental productions. Also during the period of lallation, the infant's response to others becomes more selective in that "he will not interrupt his own oral play merely because some adult is speaking to him or is near him." (Eisenson, 1963, p. 194)[5]

The fifth and final stage of prelinguistic speech is that of *echolalia*. This stage begins in about the ninth or tenth month and is characterized by the "imitation by the infant of sounds which he hears others make, but which he does not comprehend." Says Eisenson (1963), "It is unlike lallation in that another individual provides the stimulus for the repetition of a sound." As is pointed out by Eisenson, "The lallation and echolalic periods are of tremendous importance because during these stages the child acquires a repertoire of sound complexes which ultimately he will be able to produce at will, and which he must have before he can learn to speak or acquire a language in the adult sense." (p. 195)[5] To some extent, echolalic behavior continues throughout life.

The sequential character of these prelinguistic activities is one of the strongest arguments for the large biological component of language behavior. Referring to Lenneberg (1966):

> The hallmarks for maturationally controlled emergence of behavior are four: (1) regularity in the sequence of appearance of given milestones, all correlated with age and other concomitant developmental facts; (2) evidence that the opportunity for environmental stimulation remains relatively constant throughout development but that the infant makes different use of such opportunities as he grows up; (3) emergence

[5] Reprinted by permission of Appleton–Century–Crofts, New York; © 1963 Meredith Publishing Company.

of the behavior either in part or entirely, before it has any immediate use to the individual; (4) evidence that the clumsy beginnings of the behavior are not signs of goal-directed practice. (p. 220)

Studies have demonstrated that the emergence of speech and language meets these criteria.

LINGUISTIC DEVELOPMENT

The period of actual linguistic development does not divide itself readily into stages as visible as those which characterize prelinguistic development. Eisenson (1963) simply subsumes the entire linguistic development sequence under the term *verbal utterance*. This term refers to "the establishment of conventionalized speech patterns as specific responses to socially presented stimuli." (p. 195)[6] Implicit to this definition is the assumption that a period of verbal comprehension without meaningful vocal responses has preceded the emergence of actual utterances. Linguistic development for Eisenson, then, consists of gradual increases in both receptive and productive speech ability.

The period of verbal utterances can, however, be partitioned in terms of the degree to which the child's vocalizations approach an adult level of grammatical structure. According to this criterion, one may discern on an impressionistic basis three levels of linguistic development.

The first stage is that of the word sentence and lasts for several months after the child begins to speak. Single word utterances are considered to be word sentences because they serve to express a complete thought for the child. Any single "word sentence" may have a multiplicity of meanings, depending upon the type of vocal expression inflection, or situation in which it is used.

The second stage of linguistic development might be called that of the multi-word sentence. Eisenson suggests that most children reach this stage only after two years of age: "The early multi-word sentences are most likely to consist of a noun and a verb with full subject-predicate implications. 'Baby eat' or 'baby walk' are typical noun-verb combinations which may be produced by children between fifteen and twenty-seven months of age." (p. 207)[7] The multi-word sentences at this stage, however, are not correct grammatically. Under two years of age, children tend not to use articles, prepositions, conjunctions, etc.

A third stage might be delineated as the period of grammatically correct verbal utterances. This period begins around three years of age for

---

[6] Reprinted by permission of Appleton–Century–Crofts, New York; © 1963 Meredith Publishing Company.

[7] Reprinted by permission of Appleton–Century–Crofts, New York; © 1963 Meredith Publishing Company.

most children. Correct grammatical usage, of course, is acquired only gradually and therefore, it would not be applied consistently to all of the child's utterances.

As we mentioned earlier, children appear to master all of the essential grammatical structures of their language in the incredibly short period of thirty months (McNeill, 1966a). Our support for such statements is derived largely from a body of recent research which incorporates the latest advances in psycholinguistics. Says McNeill (1966a):

> The past half-dozen years have seen a great change in the study of child language. Formerly, attention was concentrated on surveys of vocabulary, frequency counts of various grammatical classes, and case histories of the gradual elimination of errors in speaking. The basic assumption appears to have been that child language was adult language filtered through a great deal of cognitive noise and impoverished of vocabulary. The scholar supposed that he knew the child's grammar in advance and that it was reasonable to use categories of adult grammar to describe child language. The change from this point of view has been simple but fundamental and mainly methodological. Recent studies look upon a young child as a fluent speaker of an exotic language. The psycholinguist's problem, therefore, is analogous to the problem faced by a field linguist. (p. 16)

Despite the many problems involved in the study of child language, investigators like Brown and Bellugi (1964), Brown and Fraser (1963), Miller and Ervin (1964) and Menyuk (1963) have managed to demonstrate that almost all of the basic structures used by adults to generate sentences are discernible in the language behavior of three-year-olds.

A study by the latter investigator examined the hypothesis that children have incorporated the generative rules of their grammar and are able to understand and produce sentences in accord with these rules, thereby extending their behavior systematically without additional instruction if additional memory aid are given. Menyuk (1963) obtained a language sample from each of her nursery school and kindergarten children in various stimulus situations: conversation with an adult, conversation with peers, and responses to the Blacky Pictures projective test. The children were then asked to repeat a set of sentences representative of the various "restricted forms"—Menyuk's term for grammatically incorrect sentences produced originally by children the same age as the subjects—and a set of sentences representative of various transformation types, i.e., sentences which go beyond the simple active, declarative type that were found in their usage of grammar.

Older children were found to be able to perform the task of repeating the sentence sets regardless of the structure of the sentences. The data appear to confirm the hypothesis that the children in this age group (three years) have incorporated most of the basic generative rules of the grammar that we have thus far been able to describe and are capable of using these rules to understand and produce sentences.

Fraser, Bellugi, and Brown (1963) attempted to determine whether understanding does actually precede productive capability in the process of language development. Twelve children ranging in age from thirty-seven to forty-three months served as subjects in this investigation. The task involved ten grammatical contrasts created by the use of two utterances which are identical for some grammatical feature. Understanding was operationalized as the correct identification of pictures named by contrasting sentences. Production was operationalized as the correct imitation of contrasting features in sentences applied appropriately to pictures. The drawings specified by the investigator followed the general principle that the representations of paired utterances should be identical in every respect except the one coded by the grammatical contrast. The pictures were mounted side by side in a transparent-loose-leafed photograph album. The order of the problems was counterbalanced and randomized. Four practice items preceded the test. Two to three sessions were necessary for all three children to do all three tasks. The remaining three took only one session. Records consisted of one on tape and one written on the scene. Two scorers independently scored all of the data (720 items).

Results indicated that production, meaning the correct production of contrasting features in sentences applied appropriately to pictures, proved to be less advanced than understanding in three-year-old children. However, production in the sense of imitation proved to be more advanced than understanding. It would appear that the highly systematic speech system is under more complete control at three years than is the less systematic and more complex referential system. The outcome suggests that children undergo considerable learning about referential patterning, the stimulus control of grammatical forms, before they produce the forms themselves.

VOCABULARY DEVELOPMENT AND PARTS OF SPEECH

The first word that makes its appearance in the child's vocabulary is usually a noun, followed shortly thereafter by verbs. Pronouns, adjectives, and adverbs appear rather late in the developmental sequence; prepositions, articles, and conjunctions are the last to appear. Even after they have been learned, these later parts of speech are often omitted in speech. According to Eisenson (1963):

> Nouns, interjections, and verbs precede the other word categories probably because these words, alone or in utterances that approximate conventional sentences, most easily express the child's feelings about his

own needs and his reactions to the potencies of words, or really, his potency as a user of words. The word forms get done what needs to get done! (p. 208)[8]

Early vocabulary development is a slow process. Following the utterance of his first meaningful word, months may pass and the child may still know a very small number of words. He reaches a stage, however, in which the acquisition of vocabulary proceeds at an accelerated pace. This occurs, according to Carroll (1964), "when in his cognitive development the child has reached the point of perceiving that things, events, and properties have 'names.'" (p. 32) During what might be called this "naming stage," the child may prove a trial for his parents and others with endless questions of "what is that?" The results of this constant quiz process, however, are evident in the following figures on vocabulary development compiled by Smith (1926):

Year Level	Mean Number of Words that Child Can Produce and Respond To
1	3
2	272
3	896
4	1,540
5	2,072
6	2,562

The child's linguistic progress is marked by features other than vocabulary growth. McCarthy (1960) reported an increase in sentence length: from an average of 1.2 words at 18 months to an average of 4.6 words at 54 months. Another investigator by the same name (Smith, 1941) noted an increase in "recognition" vocabulary from 23,000 words at the age of 6 (first grade) to approximately 80,000 words at age 17 (12th grade). The absolute validity of such figures is, of course, highly suspect; but from these and similar studies we gather a general impression that vocabulary development occurs at its swiftest rate between the ages of two and four years, thereafter proceeding at a more moderate pace.

REFERENCES

Bellugi, U. and Brown, R. (Eds.), *The acquisition of language*. Lafayette, Ind.: Child Development Publications, 1964.

---

[8] Reprinted by permission of Appleton–Century–Crofts, New York; © 1963 Meredith Publishing Company.

Brown, R. Linguistic determinism and the parts of speech. *Journal of Abnormal and Social Psychology,* 1957, *55,* 1–5.

Brown, R. *Words and things.* Glencoe, Ill.: The Free Press, 1958.

Brown, R. and Bellugi, U. Three processes in the child's acquisition of syntax. *Harvard Educational Review,* 1964, *34,* 133–51.

Brown, R. and Berko, J. Word association and the acquisition of grammar. *Child Development,* 1960, *31,* 1–14.

Brown, R. and Fraser, C. The acquisition of syntax. In C. N. Cofer and B. S. Musgrave (Eds.), *Verbal behavior and learning.* New York: McGraw-Hill, 1963.

Carroll, J. B. *Language and thought.* Englewood Cliffs, N. J.: Prentice-Hall, 1964.

Davis, K. Extreme social isolation of a child. *American Journal of Sociology,* 1940, *45,* 554–65.

Eisenson, J., Auer, J. J., and Irwin, J. V. *The psychology of communication.* New York: Appleton-Century-Crofts, 1963.

Fraser, C., Bellugi, U., and Brown, R. Control of grammar in imitation, comprehension, and production. *Journal of Verbal Learning and Verbal Behavior,* 1963, *2,* 121–35.

Hockett, C. F. The foundations of language in man, the small-mouthed animal. *Scientific American,* 1967, *217,* 141–44.

Irwin, O. C. Infant speech: Vowel and consonant frequency. *Journal of Speech Disorders,* 1946, *2,* 123–25.

Itard, J. M. G. *The wild boy of Aveyron.* New York: Century, 1932.

Jenkins, J. J. and Palermo, D. Mediation processes and the acquisition of linguistic structure. In U. Bellugi and R. Brown (Eds.), *The acquisition of language.* Lafayette, Ind.: Child Development Publications, 1964.

Lenneberg, E. H. Understanding language without ability to speak: A case report. *Journal of Abnormal and Social Psychology,* 1962, *65,* 419–25.

Lenneberg, E. H. Speech as a motor skill with special reference to nonaphasic disorders. In U. Bellugi and R. Brown (Eds.), *The acquisition of language.* Lafayette, Ind.: Child Development Publications, 1964.

Lenneberg, E. H. The natural history of language. In F. Smith and G. A. Miller (Eds.), *The genesis of language.* Cambridge, Mass.: The M. I. T. Press, 1966.

Lenneberg, E. H. *The biological foundations of language.* New York: Wiley, 1967.

McCarthy, D. *Language development and language disorders.* Yellow Springs, Ohio: Antioch University Press, 1960.

McNeill, D. Developmental psycholinguistics. In F. Smith and G. A. Miller (Eds.), *The genesis of language.* Cambridge, Mass.: The M.I.T. Press, 1966. (a)

McNeill, D. The creation of language by children. In L. Lyons and R. J. Wales (Eds.), *Psycholinguistics papers.* Edinburgh: Edinburgh University Press, 1966. (b)

Menyuk, P. A. A preliminary evaluation of grammatical capacity in children. *Journal of Verbal Learning and Verbal Behavior,* 1963, *2,* 429–39.

Menyuk, P. A. Alternation of rules in children's grammar. *Journal of Verbal Learning and Verbal Behavior*, 1964, *3*, 480–88.

Miller, G. A. Some preliminaries to psycholinguistics. *American Psychologist*, 1965, *20*, 15–20.

Miller, W. and Ervin, S. The development of grammar in child language. In U. Bellugi and R. Brown (Eds.), *The acquisition of language*. Lafayette, Ind.: Child Development Publications, 1964.

Singh, J. A. L. and Zingg, R. M. *Wolf children and feral man*. New York: Harper, 1942.

Smith, F. and Miller, G. A. (Eds.), *The genesis of language*. Cambridge, Mass.: The M.I.T. Press, 1966.

Smith, M. *An investigation of the development of the sentence and the extent of vocabulary in young children*. University of Iowa Studies in Child Welfare, 1926, No. 5.

Smith, M. K. Measurement of the size of general English vocabulary through the elementary grades and high school. *Genetic Psychology Monographs*, 1941, *24*, 344.

Weksel, W. Review of U. Bellugi and R. Brown (Eds.), *The acquisition of language*. *Language*, 1965, *41*, 692–709.

Wood, N. E. *Delayed speech and language development*. Englewood Cliffs, N. J.: Prentice-Hall, 1964.

CHAPTER 4

LINGUISTIC RELATIVITY
AND THE ADAPTATIVE FUNCTIONS
OF LANGUAGE

It has been suggested that man's greatest talent is the ability to symbolize and abstract the world around him into a conceptual system. In his dealings with this set of abstractions, he is empowered to discover relationships and then turn back to his experience with understanding.

But what of the ability to abstract itself—the system or "go-between" relating man to what he knows? To state the question is to invite consideration of the possible role that language symbols and their systematic features might play in this process. As we reflect upon differences among language codes, we are led to the further possibility—one with endlessly intriguing implications—that these differences may in some way *produce* rather than merely reflect some of the variance we discover in what is conveyed by the German term *Weltanschauung,* i.e., total philosophic outlook or "world view."

The hypothesis of *linguistic relativity,* which in the United States is identified with Edward Sapir and Benjamin Lee Whorf, is a statement about the influence upon world views of accidental linguistic characteristics of cultures. It asks what effect language (in the Saussurian connotation of *la langue*) has upon the cognitive behavior of people. It postulates that different linguistic systems impose different pictures of the physical universe.

Sapir (1921) stated the linguistic relativity thesis in the following terms:

> Human beings do not live in the objective world alone, nor alone in the world of social activity as ordinarily understood, but are very much at the mercy of the particular language which has become the medium of expression for their society. It is quite an illusion to imagine that one

adjusts to reality essentially without the use of language and the language is merely an incidental means of solving specific problems of communication or reflection. The fact of the matter is that the "real world" is to a large extent unconsciously built up on the language habits of the group. . . . We see and hear and otherwise experience very largely as we do because the language habits of our community predispose certain choices of interpretation. (p. 134)

Both Sapir and Whorf emphasized the importance of structural elements of language in the organization of perceptual and cognitive experience. Comparing English, a linguistic variant of what he called Standard Average European (SAE) language with several North American Indian languages, Whorf, for example, purported to show that the speakers of these languages formed the native SAE speaker. Although Brown (1958) has been critical of Whorf's frequent and rather questionable use of literal translation as a kind of bootstrap operation for demonstrating linguistic relativity, there is a fair amount of experimental evidence (Brown and Lenneberg, 1954; Carroll and Casagrande, 1958; Lenneberg and Roberts, 1956) which provides extralinguistic validation for certain features of the linguistic relativity hypothesis.

Relativity in the Whorfian sense refers to the larger aspect of cultural comparison in the linguistic context. But there is a kind of *intralinguistic* relativity that has much potential significance for the study of language behavior in psychopathology. This meaning of linguistic relativity derives from the referential features of language. Words, as symbols, do not merely stand for objects, but for relationships and categories. Says Weinstein (1962):

Language not only classifies the physical world but it defines identity for its speakers. The term "identity" will be used to denote the cultural orientation and social categorization through which we order our environment. The expression "sense of identity" refers to the *feeling* that things and events are what they are called. (pp. 29–30)[1]

According to this view, language is not merely a vehicle for the expression of ideas; it is a versatile instrument which performs vitally important functions in the individual's adjustment. It is this interpretation of linguistic relativity that we shall examine in the present chapter.

ADAPTATIVE AND DEFENSIVE FUNCTIONS OF LANGUAGE

In his book *Cultural aspects of delusion,* Weinstein (1962) interprets delusional formations of the psychotic patient as symbolic expressions

---

[1] Reprinted by permission of the Macmillan Company, New York.

of the patient's relationship with his sociocultural milieu. The delusion, he believes, expresses motives and feelings which are of paramountcy to the patient, but the nature of such motives and feelings is largely determined by culturally dominant themes. Thus, for instance, the prevalence of delusional content centering about children among Weinstein's Virgin Islanders correlates closely with the importance assigned to children in the social norms of that society.

In another work which reports the results of extended study of language usage among brain-damaged patients, Weinstein (1958) "examines the role of changes in language pattern as a mode of adaptation to stress." According to Weinstein:

> In situations of stress, language is more readily equated with reality by its speakers, although in fact it is less referential. The capacity for complex interaction in the environment is impaired, and the events of the physical world classified in more comprehensive black and white fashion. The number of channels of relatedness is reduced, and the speaker becomes even less aware of the inter active processes of language, regarding the product of the interaction as the very essence of reality. Language becomes highly stereotyped, and a single symbolic unit such as a cliché, delusion, confabulation, or other metaphor serves as a condensed representation of problems and relationships. Such forms of language are not only indicators of stress but measures of the adaptation. (p. 31)[2]

In this work the focus is on spoken language, and it is concluded that the patients "use" language idiosyncratically to suit their needs and shift symbolic levels as is done in humor or poetry. For example: "My home town is ten minutes from here" (actually 400 miles). Later the patient says, "It will take my brother a day of driving to get here." The statement "ten minutes from here" serves to bring the patient closer to where he wants to be, and he sees no contradiction between this and the reality which he has later acknowledged.

Weinstein says that statements "serve as modes of adaptation to stress by reason of the change in the level of interaction." They are acceptable to the patient because "one's feeling of relativity may be more closely related to one's relationship in his environment than to any more logical process."

Jaffe (1960) has supplied a number of observations on the defensive properties of formal language patterns. These are offered rather diffidently, "classified into rough categories which are arbitrary, not of the same order, somewhat overlapping, and by no means exhaustive." (p. 140) The list includes these categories: (1) names and forms of address; (2) idiomatic language patterns; (3) person and number; (4)

---

[2] Reprinted by permission of the Macmillan Company, New York.

verb tense; (5) passive constructions; and (6) exaggeration and commitment. We shall define and briefly illustrate these categories.

(1) NAMES AND FORMS OF ADDRESS

This category of language patterns deals with questions of identity, status, intimacy, and social distance. Forms of address help to define the social situation. This function of language structure is more obvious in French and German where more than one form of personal pronoun exists for addressing one's partner, e.g., "tu" and "vous." (p. 140)[3]

Brown and Gilman (1960) have pointed out that forms of address always follow rules which are understood by the whole society. The two rules of address that these authors identify as basic are those pertaining to the dimensions of solidarity and status or power. In solidarity there is a perceived similarity among members which produces liking; this liking stimulates increased interaction which in turn reinforces solidarity. On the other hand, status emphasizes the differences between members rather than the similarities. It identifies in an interpersonal situation who holds the greater power, that is, who can control the behavior of the other. The solidarity semantic is identified with the informal mode of address, e.g., the "T" form of the pronoun (as in "tu," "Du", etc.). The power semantic is identified with the "V" form of pronoun ("Vous", "Sie," etc.). American English, which presently lacks the formal differentiation conveyed in earlier times by "thou" and "you," probably accounts for a greater number and variety of linguistically or pronominally ambiguous situations than languages like French and German. One thinks, for example, of the pre-World War II practice of the German prostitute of addressing her customers as "Du" (informal) before and during sexual intercourse, at the conclusion of which she reverted to the use of "Sie" (formal).

Jaffe gives the example of the patient struggling to resolve his family ties who began to refer to his parents by their first names, rather than as "Mom" and "Dad." Also:

> The analyst's mode of addressing the patient can mobilize affect in striking fashion. Use of the patient's first name may foster generally positive and dependency feelings due to similarity to the forms used by parents and friends. It is also reminiscent of the mode of address used by teachers in elementary schools. This latter type of transference is marked in early group therapy meetings, where patients' first names are used by convention. They may develop a conflict over the reciprocal mode of

---

[3] From Formal Language Patterns as Defensive Operations, in D. A. Barbara (Ed.), *Psychological and psychiatric aspects of speech and hearing,* 1960. Courtesy of Charles C Thomas, publisher, Springfield, Illinois.

address which elicits new information about the doctor-patient relationship. One patient became panicky, warning me that he could not continue to call me "Doctor" if I used his first name in the group because, "It would be too humiliating, like being a child." Feelings revolving about mode of addressing patients are also fruitful areas for countertransference analysis. My preferences for certain forms with specific patients have revealed aspects of the relationship of which I was unaware. (p. 142)[4]

Included in this general category are honorities which can function as verbal defense mechanisms, e.g., when used in sarcasm, and euphemisms which are pleasant-sounding terms substituted for harsh or unpleasant ones, e.g., "passed away" for "died."

(2) IDIOMATIC LANGUAGE PATTERNS

The word idiom is here used in the sense of "the language peculiar to a people (a tongue), or to a district, community or class (a dialect)." (p. 143)[5]

Language-switching during psychoanalysis has been investigated by Krapf (1955). When the patient speaks about certain subjects, there is a spontaneous and often compulsive change from one language to another —as in the case of the polyglot adolescent reported by Ostwald (1963) who could curse in several languages but not in English, his mother tongue, which had to be kept clean. Krapf concludes that "the common denominator of the motivations that underlie the choice of language in polyglot psychoanalysis is in general a tendency to avoid anxiety. The individual uses the language that in a particular situation is least likely to provoke a feeling of anxiety, or conversely, most likely to give him a feeling of security." (p. 356)

(3) PERSON AND NUMBER

Changes in the person of pronouns are related to intimacy, commitment, and social distance. First and second person (I, you, we) are more direct than third person (someone, they). Changes in number (singular, plural) may serve similar functions, and are also comments on interpersonal relatedness. . . . (p. 144)[6]

Jaffe cites the example of the patient who, as the leader of a contending faction within an organization, expressed his fear in the form: "I will fail." Following the successful outcome of the contest, his opening words

---

[4] *Ibid.*
[5] *Ibid.*
[6] *Ibid.*

to the therapist were: "Well, *we* won." Jaffe's analysis emphasized that the verbal pattern served to deny ambition and ward off possible disappointment.

(4) VERB TENSE

The defensive function of tense has long been recognized in the psychoanalytic rule of technique which says, in effect, "When the patient speaks of the past the analyst should speak in the present, and when the patient speaks in the present the analyst should speak of the past." (pp. 145–46) [7]

The author relates the case of the obsessional patient who reported his hostile and aggressive dreams in the past tense. When asked to "translate" his dreams into the present tense, the patient demurred, saying "I have a feeling that in the present tense I *might begin to act it out in reality.*"

(5) PASSIVE CONSTRUCTIONS

These are grammatical distinctions which indicate the relation of the speaker to the action expressed. (p. 147) [8]

The use of passive voice constructions in situations where the action would usually be expressed by the active voice is defensive in nature. Jaffe mentions the patient who changed his statement describing a visit from, "I *went* there" to "I *found* myself there." In somewhat the same vein were the two women patients of Jaffe who spoke of putting their contraceptive diaphragms "on." When asked why they said "on" rather than "in," one of them replied, "Putting it *in* is too literal, it would be like inserting it here, exposing myself. I'd rather refer to it as a garment."

(6) EXAGGERATION AND COMMITMENT

Included in this category are language patterns which Jaffe views as characteristic of hysterics and obsessives, respectively. In the former case, the hysteric habitually uses vivid, hyperbolic, emotionally hued words to dramatize his personal situation. In the latter case, the formal language patterns of the obsessive patient reveal habitual overqualification, denial, and indecisiveness.

Jaffe sees an area of common interest between psychoanalysis and psycholinguistics in the exploration of formal patterns or "styles" of symbolic behavior. Referring to the continuous interplay between language and experience, Jaffe indorses the proposition that "the structure of the

---

[7] *Ibid.*
[8] *Ibid.*

language habitually used influences the way in which the environment is apprehended." (p. 149) Thus we are brought back to the concept of linguistic relativity. Jaffe contrasts two hypothetical personalities, both speakers of English:

> The first has been reared in a language environment characterized by decision, commitment, and absolutes. His voice is assertive, and his speech abounds in clear-cut "either-or" constructions. He speaks in absolutes, and uses few qualifying adverbs such as "perhaps" and "maybe." The latter make him uneasy because they seem vague, and indefinite. He is intolerant of ambiguity, non-introspective, a man of action. His verbal structure may be said to "express" his mode of experience of himself and the world. In his logical structure any assertion implies the negation of its alternatives. However, this person lacks the verbal, and presumably the conceptual tools to make subtle discriminations. A whole dimension of phenomenal experience is beyond him.
>
> The second person has always been forced to be aware of shades of meaning, and of inconsistencies. His voice is hesitant, and he prefers to speak in the third person, with subjunctives and qualifiers as in the sentence, "One might perhaps consider that." He is overintellectualized and introspective. Clear-cut alternatives distress him for they never seem to do justice to the complexity of the facts. His language is said to "express" a more tentative inner state. But more than this, for his linguistic and conceptual structure do not admit the possibility of commitment. He cannot give an unequivocal "yes" or "no." A firm stand is impossible since he can always identify to some extent with the opposition. His is a relative world, devoid of strong beliefs. He is indecisive and action-inhibited. He cannot experience powerful, uncomplicated emotion welded to action. (pp. 149–50)[9]

Carroll (1958) differentiates between what he calls "mold theory" and "lattice theory." The former states that the language we have learned maintains strict control over our cognitive behavior, i.e., the position held by Whorf (1956) and Sapir (1921). The "lattice theory" involves a genetic approach, implying that a latent structure develops in the process of learning and using a language that allows focusing on some areas and a tendency to blur others. The patient's use of language to "make" reality seems to suggest the latter.

The individual's personal variety of the community language, the sum total of personal usage of language—*la parole* in the Saussurian connotation—we call *idiolect*. With the aid of contextual methods of analysis, Laffal (1965) attempts to interpret the language of a patient. He manages a long-term recording of associations to different words in a single

---

[9] *Ibid.*

psychotic's speech and from this is able to "translate" the patient's symbolism, as shown below:

AN ANALYSIS OF CONTEXTUAL
ASSOCIATES AND "TRANSLATIONS"

"It is hard to speak with a language which has an idiom of opposition."

Is interpreted to mean: "I find it difficult to speak with the oppositional language of Mother."

"I mean insofar as there are so many bulwarks in historical, in historical content representative of a, the revolutionary victory won over an English prosidium."

Is interpreted to mean: "Mother has been overthrown in the past by force."

"It's made this country great in its self-containment."

Is interpreted to mean: "The victory has led to great independence." (p. 146)[10]

Fishman (1960) has cut the linguistic relativity hypothesis into a 2 x 2 table. The deterministic part is split on the dimensions of semantic characteristics of language versus grammar and the resulting behavior on a language and cultural theme dimension versus nonlinguistic behavior. The table can be adapted to by adding a language-idiolect differentiation to the deterministic variables, as shown in Figure 3. The possible causal route of language to idiolect and thence to criterion is important. Also important is the fact that the whole figure now refers to a limited psychotic "culture." As Sapir (1921) has suggested, it is important to realize that langauge may not only refer to experience or even help to shape and interpret experience; it also substitutes for experience in the sense that speech and action supplement each other in those sequences of interpersonal behavior which constitute the greater component of our everyday lives.

Whatever the nature of the extralinguistic pathological processes in psychosis, a contributory role must be assigned to language functions. One engages in a considerable amount of reality testing via the linguistic context in social interaction; and it is the feedback that one receives in such exchanges that substitutes for direct experience in many areas of human existence. At the same time, social interaction is the means whereby idiolect and language are kept from excessive divergence.

Korzybski (1941) emphasized the pathogenetic consequences of mistaking the map for the territory, i.e., of mistaking the world of linguistic symbols for the world of physical and social reality. Painful, traumatic, self-deprecatory meanings assume potentially catastrophic

---

[10] Reprinted by permission of the publishers, Atherton Press, Inc. Copyright © 1965 Atherton Press, New York, all rights reserved.

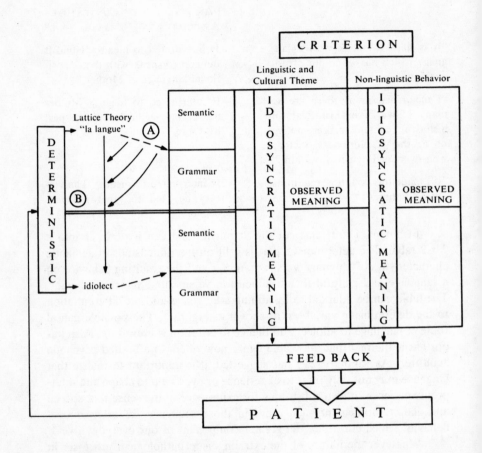

The change from A to B in the above diagram signifies
the acquisition of psychosis.

FIGURE 3

Fishman's (1960) Model of Linguistic Relativity Adapted to Psychotic Language

significance for an individual, and they can only be replaced by positive emotional referents in the communicative setting. But anxiety, guilt, hostility, and other strong negative affects lead to withdrawal and increasing social isolation. Bit by bit, the individual's idiolect, his language habits, shows estrangement from the language code of his community; eventually it might even acquire bizarre properties. With growing pressure, even grammatical habits of lifelong standing give way. Grammar, it may be hypothesized, is the last area to show disintegration, except in cases of actual brain damage.

According to this view, psychosis would be characterized in terms of several stages: (1) conceptualizations that evoke profound anxiety, guilt, hostility, etc.; (2) the progressive spread of misdefinition of other concepts in an attempt to escape anxiety; (3) the development of a psychotic delusion, consisting of semantic and/or grammatical misdefinition; and finally, if the reaction formation of Step 3 does not halt the process, a gradual increase in bizarreness of the idiolect until all rules of grammar are abandoned and any remaining "correct" semantic concepts are lost in a formless pile of associations. Psychosis in the most acute state is tantamount to a complete disruption of symbolic behavior. The patient is trapped, in that he can no longer understand or cope with the world or even the reality of his own existence.

REFERENCES

Brown, R. *Words and things.* Glencoe, Ill.: The Free Press, 1958.

Brown, R. and Gilman, A. The pronouns of power and solidarity. In T. A. Sebeok (Ed.), *Style in language.* Cambridge, Mass.: The Technology Press, 1960.

Brown, R. and Lenneberg, E. H. A study in language and cognition. *Journal of Abnormal and Social Psychology,* 1954, *49,* 454–62.

Carroll, J. B. Some psychological effects of language structure. In P. H. Hoch and J. Zubin (Eds.), *Psychopathology of communication.* New York: Grune and Stratton, 1958.

Carroll, J. B. *Language and thought.* Englewood Cliffs, N. J.: Prentice-Hall, 1964.

Carroll, J. B. and Casagrande, J. B. The function of language classifications in behavior. In E. E. Maccoby, T. M. Newcomb, and E. L. Hartley (Eds.), *Readings in social psychology.* New York: Holt, 1958.

De Saussure, F. *Course in general linguistics.* W. Baskin (Trans.). New York: Philosophical Library, 1959.

Fishman, J. A. A systematization of the Whorfian hypothesis. *Behavioral Science,* 1960, *5,* 323–39.

Jaffe, J. Formal language patterns as defensive operations. In D. A. Barbara (Ed.), *Psychological and psychiatric aspects of speech and hearing.* Springfield, Ill.: Charles C Thomas, 1960.

Korzybski, A. *Science and sanity.* New York: Science Press, 1941.

Krapf, E. E. The choice of language in polyglot psychoanalysis. *Psychoanalytic Quarterly,* 1955, *24,* 343–57.

Laffal, J. *Pathological and normal language.* New York: Atherton Press, 1965.

Lenneberg, E. H. and Roberts, J. M. The language of experience: A study in methodology. *International Journal of American Linguistics,* 1956, Supplement to Vol. 22, No. 2.

Sapir, E. *Language.* New York: Harcourt, Brace and World, 1921.

Weinstein, E. A. Changes in language patterns as adaptive mechanisms. In P. H. Hoch and J. Zubin (Eds.), *Psychopathology of communication.* New York: Grune and Stratton, 1958.

Weinstein, E. A. *Cultural aspects of delusion.* New York: The Free Press of Glencoe, 1962.

Whorf, B. L. Science and linguistics. In J. B. Carroll (Ed.), *Language, thought, and reality.* Cambridge, Mass.: The Technology Press and John Wiley and Sons, 1956.

PART 2

LANGUAGE BEHAVIOR IN SPECIFIC SYNDROMES

CHAPTER 5

LANGUAGE BEHAVIOR
IN MENTAL RETARDATION

Heber (1958) defines mental retardation as "subaverage general intellectual functioning which originates during the developmental period and is associated with impairment in adaptive behavior." The point of view presented here is that mental retardation is a reversible condition, provided that techniques of general remediation are discovered and applied appropriately. It should be noted that this view of mental retardation is a recent one. Doll, as late as 1947, held that mental retardation was "incurable." This is essentially the classical, medical (and pathological) orientation which has tended to dominate the field of mental retardation. At one time such an "incurable" interpretation was further supported by the dogma of "I.Q. constancy" in the field of psychological measurement. The inherent pessimism of such a pathological orientation all but obliterated the meager attempts to treat mental subnormality prior to the 1960's. The custodial and nonacademic educational approaches were direct corollaries of such a narrow interpretation of all mental retardation. It is highly questionable whether or not the medical diagnoses of mental retardation as resulting from "brain-damage" or "neurological dysfunction" are empirically justified in the less extreme cases of intellectual impairment. Such classifications have few, if any, pragmatic implications for the treatment of the behavioral problems of concern here. Rather, a new emphasis is in order which concentrates upon both the abilities and disabilities of the mentally retarded, and the improvement or facilitation of the latter through the former.

Until a more reliable and valid system of classification is developed, the mentally retarded must continue to be differentiated on the basis of their performance on standard tests of general intelligence. In terms of this criterion, the mentally retarded have traditionally comprised that group of individuals with tested I.Q.'s of about 70 or below. There are four levels of mental retardation suggested by the American Association of Mental Deficiency (Heber, 1958, p. 57). These are *profound, severe, moderate,* and *mild* retardation. The profoundly mentally retarded have I.Q.'s of below 20; the severely retarded I.Q.'s of 20–35; the moderately retarded an I.Q. range of 36–52; and the mild retardates I.Q.'s of 53–68.

Stevens (1964) has characterized the profoundly retarded as exhibiting extensive impairment of the central nervous system and has noted the presence in this group of considerable organic pathology. Handicapping conditions other than mental retardation (e.g., blindness, deafness, epilepsy, etc.) are also present in the profoundly retarded. Motor development among these individuals is very poor and speech is absent. The profoundly retarded are considered "incapable of profiting from any type of training or education" and most "require life-long residential care." (p. 4)[1]

The severely retarded share some of the same characteristics of the profoundly retarded, but to a lesser degree. Many of the severely retarded may also require intensive care. Language, speech, and motor development are also retarded in the severe group. Stevens notes further that many severely retarded individuals, particularly those with intelligence quotients between 25 and 35, can respond to and profit from systematic training in self-help skills.

The moderately retarded group presents a less complicated neuropathological picture and fewer additional handicaps than the profoundly and severely retarded groups. Language and speech show capabilities of being "developed" and potentialities for motor behavior approach normal. Self-help skills and social awareness can be taught to this group with organized formal programs of systematic training.

The mildly retarded make up the largest group among the mentally retarded—possibly as many as 85 per cent of all retardates. According to Stevens:

> They are usually slow in development in walking, talking, feeding themselves, and toilet training . . . handicapping conditions appear in a frequency higher than in the average general population. Motor development is relatively normal. Eye-hand coordination is somewhat retarded below normal expectancy. (p. 5)[2]

Stevens suggests that carefully structured educational programs may help in the development of social and communication skills:

> The mildly mentally retarded can also profit from systematic training in arts and crafts and arithmetic at the elementary education level. They

---

[1] From Stevens and Heber, *Mental retardation: A review of research.* Copyright © 1964 University of Chicago Press.

are incapable of completing secondary school requirements although many can participate in a special class program located in a secondary school. (p. 5)[2]

A system of I.Q. classification similar to the above system has been used in educational circles. It includes the "custodial class" of retardates (I.Q. below 25), the trainable retardates (I.Q. between 25 and 50) and the educable retardates with I.Q.'s of 50 to about 75 (Kolburne, 1965).

Before considering language and speech, it would be relevant to consider first some of the characteristics of the mentally retarded which speech and language specialists see as being related to the problem of language behavior development. Schlanger (1963) has listed the characteristics which he considers important in this regard. Schlanger notes that besides being retarded in the linguistic functions of "generalizing, associating, discriminating and manipulating verbal concepts," the mentally retarded have the following characteristics:

1. Poor auditory retention span (auditory memory).
2. Short attention span developed through negative training and/or inherent in the biological mechanism.
3. Linguistic ability deficient as demonstrated by poor grammar and minimal content.
4. Perseveration in oral expression.
5. Inability to transfer meanings.
6. Absence of self-criticisms.
7. Poor evaluation and organization of perceptual clues.
8. Frustration in communication activities leading to withdrawal and lowered thresholds of frustration.

Any one of the above or their combination could result in delayed language behavior development. As Schlanger views it, the multiple possibilities for "noise" in the expressive and receptive communication processes of the mentally retarded alone can cause language problems, not to mention their "inner language" retardation also.

THE ASSESSMENT OF RETARDED
LANGUAGE DEVELOPMENT

Schiefelbusch (1963) has defined delayed language and speech as a "marked deviation from the anticipated stages" of speech development. Perhaps a more comprehensive view is afforded by McCarthy's (1964b) threefold categorization. McCarthy suggests that:

...three languages must be acquired by a minimally sophisticated language user: receptive language, inner language, and expressive lan-

---

[2] *Ibid.*

guage. Receptive linguistic ability can be defined as the facility with which linguistic symbols are comprehended. Inner linguistic ability can be defined as the facility with which ideas can be expressed by linguistic symbols. (p. 3)

Delayed language development represents a clinical judgment based on multiplicity test scores and observational data. In terms of the above considerations, language retardation might be the result of deficiency in any one of the linguistic areas designated as receptive, inner, or expressive linguistic ability. With the mentally retarded, however, delayed language and speech are most likely to be the result of an overall deficiency in all three areas, though one may be less deficient than the others.

The most objective way at present of diagnosing delayed speech and language is by means of available standardized tests which tap the three linguistic abilities from various angles. The Stanford-Binet I.Q. is, from this point of view, a composite score reflecting verbal comprehension (receptive linguistic ability), verbal problem-solving ability (inner linguistic ability), and fluency (expressive linguistic ability). The same is true of the WISC total score I.Q., but the performance scale subscore is probably more a test of receptive and inner linguistic than expressive ability. Both the Ammons Full-Range Picture Vocabulary Test and the Peabody Picture Vocabulary Test are fairly good measures of receptive and inner linguistic ability as they require little expressive ability aside from pointing. Although only in experimental form, the Illinois Test of Psycholinguistic Ability tests the communication channels of auditory or visual stimuli and motor or vocal responses. The ITPA also tests inner linguistic ability by means of memory items.

Delayed speech and language can be operationally defined with reference to all the tests mentioned above. The least ambiguous definitions would probably be in terms of the nonintelligence tests since they are most purely measures of linguistic ability. According to the Ammons, Peabody, or ITPA, language and speech delay would refer to total performance which, when converted to age norms, showed the individual to be deviating markedly from his age group. Still, a clinical judgment is necessary. However, in most cases of mental retardation, there seems to be a significant overall deficiency in the three linguistic abilities. The limited research suggests that inner linguistic ability may be the most limited of the mental retardate's linguistic skills.

LEARNING IN THE MENTALLY RETARDED AND ITS RELATIONSHIP TO LANGUAGE AND SPEECH DELAY

The experimental literature in the area of learning in the mentally retarded is neither very complete nor consistent. Conflicting results which show the retardate as better than, equal to, or worse than his normal counterpart, are at least in part a reflection of differing experimental tasks, procedures, designs, and samples. Nonetheless, we must attempt to evaluate the importance of these studies for understanding language and speech delay in the mentally retarded.

Denny's (1964) excellent paper discusses in detail the available research with the mentally retarded in the areas of both classical and instrumental learning. Under instrumental learning, Denny discusses operant learning, maze learning, discrimination learning, complex instrumental learning, rote learning, as well as verbal learning. Denny also discusses performance research in regard to the areas of motor skills, reaction time, and basal skin conductance.

In the summary of his review, Denny makes a few concise statements concerning both the deficits and relative strengths of the mentally retarded as compared to normal individuals. In regard to the "performance deficits" of the mentally retarded, the author makes the following observations:

1. An inhibition deficit is manifested by increased resistance to extinction in classical conditioning, difficulty in discrimination learning (including differential conditioning) and special susceptibility to disinhibition or distraction.
2. A defect in complex learning is exhibited in poor performance on learning set, delayed reaction, and double alternation.
3. Difficulty in verbal learning is reflected in poor performance in verbal rote learning and abstraction tasks.
4. A lack of verbal control of the motor sphere is congruent with poor semantic conditioning, difficulty in following verbal instructions, ease of learning and lack of verbalization in discrimination reversal, possibly with poor performance on a shielded usage, and possibly with the ease of conditioning finger withdrawal. (pp. 135–36)[3]

Denny also comments in regard to the positive side of the mental retardate's performance:

1. When matched on CA with normals, retardates do very poorly at the onset on motor skill tasks but with continued practice show a rapid rate of improvement and, if the task is not too difficult, may even catch up with normals (can learn if properly motivated or make the required responses).
2. In rote learning, if familiar nonverbal material is used, an association seems to be established as quickly and retained about as well as in the normals, at least for noninstitutionalized subjects.
3. There is little evidence of appreciable retention deficit in any performance area.

---

[3] *Ibid.*

4. The retarded can learn to use verbal mediators when specifically trained to do so. (p. 137)[4]

Denny concludes his article by noting that "the outlook for the mentally retarded is surprisingly optimistic—at least theoretically." Denny also suggests that it "should be possible to develop appropriate motivational procedures and special training techniques to overcome an appreciable portion of the retardates' difficulties, at least to the extent that they relate to the closely connected deficits in incidental learning, attention, and verbal control." More specifically, Denny comments that "these defects might be amenable to correction by (1) long-term training to attend or orient to stimuli, especially verbal stimuli, and (2) motivating the retarded children sufficiently and building in what they failed to learn incidentally during the early years, as, for example, with specially designed and programmed teaching machines." (p. 137)

Before considering the implications of the previous discussion for language and speech delay, it should be noted that the more recent research on learning seems to support firmly Denny's conclusions. For example, Prelun (1966) in his study of paired associate learning with meaningful and nonsense verbal stimuli, found public school retardates to be slower in acquisition than the normals. Such a finding offers support for the inhibition deficit hypothesis suggested by Denny. The research in overlearning and retention by Lance (1966) and Vergason (1964) showing slower acquisition with retardates lends additional support to this inhibition deficit hypothesis. Lance and Vergason also found no appreciable short-term retention deficit in retardates, with adequate overlearning. Rossi (1963) and Stedman's (1963) findings that retardates cluster less in recall of verbal stimulus also underlines Denny's conclusion that the mentally retarded are deficient in verbal learning ability. Milgram and Furth's (1963) findings, that retardates do more poorly than normals in applying an acquired language concept, give still further support to Denny's conclusions regarding complex behavior and verbal learning deficiencies.

What then seem to be the implications of these learning characteristics for the interpretation and training of the mentally retarded's delayed speech and language? It seems obvious that the inhibition deficit of the retarded is most relevant to delayed language and speech. This inhibition deficit slows down all learning in the retarded because it prevents him from readily concentrating his responses to a specific task or stimulus dimension as the normal individual does. In regard to speech development, the retardate's poor attending ability makes him unable to inhibit

---

[4] *Ibid.*

his responding to the "noise" stimuli in the verbal learning situation. The retardate's attention or orienting responses are thus more *elicited* than emitted, in comparison with normals. When motivated to do so, the normal child can direct his attention to specific stimuli. In the mentally retarded, such selective orientation responding has to be taught to be readily acquired. It does not seem to be learned incidentally as with normal children. Without specific listening training, the mentally retarded tend to respond randomly to all impinging auditory stimuli even when directed to listen for specific kinds of sounds.

In view of the fact that attention is a necessary condition for learning any discrimination, verbal or otherwise, the delayed acquisition of speech and language of the retardate seems to be a direct function of the inhibition deficit. Learning speech and language requires the acquisition of many fine discriminations among external stimuli, and the retardate simply learns these more slowly than does the normal individual.

The fact that the retarded show slower acquisition of verbal responses and no retention deficit with sufficient overlearning suggests that the failure of treatment attempts with delayed language and speech is a function of the techniques rather than the subjects. More specifically it seems that a highly structured learning situation is required with much opportunity for overlearning. The learning tasks should be simple enough to provide a great deal of success as compared to failure, since more incentives are required to sustain the slower acquisition of the retardate. Insufficient overlearning, too much failure, or insufficient motivation rather than I.Q. may explain the negative results obtained in many language and speech remediation studies with the mentally retarded. In any case, increased optimism is in order regarding treatment of the retardate's speech and language handicaps. As the next section of his chapter will try to show, successful treatment techniques are available and are presently in use.

THE TREATMENT OF LANGUAGE AND SPEECH DELAY

The rather substantial literature on the treatment of language and speech delay in the mentally retarded has been very comprehensively reviewed by McCarthy (1964b). In the first part of his review, McCarthy provides a convenient summary of the research on mentally retarded language under the three headings of receptive, inner, and expressive linguistic ability:

RECEPTIVE LINGUISTIC ABILITY

The bulk of the research on receptive language ability in the retarded is devoted to sensory function, chiefly auditory. Most studies of learning impairment have been done on institutionalized retardates and estimates of hearing impairment have ranged from 9 to 34 per cent of the samples studied. The high incidence has been credited to the sterile atmosphere of institutions; to the possibility of brain-injury in many retardates; and more recently (and convincingly) to the lack of training for audition among many institutionalized retardates. Few studies were located concerning either retardates or the more central aspects of receptive language (e.g., auditory perception). Further, there appears to be little recent research interest in either the peripheral or central aspects of visual receptive language. (p. 6)

INNER LINGUISTIC ABILITY

Studies were reviewed which appeared to be related to the "inner language" of the retarded. Generally, verbal ability appears to be related to MA; retarded children are uniformly poorer than mentally normal children in linguistic ability (except in "paired-associative studies"); and certain techniques, such as the use of verbal mediators and practice in associative clustering, appear to be useful devices for improving the inner linguistic ability of the retarded. One cannot read these studies without developing a conviction that there is a strong, perhaps causal, relationship between language—especially inner language—and intelligence; yet, there is a substantial area of uniqueness. This point was made convincing by Furth (1963) who clearly distinguished between Luria's "verbal control of behavior" and what Furth described as "conceptual control of behavior." (p. 8)

EXPRESSIVE LINGUISTIC ABILITY

The literature on expressive language ability in the retarded has been concerned chiefly with the evaluation of speech skills. Retarded children appear to develop these skills in the same sequence as nonretarded children, but at a slower pace. Factors such as etiology, intelligence, and effects of environment must be taken into account when considering the speech defects of the retarded. Generally, the familial, educable, community child seems to have the lowest percentage of defects among the retarded population. The importance of oral language for institutionalized retardates was stressed. The influence of environment on expressive linguistic ability has been demonstrated in studies by Sievers and Essa (1961) and Blessing (1964). The "speaker-listener" studies by Siegel (1963) and Siegel and Harkins (1963) are promising because of their methodological and theoretical continuity; additionally, they focus on the important communicative process about which surprisingly little is known. Copeland's study on delayed feedback appears to suggest possibilities for increasing verbal output. For this reason alone, the present writer would attach significance to further inquiry along this line.

The area of expressive linguistic ability in the retarded appears to be in great need of further research; and, judging from present studies, one in which such an effort would be rewarding. (pp. 9–10)

McCarthy points out that since 1955 there has been a gradual decrease in emphasis on speech therapy techniques with the mentally retarded in practice and in the literature. Articulation therapy has been losing ground as "the" approach to the linguistic problems of the retardate. To take its place, a number of language and speech development procedures have been developed. In practice, speech therapy is still used with retardates, but only as a supplementary procedure for special cases. Thus specialists in the fields dealing with the treatment of language and speech delay have come to recognize the retardates' linguistic or language deficit as the more fundamental problem than the phonetic deficit.

Before looking at the relatively few experimental studies of language development methods, note should be taken of Mecham's (1955) experimental study on speech therapy with the mentally retarded. Mecham reported a quantitatively evaluated study of the effectiveness of speech therapy using control groups. However, the significant positive results on tests of articulation, auditory digest span, auditory discrimination, and oral language development that Mecham found are not necessarily valid. Since subjects were chosen for the treatment group because of "need," there is the possibility that the results are in part attributable to a selection-treatment interaction effect. Depending on one's vested interests and scientific sophistication, Mecham's study may be considered as at least some "proof" of the validity of speech therapy with the retarded. The effectiveness of speech therapy is still scientifically undemonstrated with low I.Q. retardates (below I.Q. of 40). In Mecham's study, the treatment group had a mean I.Q. of 67.7.

An experimental study of the effectiveness of language and speech development programs was reported by Kolstoe (1958). After five and one-half months of language training with fifteen institutionalized mongoloid children (mean I.Q. of 24), the treatment group showed a significantly smaller decrease in Kuhlmann I.Q. scores than the controls (matched on MA). There were also significant increases in subtest scores on the Illinois Language Facility Test, for labeling of pictures, labeling of mutilated pictures, object association and gestural sequential matching. Kolstoe also reported that the higher I.Q. children seem to profit more from training. The decrease in mean I.Q. found in both groups may have been the result of the unequal variabilities of the norms for different age levels in the ratio I.Q.'s used by Kolstoe.

Another experimental evaluation of the language development approach was reported by Johnson, Capobianco, and Miller (1960). This study, however, reported no significant improvement in the treatment group after one year of language training. Language proficiency in this study was measured with the Illinois Test of Language Ability (ITLA). A significant criticism is that its measuring instrument, the ITLA, may be much too insensitive for testing the language ability of a trainable retarded child. The ITLA was standardized on an unrepresentative sample of above average children (no I.Q. below 90). The item selection based on this sample thus resulted in high difficulty items unsuitable for measuring the linguistic ability of the rather profoundly retarded. The norms, of course, would also tend to underestimate the actual progress which may have been made. Thus progress may have occurred in this study but the instrument used to measure it may have had too high a "floor" to reflect it.

The third study which will be discussed is that done by Smith (1962). The results of this experiment were statistically significant and positive. Smith worked with educable retardates in small groups of eight for forty-five minutes a session, three times a week for three months. Smith's treatment group showed an average gain of seven months in language age over the control group as measured by the Illinois Test of Psycholinguistic Ability (ITPA). Mean subtest language gains for the treatment group ranged from three months to thirteen months. These results seem very significant, pragmatically speaking, in that they show that language training can accelerate language development quite a bit with the educable retarded. It should also be noted that Smith also gives a well detailed description of his group language techniques.

The last study to be considered here is that by Bradley, Maurer, and Hindziak (1966). These researchers did a rather thorough study from a measurement standpoint in evaluating the combined effect of both milieu therapy and language training. The ITPA and eight other psychological and educational tests were used in this pre-post design, including the WISC. Using the various subtest and total scores, Bradley *et al.* found seventeen of thirty-eight comparisons of control-experimental groups gain score means to be positive and significant at greater than the .05 level. There were significant differences on six of the subtest scores of the ITPA as well as on the WISC verbal scale I.Q. The treatment subjects showed a mean WISC total I.Q. score gain of 14.33 while the controls gained only 1.80 points.

These results overall seem almost phenomenal considering the language training and milieu therapy program lasted only seven months and the group mean I.Q. for the experimental and controls was reported as 37 on the Stanford-Binet. However, the results must not be interpreted as showing the effectiveness of the language training program alone. The results could be attributed to either the milieu therapy or language training or to the interaction of the two. Still, the results taken together with those reported by Kolstoe (1958) and Smith (1962) suggest that language training or developmental langauge approaches have more validity than the speech-therapy approach. The raising of I.Q.'s through language training seems to be a particularly promising approach to the treatment of mental retardation.

CONCLUDING COMMENTS

In this final section, some of the issues and trends as well as some suggestions for future research will be noted briefly in relation to what has already been discussed.

In terms of methodology, speech and language delay research studies were until only recently, scientifically weak. Approximately 75 per cent of all the studies in the literature have made no use of quantification or control group design. Procedures followed during "therapy" and measurement methods are often inadequately described. For example, Johnson, Capobianco, and Miller (1960) talk about matching for mental age but say nothing about which intelligence test was used. They also took no measure of I.Q. in the post-treatment measurement phase of the study, when easily such a procedure might have yielded positive results. As another example of poor methodology, the Bradley, Maurer, and Hindziak (1966) study might be noted. Despite the extensive measurements, no attempt was made to use a control group design which would have allowed them to evaluate the relative effectiveness of milieu and language therapy separately and in their possible interaction. The tendency in these studies is clearly an "applied science" approach which yields unclear results. Future research needs to concentrate more on possible important parameters in language-training programs such as motivation levels, social versus material rewards, mixed versus homogeneous I.Q. groups, etc. Various techniques of teaching auditory discrimination and memory must be compared with different I.Q. and age groups of retardates.

Another aspect of methodology which seems very important is that of developing reliable and valid instruments to measure the linguistic ability in the retarded. For instance, there is very limited evidence of the reliability of the Illinois Test of Psycholinguistic Ability when used with the lower-grade mentally retarded. The ITPA as Werner, Barrett and Semmel (1966) have noted was developed on a normal I.Q. range standardization sample. Thus, its items probably do not have sufficient floor to test improvement with the lower I.Q. range. The ITPA subscales have fairly low reliabilities and would probably benefit by adding a few easier items selected using a mentally retarded sample. In regard to the ITPA total scale language age as used by Smith (1962) to measure overall linguistic improvement, it should be noted that this score as derived according to the manual reflects differential weighting which was not taken into account by the test constructors (Werner *et al.*). Because there are unequal variabilities for subscale scores at different ages, the composite score differentially weights the nine subscales depending on the different age levels for which it is computed. One hopes such measurement deficiency will be corrected in the coming revision of the ITPA. The above considerations are highly important because the ITPA is the most popular instrument in the measurement of linguistic ability. There is a rather urgent need therefore for more sophisticated test construction aimed at measuring both normal and deficient language ability. One good instrument is not sufficient for research or diagnostic purposes.

Last but not least, a few additional comments are in order regarding the pessimism which tends still to hang on with regard to the speech and language delay of the retarded. In view of the experimental research on treatment possibilities and the learning characteristics of the mentally subnormal, a new and more intensive effort than ever before is called for in the area of delayed speech and language. Studies cited indicate that the mentally retarded are probably most educable with respect to language development, despite their inhibition deficit. It is suggested that they might also be most motivated in this particular sphere of activity. It has been shown that a creative and systematic approach to language development can increase communicative ability and consequently help raise the I.Q. of the mentally retarded (within limits) and probably with more efficiency than most other educational approaches.

The model of language and speech development presented earlier suggests that spoken language should be taught only after echolalic behavior has evolved. Potentially, there is much that might be attempted in terms of the operant conditioning paradigm. Considerable success has been reported in the modification of behavior in mental retardates by means of operant procedures. Most of these studies, however, have dealt with the abatement of undesirable behavior or the institution of self-help skills such as feeding, grooming, and toileting among the severely and profoundly retarded. Thus far, it would appear that only limited use has been made of operant conditioning techniques in the area of language behavior.

REFERENCES

Blessing, K. R. An investigation of a psycholinguistic deficit in educable mentally retarded children: Detection, remediation, and selected variables. Doctoral dissertation, University of Wisconsin. *University Microfilms,* 1964, *25,* 2372–73.

Bradley, B. H., Maurer, R., and Hindziak, M. A study of the effectiveness of milieu therapy and language training for the mentally retarded. *Exceptional Children,* 1966, *33,* 143–50.

Denny, M. R. Research in learning and performance. In H. A. Stevens and R. Heber (Eds.), *Mental retardation: A review of research.* Chicago: University of Chicago Press, 1964.

Furth, H. G. Conceptual discovery and control on a pictorial part-whole task as a function of age, intelligence, and language. *Journal of Educational Psychology,* 1963, *54,* 191–96.

Heber, R. (Ed.) A manual on terminology and classification in mental retardation. *Monograph Supplement of the American Journal of Mental Deficiency,* 1958, *64,* No. 2.

Johnson, G. O., Capobianco, R. J., and Miller, D. Y. Speech and language development of a group of mentally deficient children enrolled in a training program. *Exceptional Children,* 1960, *27,* 72–77.

Kolburne, L. L. *Effective education for the mentally retarded child.* New York: Vantage Press, 1965.

Kolstoe, O. P. Language training for low-grade Mongoloid children. *American Journal of Mental Deficiency,* 1958, *63,*17–30.

Lance, W. D. Effects of meaningfulness and overlearning on retention in normal and retarded adolescents. *American Journal of Mental Deficiency,* 1966, *70,* 270–75.

McCarthy, D. *Language development and language disorders.* Yellow Springs, Ohio: Antioch University Press, 1960.

McCarthy, J. J. The importance of linguistic ability in the mentally retarded. *Mental Retardation,* 1964, *2,* 90–96. (a)

McCarthy, J. J. Research on the linguistic problems of the mentally retarded. *Mental Retardation Abstracts,* 1964, *1,* 3–27. (b)

Mecham, M. J. The development and application of procedures for measuring speech improvement in mentally defective children. *American Journal of Mental Deficiency,* 1955, *60,* 301–60.

Milgram, N. A. and Furth, H. G. The influence of language on concept formation in the educable mentally retarded child. *American Journal of Mental Deficiency,* 1963, *67,* 733–39.

Prelun, H. J. Associative learning in retarded and normal children as a function of task difficulty and meaningfulness. *American Journal of Mental Deficiency,* 1966, *70,* 860–65.

Rossi, E. L. Associative clustering in normal and retarded children. *American Journal of Mental Deficiency,* 1963, *67,* 691–99.

Schiefelbusch, R. L. The development of communication skills. In R. L. Schiefelbusch and J. O. Smith (Eds.), *Research planning conference in speech and hearing for mentally retarded children.* Lawrence: University of Kansas Press, 1963.

Schlanger, B. B. Issues for speech and language training of the mentally retarded. In R. L. Schiefelbusch and J. O. Smith (Eds.), *Research planning conference in speech and hearing for mentally retarded children.* Lawrence: University of Kansas Press, 1963.

Siegel, G. M. Verbal behavior of retarded children with preinstructed adults. *Journal of Speech and Hearing Disorders Monograph Supplement,* 1963, *10,* 47–53.

Siegel, G. M. and Harkins, J. P. Verbal behavior of adults in two conditions with institutionalized retarded children. *Journal of Speech and Hearing Disorders Monograph Supplement,* 1963, *10,* 39–46.

Sievers, D. J. and Essa, S. H. Language development in institutionalized and community mentally retarded children. *American Journal of Mental Deficiency,* 1961, *66,* 413–20.

Smith, J. O. Group language development for educable mental retardates. *Exceptional Children,* 1962, *29,* 95–101.

Smith, M. An investigation of the development of the sentence and the extent of vocabulary in young children. *University of Iowa Studies in Child Welfare,* 1926, No. 5.

Stedman, D. J. Associated clustering of semantic categories in normal and retarded subjects. *American Journal of Mental Deficiency,* 1963, *67,* 700–704.

Stevens, H. A. Overview. In H. A. Stevens and R. Heber (Eds.), *Mental retardation: A review of research.* Chicago: University of Chicago Press, 1964.

Van Riper, C. *Speech correction: Principles and methods.* Englewood Cliffs, N. J.: Prentice-Hall, 1963.

Vergason, G. A. Retention in retarded and normal subjects as a function of original training. *American Journal of Mental Deficiency,* 1964, *68,* 623–29.

Werner, P., Barrett, L., and Semmel, M. A critical evaluation of the Illinois Test of Psycholinguistic Ability. *Exceptional Children,* 1966, *33,* 373–79.

Wood, N. E. *Delayed speech and language development.* Englewood Cliffs, N. J.: Prentice-Hall, 1964.

CHAPTER 6

LANGUAGE BEHAVIOR
IN AUTISM

Autism is a psychotic disorder of childhood and forms part of the psychopathology of schizophrenia. Berkowitz (1960) designated two categories of childhood schizophrenia: autism and pathological symbiosis. The latter form of emotional disturbance is characterized by an initial development of communication patterns. The source of difficulty comes from a mother-child relationship of such a degree of closeness that the two function as one. As Wood (1960) stated: "It is as if the child has not yet been born." (p. 44) There is no gradual increase of independence from one another. This relationship is disrupted as the child develops psychosexually and the enforced intimacy with the mother provokes a break which leaves the child on his own for the first time. The problem is that he has not developed the ability to become independent and build up defenses for self-protection because the mother has done everything. Anything the child has done has been for her. Consequently, the child cannot cope with the situation and reacts violently in one of two ways: (1) he panics and goes into periods of self-inflicted injury, or (2) there is a revulsion of the mother with accompanying sadistic hostility which the mother cannot overcome. If she attempts to reestablish the relationship, the child becomes panicky, but if she does not try to reestablish the relationship, he withdraws even more. Both of these reactions are accompanied by elective mutism. The play behavior of such children reveals the inability to alter the dependence on the mother as the child imitates all that she does. Speech and language generally reappear at a later period either gradually, when the child goes through the entire developmental sequence, or suddenly, when the child begins speaking at the level he ceased speaking.

The autistic child is unable to establish contact and to relate to people. He is capable of understanding and using language, but often employs language for purposes of concealment rather than communication. For example, he may possess a vocabulary that is advanced in comparison with that of a normal child. He uses this development, however, to produce bizarre noises, talk in a repetitious fashion to himself, to an object such as a television set or to a nonexistent person. In addition to language abnormality, such a child often has an obsessional preference for relationships with objects and fragments of things that he has destroyed. Consequently he fails to develop an adequate self-concept and ego-strength. He cannot endure change in his environment and becomes extremely difficult to manage if sameness is not maintained.

Kanner (1943) first described the syndrome which he called "early infantile autism." He applied this term originally to children who exhibit "an inability to relate themselves to people and to situations from the beginning of life." (p. 217) Later he extended the concept of autism to include children who seemed to have experienced normal development for the first year and a half of life, only to undergo at this point a waning of interest in normal activities, severe withdrawal of affect, arrested social development, and marked disturbances of language and communication. Among the criteria which Kanner (1956) considered most significant for autism were (1) "An extreme self-isolation, or an inability to relate themselves in the ordinary way to people or situations from early in life"; and (2) "An obsessive insistence on the maintenance of sameness." The failure to react normally to the sound of the human voice, as well as to other familiar sounds in his environment, may create an erroneous impression of mental retardation or severe impairment of hearing. Says Eisenson (1963), "Many autistic children have histories of being quiet from birth. Parents often report little crying and almost a complete absence of sound play." (p. 21)

Cunningham and Dixon (1961) describe some of the characteristics of language in autistic children:

> There may be no speech at all. In those who do speak, there is often a failure to use language to convey meaning to others. There is a tendency to repeat the same phrases, rather than to construct original remarks. Immediate echolalia may be present, or delayed echolalia. Affirmation is indicated by the repetition of a question. It takes many years before such a child can use the word "yes." Reversal of pronouns occurs. Kanner's explanation of this phenomenon is worth quoting: "The absence of spontaneous sentence formation and the echolalia type of reproduction give rise to a peculiar grammatical phenomenon. Personal pronouns are repeated just as heard, with no change to suit the altered situation. The child, once told by his mother: 'Now I will give you your milk,' expresses the desire for milk in exactly the same words. Consequently he comes to

speak of himself always as 'you,' and of the person addressed as 'I.' "
(pp. 193–94)

The autistic child may invent his own words for various objects and situations, or he may use conventional words in such an idiosyncratic fashion that he is unintelligible to others. A parent may acquire a limited capacity for "understanding" some of the autistic child's verbal responses by carefully noting the recurrent situations in which his "words" are used.

On occasion, says Eisenson, one may be able to understand the bizarre language of autistic children:

> Their responses may be delayed for long periods and be produced with either absence or inappropriateness of affect. The result is that one may be unable to make the association between the presented situation and the elicited response. If, for example, the autistic child is presented with a ball, a crayon, and a pegboard, he may seem to ignore all the objects. Later, perhaps, when involved in another activity, he may return to the ball and even name it. Anticipation of this form of delayed response may provide an interpretation for the bizarre language behavior. (pp. 21–22)[1]

The nonverbal behavior of the autistic child also shows considerable disturbance. For instance, the child may make contorted faces, flop his arms, waggle his fingers, or cover his head. Often his face is masklike and expressionless.

Family life is usually of a cold, formal type and the child has received very little fondling, cuddling, or warm and genuine expressions of parental affection. The mother's behavior is mechanical and does not convey love. When a child with early autism is brought to the clinic, his parents readily volunteer the opinion that he is severely retarded and should therefore "be put away." It is a rather frequent finding that the parents of autistic children are often intelligent, successful people in better-than-average income circumstances, but who seem to be obsessively preoccupied with abstractions of a scientific, literary, philosophical, or artistic nature.

FORMAL CHARACTERISTICS OF AUTISTIC LANGUAGE

Pronovost (1961) conducted a descriptive study of the speech and language comprehension of twelve autistic children who were observed over a period of two years in a residential setting. The author noted in his introduction a few of the problems encountered in dealing with autistic children: "The highly variable behavior of the autistic children precluded

---

[1] From J. Eisenson, *Journal of Pediatrics*, 1963, *62*, 20–24; The C. V. Mosby Company, St. Louis.

the use of formal testing procedures. In addition, no behavior rating scales that could appropriately describe the details of the behavior of autistic children were available." (p. 228) Finding it impossible to devise a situation which would dependably elicit speech from his autistic patients, Pronovost obtained speech samples from the tape recordings of regular therapy sessions. These samples were then subjected to analysis in order to obtain descriptions of the children's speech.

Among the five children on whom Pronovost reported briefly, there was a wide range of inter- and intra-subject variation in language behavior: babbling, echolalia, perseverative repetition of unidentifiable sounds, and rote repetition of number sequences, rhymes, or scraps of song. On the other hand, at least one of the children was able to produce complete sentences with well-articulated sound patterns, but in sentences that were totally irrelevant to the situation.

As part of his pilot study, Pronovost developed a rating scale to take the place of standard tests of linguistic comprehension which, for obvious reasons, could not be used with these children. According to the author, "The items of the scale are questions which may be answered by observation of the children and were designed to explore certain aspects of auditory discrimination of environmental sounds, response to gestures, and response to music, as well as to various aspects of spoken language." (p. 230) Observations were supplied by the three therapists who were in daily contact with the children. Pronovost's rating scale follows:

TENTATIVE SCALE FOR RATING CERTAIN ASPECTS OF LANGUAGE[2] COMPREHENSION IN AUTISTIC CHILDREN

INSTRUCTIONS—*Observe the child in your contacts with him. Check each item for which you can answer "yes." Make more than one observation so that you have some confidence in your answer.*

I *Discrimination of sounds:* Can the child recognize any of the following specific environmental sounds?

1. Lunch bell	6. Noises of toys
2. Telephone	7. Clapping
3. Whistling	8. Fire or police siren
4. Dog barking	9. Car approaching
5. Radio static	10. Car horn

II *Awareness and comprehension of spoken language of others:*
    11. Does the child show an awareness that someone is speaking?
    12. Can the child distinguish the speaking voices of specific adults?
    13. Can the child distinguish the voices of specific children?

---

[2] Reprinted with permission, from W. Pronovost, The speech behavior and language comprehension of autistic children, in *Journal of Chronic Diseases,* 1961, *13,* 228–33, Pergamon Press.

14. Does the child recognize differences in the emotional tone of the speaking voice?
15. Does the child recognize his own name when called?
16. Does the child recognize the names of specific adults or children?
17. Does the child recognize the names of actual objects?
18. Does the child recognize the names of actual pictures?
19. Does the child recognize verbs as walk, run, jump, etc.?
20. Does the child recognize the names of colors?
21. Does the child understand words which express spatial relationships such as up—down, in—out, etc.?
22. Does the child understand words which express time relationships such as early, late, etc.?
23. Does the child understand number concepts?
24. Does the child understand simple phrases and sentences where comprehension of more than one key word is required?
25. Does the child follow verbal suggestions?
26. Does the child obey verbal commands?
27. Will the child listen to a story told by an adult?
28. Will the child listen to a story read aloud by an adult?
29. Does the child recognize differences in a story retold incorrectly?
30. Does the child anticipate parts of the story?

III *Awareness and comprehension of certain aspects of visual language:*
31. Does the child respond to directions given by gestures?
32. Does the child recognize different geometric forms?
33. Does the child recognize different letters?
34. Does the child recognize different written numbers?
35. Does the child recognize different pictures?
36. Can the child recognize printed words which are the names of objects or people?
37. Can the child recognize printed words that name actions?
38. Can the child recognize abstract words?
39. Can the child read phrases?
40. Can the child read sentences?

IV *Response to music:*
41. Does the child recognize music?
42. Does the child distinguish between the singing voice and the speaking voice?
43. Does the child distinguish between vocal and instrumental music?
44. Does the child distinguish different instruments?
45. Does the child distinguish between live and recorded music?
46. Will the child watch television or movies?
47. Can the child recognize specific melodies?
48. Can the child distinguish different rhythms?
49. Does the child react differently to familiar as opposed to unfamiliar tunes?

50. Will the child listen to music for a longer period than story-
telling?
51. Will the child perform actions suggested by the lyrics of a song?

On the basis of information supplied by the therapists using the
rating scale, Pronovost offers the following conclusions:

> The observed autistic children exhibited definite ability in certain
> aspects of language comprehension. They were able to discriminate en-
> vironmental sounds and voices of adults. They were able to recognize
> the names of people, objects and actions. However, comprehension of
> abstract or complex language expressed in sentences was less noticeable.
> Response to written language was extremely limited, except in the case
> of one child who had developed the ability to read words by matching
> them with pictures. This child had limited response to environmental
> sounds and none to music. All other children exhibited considerable
> interest in and response to musical sounds. (pp. 231–32)[3]

Pronovost identified his project as a pilot study; and there is no particular point in conducting a detailed criticism of its many shortcomings
and weaknesses—the lack of adequate identifiying information on his
autistic patients, the absence of obvious controls, the failure to impose
reliability checks on his raters, the lack of quantification, etc. In these
respects, Pronovost's study is typical of many descriptive studies in the
clinical area which originate, one strongly suspects, in the ready and convenient access of the investigator to a particular group. Unfortunately,
even when they are properly conceived and executed, they are often no
better than suggestive; at worst, they can be definitely misleading.

Cunningham and Dixon (1961) reported a study of the language
behavior of a single autistic boy (aged seven years) in a standard situation
like that employed by McCarthy (1930) and Sampson (1945) in their
studies of language development in normal children. As Wolff and Chess
(1965) have stated:

> Both Sampson and McCarthy found that quantitative and qualitative
> aspects of language were closely related. As children grow older they
> produce more words, more different words and longer utterances, and
> their language changes in quality such as the completeness of sentences
> and the parts of speech used. Adopting Piaget's (1959) functional class-
> ification of language into egocentric and socialized, McCarthy found that
> quantitative changes are closely related to functional changes. Both
> authors conclude that the total number of words uttered by a normal
> child in a standard situation is a good index of his general level of lan-
> guage development. It is interesting to note Sampson's observation that
> strong feeling often increased the motivation of normal children to com-

---

[3] *Ibid.*

TABLE 5

COMPARISON OF AUTISTIC CHILD AND NORMS FROM McCARTHY STUDY

(After Cunningham and Dixon, 1961)

	McCarthy			Autistic Child			
	24 Months	30 Months	36 Months	1st Four Interviews	2nd Four Interviews	3rd Four Interviews	All 12 Interviews
Length of sentence*	1.8	3.1	3.4	1.9	2.5	3.0	2.4
Variety of words used†	29.1	51.0	62.8	25.8	34.0	43.5	34.4
Percentage of incomplete sentences‡	25.1	18.1	16.2	39.1	33.6	46.1	40.0
Percentage of incomprehensible responses	33.0	11.0	7.0	6.5	8.8	9.1	8.4

*Mean no. of words per response (comprehensible responses only).
†Mean no. of different words used in first 50 responses of each interview.
‡Comprehensible sentences only.

TABLE 6

PERCENTAGES IN VARIOUS CATEGORIES OF FUNCTION*

(After Cunningham and Dixon, 1961)

	McCarthy			Autistic Child			
	24 Months	30 Months	36 Months	1st Four Interviews	2nd Four Interviews	3rd Four Interviews	All 12 Interviews
Egocentric responses	6.5	4.0	3.6	35.0	31.0	21.8	28.3
Emotionally toned responses	18.3	14.2	9.4	24.6	23.4	35.1	27.9
Responses giving information	40.8	57.7	50.9	29.7	31.0	28.5	29.7
Questions	13.9	3.5	13.2	0.0	0.3	0.0	0.1
Answers	16.6	14.6	19.1	7.4	6.6	8.6	7.6

*Comprehensible responses only.

municate, and that this improved their standard of verbal expression.
(p. 29)

Over a period of six months, Cunningham and Dixon collected observations of the language behavior of their autistic child and conducted
qualitative and quantitative analyses of the data in accordance with the
functional classification schema of Piaget. The results presented in Table
5 and Table 6 indicate a markedly lower level of development, despite
the resemblance of the autistic child's language to that of a normal twenty-
four- to thirty-month-old child in certain quantitative respects (length
of utterance, variety of words used, etc.) and in many qualitative respects
(monotony, frequency of incomplete sentences, frequency of use of nouns,
rarity with which questions were asked or information given). Also, egocentric speech appeared much more frequently than is common in the
speech of a normal child of two-and-a-half to three years. The authors
made the concluding observation that their autistic child showed some
progress during the six-month period of the study as gauged by McCarthy's and Sampson's criteria.

Wolff and Chess (1965) conducted a study of language behavior
in schizophrenic children which presents certain innovations and refine-
ments in approach and technique over the preceding studies. Their sample
of 14 children included 12 boys and 2 girls, all of whom were less than
eight years of age. The diagnosis of childhood schizophrenia was based on
the independent judgments of two psychiatrists—and it seems worth noting that this is one of the few studies in the literature in which the authors
give an explicit statement of their selection criteria.

Information on language behavior was collected from two sources:
a series of two or three intensive interviews with the mother of the schizophrenic child, and a direct observation of the child's classrooom behavior
over a period of one and a half hours. According to the authors:

> During the interviews systematic questions were asked in a set order,
> following a protocol, about the child's behavior in all aspects of daily
> living, e.g., sleeping, getting to bed, awakening, dressing, eating, toileting,
> play, reaction to pain, verbalization, awareness of body, reaction to new
> situations, etc. For every item of enquiry the mother was asked to pro-
> vide details of the situations presented to the child and of what the child
> did or said in those situations. Interpretations of possible meaning of
> behavior were not accepted as basic data. Instead, the emphasis was on
> the stimulus presented to the child and his actual response to it, verbal or
> otherwise. (p. 30)

The material gathered in both the history (H) and the observation
(O) sessions was prepared in typescript. Before any analyses of the data
were conducted, however, the children were rank-ordered in severity
of illness, from 1 (most severe) to 14 (most normal). With the exception

of obsessional behavior, which clustered in the middle of the scale and was infrequent at the extremes, all of the behavioral abnormalities showed a regular pattern of variation.

Separate analyses of the (H) and (O) protocols afforded a means of assessing the validity of maternal observations. Also, comparisons were made between the children's rankings on severity of illness and qualitative and quantitative features of their language behavior.

The authors reported significant correlations between (H) and (O) protocols on three verbal categories: total number of words, total number of words corrected for length of protocol, and average length of utterance. In addition, the quantitative aspects mentioned above correlated significantly with clinical status, as designated by rank-order of severity of illness.

With regard to qualitative considerations, Wolff and Chess found that their data best fit a functional classification which included the following categories:

1. *Noncommunicative repetition.* This was described as "speech not apparently directed at another person and serving no evident purpose" (p. 35); included in this category were both immediate repetition (echolalia) and deferred repetition.

2. *Communicative repetition.* This consists of phrases the child has heard someone else use and which he then repeats with the grammatical structure unchanged. The result, according to the interpretation of Wolff and Chess, is that "the child's utterance does not make it clear that he views himself as the subject" (p. 35), thus accounting for such phenomena as the pronominal reversal which Kanner regarded as pathognomonic of autism.

3. *Original, communicative speech.* Despite oddities of syntax and vocabulary, this category includes speech which does not consist of mere repetition of utterances the child has heard someone else use. Included may be instances of metaphorical speech such as that noted by Kanner.

The authors add that all of the children in their sample showed retardation in language development: "Severely ill children were very grossly retarded and the two linguistically most advanced attained to only 75 per cent of the level expected for their age." (p. 39) When quality of utterances is taken into consideration, retardation was even more evident. Wolff and Chess conclude with the following interpretative comments:

> Kanner . . . suggested that affective withdrawal and obsessive insistence on sameness are the primary symptoms of early infantile autism, and that the defects of language and the motor abnormalities are secondary. He also stressed (1946, 1947) the symbolic and metaphorical aspects of the language of autistic children. All the clinical features he described were

present in our children, but in the light of our other findings we evaluate them differently. The unusual use of metaphor and symbolic language, which we found in our least severely ill children, appear to us to be the outcome of a relatively advanced level of language development distorted by repetitive clinging to former modes of expression and to former phrases and ideas, and the inability to attend adequately to external cues and to modify behavior accordingly. Our findings suggest that the basic behavioral disturbance, overshadowing the child's general development and activities to a greater or lesser degree, is the persistence of remnants of repetitive behavior, appropriate to a previous developmental level, or to a previous environmental context to the exclusion of manifestations of initiative and experimentation and of normal responsiveness to changing environmental stimuli.

The findings of these several descriptive studies, as summarized in Table 7, show a kind of consistency that is not often encountered in this area of inquiry. Despite differences in approach and observational methods, Cunningham and Dixon, Pronovost, and Wolff and Chess have succeeded in verifying the reliability of Kanner's pathognomonic signs on autism. We must regard this achievement as an auspicious and significant beginning—but only a beginning. The next step is clearly indicated in the conclusion to the Wolff and Chess report, namely, an attempt at the *interpretation* of the more basic pathological processes which appear to manifest themselves in these aspects of language behavior.

VOCAL PATTERNS IN SCHIZOPHRENIC CHILDREN

The studies reviewed in the preceding section were primarily concerned with gross characteristics of language behavior in autistic children, ab-

TABLE 7

FINDINGS FROM DESCRIPTIVE STUDIES OF AUTISTIC LANGUAGE

Investigator	Linguistic Characteristics Reported
Kanner	Elective mutism, verbal negation, literalness, self-absorbed inaccessibility, echolalia, pronomial reversals, "irrelevancies" due to personal metaphor.
Pronovost	Echolalia, uncommunicative vocalizations, rote repetition, babbling, irrelevancies.
Cunningham & Dixon	Egocentric speech, repetitions, monotony, incomplete sentences, echolalia, diminished use of personal pronouns, incomprehensible responses.
Wolff & Chess	Incommunicative repetition, communicative repetition (including Kanner's "verbal negation," pronomial reversal), metaphorical substitutions.

normalities of syntax and semantic content. We shall now examine the findings of research on some nonlexical aspects of language behavior in schizophrenic children. The first of these studies represents one in a series of investigations on speech patterns in the schizophrenic conducted by Goldfarb and his associates.

In the introduction to their report, the authors (Goldfarb, Braunstein, and Lorge, 1956) expressed dissatisfaction with the instruments available at that time for the objective analysis of speech and voice production, "except for specific articulatory deviations," and cited their justification for selecting instead a speech pathologist to serve as listener-recorder in their study: "In the last analysis, judgments regarding speech rest on a recognition of the hypothetical normal as a referent. It was presumed that the speech expert had had wide experience with normal speech and was capable of reacting to deviations from such normal speech." (p. 545)[4]
permission.

Subjects included 12 schizophrenic children and 6 with "reactive behavior disorders." The median age in each group was slightly over eight years of age. Diagnostic criteria were not stated by the authors.

The primary data for the study consisted of tape recordings of spontaneous utterances, together with observations of the communication behavior of the children in a variety of individual and group settings. Records were phonetically transcribed, then subjected to an intensive analysis by the speech pathologist for purposes of identifying patterns of articulation. It should be noted that the speech expert's examination was a "blind analysis," i.e., made without knowledge of the clinical status of the subject.

The results of the analyses are presented in Table 8. Comparison of the two groups indicates that the schizophrenic children exceeded the children with reactive behavior disorders in every category of speech deviation except voice quality. The authors noted that vocal qualities such as breathiness, hoarseness, nasality, throatiness, etc., do not appear to differentiate the two groups. However, they did note that "a kind of speech flatness" seems to characterize the schizophrenic children. They described their voices as "dull and wooden."

Flatness of voice refers to the fact that the schizophrenic children were not effective in communicating feeling to the listener by means of voice qualities. According to the authors: "Flatness appears to be compounded of insufficiency of volume, pitch, rhythm, stress, and intonation." (p. 550)[5]

---

[4] Copyright, the American Orthopsychiatric Association, Inc., reproduced by permission.

[5] Copyright, the American Orthopsychiatric Association, Inc., reproduced by permission.

TABLE 8

SPEECH DEVIATIONS FROM EXPECTED NORMAL IN SPECIFIED AREAS
OF SIX CHILDREN WITH REACTIVE BEHAVIOR DISORDERS
AND TWELVE CHILDREN WITH CHILDHOOD SCHIZOPHRENIA

(After Goldfarb, Braunstein, and Lorge, 1956)

Deviation in:	Reactive Behavior Disorder	Childhood Schizophrenia
Phonation		
Quality	6	12
Volume	0	9
Pitch	1	9
Duration	1	9
Rhythm	0	8
Intonation	1	8
Articulation	1	9
Facial and body reinforcements	0	12

It is interesting to compare the above account with the "acoustic stereotype" described as a flat voice by Ostwald (1963). The flat voice, according to Ostwald, "is the sound of patients who are listless, resigned, and depressed. No matter how convincingly such patients tell you (in words) that there is nothing wrong with them, their soundmaking says the opposite." (p. 67) Ostwald suggests that such a sound pattern seems to announce paralinguistically the patient's helplessness and dependency. In terms of the physical description, Ostwald says:

> One might think of this configuration as acoustic energy which is smeared out rather evenly across a broad portion of the frequency spectrum. Flatness of the curve denoting this energy portion seems to be the distinguishing characteristic of the acoustic stereotype we are here dealing with. (p. 70)[6]

Examples of the flat voice are given in Figure 4. The common factor which identified the 6 patients whose speech samples provided these curves is depression.

The reason for this discrepancy between these two interpretations of what characterizes a "flat voice" seems to lie in the acoustic dimensions employed by the respective investigators. Ostwald's analysis plots sound intensity against frequency; Goldfarb employs, in addition to volume and pitch, the variables of rhythm, stress, and intonation. On a purely impressionistic basis, one is tempted to say that minimal variation in the

---

[6] From Peter F. Ostwald, *Soundmaking,* 1963. Courtesy of Charles C Thomas, publisher, Springfield, Ill.

FIGURE 4

EXAMPLES OF HALF-OCTAVE BAND MEASUREMENTS OF SOUND FROM SIX
DIFFERENT PSYCHIATRIC PATIENTS

(After Ostwald, 1963)

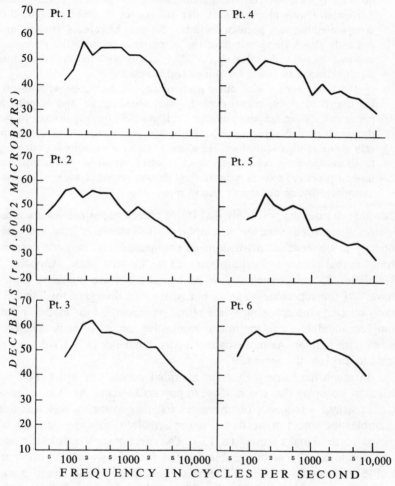

DECIBELS (re 0.0002 MICROBARS)

FREQUENCY IN CYCLES PER SECOND

Courtesy of Charles C Thomas, publisher, Springfield, Ill.

latter three would tend to elicit judgments of flatness, even when peaks
are noted in the middle of the spectrum of sound energy.

Ostwald (1963) has provided a detailed description of an eight-year-
old autistic child, a boy named Bob. Says Ostwald:

> From a soundmaking point of view, the most remarkable thing about
> Bob is his very personal use of spoken language. When he speaks it is
> not with the sentence or word patterns one customarily hears in conver-

sation. He does not ask questions, give replies, render descriptions, or make complaints. Instead, emission of speech sounds appears to be mainly a self-directed activity. Bob's soundmaking seems to be a kind of acoustic game, much like the babbling of babies which has little to do with the sort of communication aiming for outsider participation. Particularly with proper nouns, like the names of other persons, Bob does something very peculiar for a boy his age: he repeats, rhymes, and endlessly shuffles and reshuffles the component sounds (the phonemes and morphemes) of the words. In effect, in this boy's mouth, names lose all significance as labels for things and people.

Bob also tampers with other parts of speech. By incessantly distorting the rhythmicity, intensity, pitch, tone, speed, shape, and orderliness pattern of spoken language he make it impossible for any listener to put the linguistic cues—phonemes, morphemes, and words—into any properly meaningful relationships. He seems to lack the capacity for adhering to those linguistic constraints which control verbal soundmaking, but instead produces sounds because they rhyme, resemble each other onomatopoeically, or are simply fun to mouth. (p. 129)[7]

Ostwald rules out the possibility that Bob's speech abnormalities are a reflection of retarded language development. Bob shows at least a normal capacity to understand instructions or commands; and he even demonstrates verbal precocity in the playing of his favorite game, "alphabet." He mimics TV advertising slogans and jingles ("I use pumolive rapinshave," "I use superblue blade"), but with a fine disregard for linguistic precision (e.g., the dropping of the plural phoneme /z/ in "blades") and complete indifference to the uncommunicative impact of such constructions on his auditor. As in the case of poets, the meter in Bob's discourse fights to displace the argument.

In much the same manner as a skilled double-talk artist, Bob indulges in wordplay that comes close to pseudolanguage. As Ostwald puts it, "He strings a sequence of phonemes together in such a way that this resembles the sound of words but never actually comes close enough to known words to make sense." (p. 130) The effect of such pseudolanguage is to create an almost intolerable conflict for others—an "ambivalent, double bind situation"—in which Bob seems simultaneously to invite and reject communication with his plausible sounding but meaningless utterances.

On the other hand, there are times when Bob seems to experience a sense of frustration from his inability to use language normally. At such times he may go through an insistent, repetitive pattern of soundmaking which involves, as Ostwald calls it, "one of his typical phoneme-salads," (e.g., /aiskob-aiskob-aiskob/) or engage in acoustic outbursts which sug-

---

[7] *Ibid.*

gest a desire to be relieved of some intensely felt internal pressure. Figure 5 depicts a half-octave band measurement of Bob's speech before and during one of these outbursts, which partly resemble a baby's crying. Ostwald analyzes the pattern as follows:

FIGURE 5

HALF-OCTAVE BAND MEASUREMENTS OF TWO TYPES OF SOUND PRODUCED BY AN AUTISTIC CHILD

(After Ostwald, 1963)

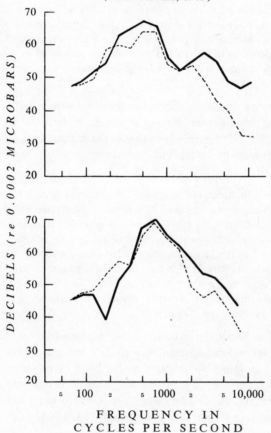

Courtesy of Charles C Thomas, publisher, Springfield, Ill.

A dashed curve denotes the linguistically comprehensible utterance "where is my doctor," uttered in a blunt, aggressive-sounding flat voice. Acoustically, this sound shows motant 1 rather broad and centered at 250 cps; motant 2 is flat-topped in the center of the acoustic spectrum; motant 3 comes to a peak at 2,000 cps. Compare this with the solid curve which denotes a robust cry-like outburst "I use a razor" that comes to a climax on the first syllable of "razor": Motants 1 and 2 are fused into one large area of acoustic energy concentration centered at 500 cps which reaches a level of 67 decibels. There is a second very prominent area of energy concentration centered at 2,860 cps. The cry-like sound (8.3 sones) is 25 per cent louder than the more normal sound (6.2 sones).

Half-octave band measurement of some of Bob's nonsense jargonizing [bottom half of Figure 6.2] shows even more clearly the resemblance between this patient's soundmaking and the cry-sound of young babies. The fragment denoted here is the sound /aiskob/. The first part, /ais/, is emitted in a scream-like manner that shows no clear differentiation of motants but simply a sharp peaking of acoustic energy at 715 cps (solid curve). The second part, /kob/, has more the acoustic characteristics of speech in that the fundamental tone is defined as motant 1 at 250 cps, while resonance energy is found in motant 2 centered at 715 cps (dashed curve). (pp. 131–33)[8]

The importance of kinetic factors in the total behavioral picture of the autistic child is apparent in the accounts of both Goldfarb and Ostwald. Goldfarb (1956) reminds us that in the normal situation spoken language is reinforced by facial and body gestures. With regard to the subjects in his study:

Inadequate and unrelated language reinforcements characterize each of the 12 schizophrenic children and never characterize the 6 children with reactive behavior disorders. The schizophrenic children show what has ofttimes been called wooden features and, often, staring, unseeing eyes. Not only are the larger muscles of the face unmoving, but also the pupils usually are rigidly fixed in an almost pathognomonic and persistent dilatation. Facial and body gestures unrelated to the spoken word are evident in the inappropriate smile, bizarre mannerisms, giggling and "pogo-stick" jumping. (p. 548)[9]

Ostwald (1963) similarly talks of the grimace-like quality of his patient's facial expressions, his tendency to dart around the room or remain too long in an immobile posture, or his habit of moving his hands in a strange and repetitive way, "suggesting that he is engaged in doing something meaningful, but that he cannot get others to share this meaning by communicating it in a code they understand." (p. 129)

SCHIZOPHRENIC CHILDREN AND MATERNAL SPEECH

While patterns of language behavior in schizophrenic children have engaged the attention of researchers, the speech of the mothers of schizo-

---

[8] *Ibid.*
[9] Copyright, the American Othopsychiatric Association, Inc., reproduced by permission.

phrenic children has failed to receive its share of systematic scrutiny. The potential importance of such study can scarcely be exaggerated. Not only does the maternal parent function as the primary model for imitative speech efforts in the child (McNeill, 1966), but also a substantial body of psychiatric opinion supports the position that the incompetence of these mothers in communicating thought and feeling is a major pathogenic factor in the development of schizophrenic disorders (Bateson *et al.,* 1956).

The recent publication of a paper by Goldfarb, Goldfarb, and Scholl (1966) provides the first empirical study in what one hopes will be a series of fruitful investigations of this hitherto largely speculative issue.

As in the study discussed previously (Goldfarb *et al.,* 1956), the present investigation employed the services of a speech pathologist as judge/analyst in assessing such factors as volume, rate, pitch, phrasing, intonation, and the communication of mood and meaning. These aspects of speech and language were rated on a 5-point scale: (1) very poor, (2) poor, (3) fair, (4) good, (5) excellent. The material used in the ratings consisted of children's speech samples (normal and schizophrenic) obtained in a structured situation—reading, naming pictures in a story, etc.—and the last five minutes of an open-ended interview with the mothers (of normal and schizophrenic children) regarding their perception of the maternal role. According to the authors, identifying information was removed from the tapes and the material was presented to the speech pathologist in random fashion.

Table 9 shows the results of the comparison between normal and schizophrenic children and the mothers of normal and of schizophrenic

TABLE 9

GENERAL ESTIMATES OF SPEECH AND LANGUAGE OF MOTHERS OF NORMAL CHILDREN, MOTHERS OF SCHIZOPHRENIC CHILDREN, NORMAL CHILDREN AND SCHIZOPHRENIC CHILDREN

(After Goldfarb, Goldfarb, and Scholl, 1966)

QUALITY	Number of Mothers of		Number of Children	
	Normals	Schizophrenics	Normals	Schizophrenics
TOTAL	23	23	23	23
Excellent	0	0	2	0
Good	4	1	7	0
Fair	13	5	8	1
Poor	4	9	4	14
Very Poor	2	8	2	8

Reprinted by permission of *American Journal of Psychiatry.*

children with regard to general evaluations of speech quality. According to the conclusions of Goldfarb *et al.* (1966):

> The present study supports the hypothesis that one factor affecting the aberrant speech of schizophrenic children is the influence of poor speech and communicative capacity in one of their earliest objects available for emulation and as a source of reinforcement, namely, their mothers. (p. 1227)[10]

Klein and Pollack (1966) have taken exception to this conclusion. Their argument is as follows:

> Laudably, systematic attention was paid to eliminating rater bias by blind-rating procedures. Not so laudably, very little attention was paid to the overriding question of matching the maternal samples for age, education, I.Q., social class, and special interests, since these factors have overwhelming importance for speech and language. We are told only that the schizophrenic children were age- and sex-matched with the normal children who were "in attendance in average classes at a public school which was selected because its population is culturally and economically comparable to that of the Ittleson Center population."
>
> There is no further information as to the mode of selection of these normal children and mothers. Obviously, unless proper sampling techniques were employed, it would be possible to inadvertently select 23 specially endowed mothers from a normal school sample. This would be likely if the selection of the "normal children" sample depended on the volunteering of cooperative, psychologically oriented parents. Such mismatched maternal samples would vitiate any comparisons.
>
> The authors' conclusion implies that there is a correlation between the degree of deviant speech and language in schizophrenic children and their mothers' speech deviations. Unfortunately, no correlation coefficients were presented, and thus we have no way of evaluating the strength of the relationship: i.e., did the mothers with the poorest speech have the children with the poorest speech? The same question should be asked of the relationship of the speech and language of normal children to their mothers! (p. 232)[11]

Professional interest in familial factors in the pathogenesis of mental illness has never been greater. But as Klein and Pollack caution, there is no substitute for "meticulously performed and presented studies" in providing answers to the complex problems surrounding the role of the maternal parent in the development of psychotic and neurotic disorders.

---

[10] Reprinted by permission, from *American Journal of Psychiatry*, 1966, *133*, 1220–27.

[11] Reprinted by permission, from *American Journal of Psychiatry*, 1966, *123*, 232.

MODIFICATION OF LANGUAGE BEHAVIOR IN AUTISM

Autism and other forms of severe language retardation have long been resistant to treatment by traditional approaches. Several investigators, however, have reported initial success in the establishment of language behavior in autistic children through the use of operant conditioning procedures (Hewett, 1965; Lovaas, Freitag, and Kinder, 1966; Lovaas, 1966).

The procedures employed in these studies are similar to those used in animal research, which probably accounts for their effectiveness: We are dealing with children who *behaviorally* resemble the infrahuman subjects of the operant laboratory. The conditioning methods follow the operant experimental paradigm of successive approximations and include:

1. Determination of the reinforcer to be used (which is then empirically verified).
2. Magazine training, during which the positive reinforcer is paired with a highly discriminable stimulus (e.g., a buzzer) in order to produce an effective conditioned reinforcer.
3. Reinforcement of any verbalization. As soon as verbalizations begin to occur in increasing frequency, imitative verbal conditioning is initiated.
4. Reinforcement of imitative verbalizations. In this stage of the program, the psychologist says a word or utters a sound (depending on the known response repertoire of the child). Initially, *any* verbalization following the word or sound uttered by the psychologist is reinforced. These verbalizations are gradually shaped so that the child is reinforced only for speech which is in direct imitation of that of the psychologist.
5. Reinforcement for imitative object identification. After imitative verbalization is brought under stimulus control, imitative verbal identification of simple objects is initiated. In this stage of the program, the psychologist presents a small toy object, such as a ball, to the child and names the object. The child is then reinforced for repeating the name of the object.
6. Reinforcement for spontaneous object identification. As soon as the subject is imitating the names of objects consistently, the objects are presented to the child and he is asked, "What is it?" He is reinforced for correct identification. If the child does not name the object correctly, the psychologist identifies it for him. Then the child is asked again to name the object. These prompts by the psychologist are gradually faded out as the subject correctly identifies the objects.

7. Reinforcement for functional application of conditioned speech. Once spontaneous object identification has been conditioned, the child is then reinforced for using speech functionally in sentences, e.g., repeating "put the ball in (on, under) the box," and then, following the instructions properly.

Lovaas *et al.* (1966) reported a study involving two autistic children who were both limited to echolalic behavior prior to the project, and who exhibited the usual bizarre symptoms of autism. The work of Lovaas and his colleagues was done within a reinforcement paradigm, but they added a few unique modifications.

They instituted a rather intensive program. The children "worked" from 8:00 to 11:30 A.M., with three 10-minute recreation breaks; another rest period from 11:30 A.M. to 1 P.M.; then another "working" period from 1:00 to 5:00 P.M., with four 10-minute breaks, for six days a week. The training was carried out in ward bedrooms which were familiar to the children. The adult and child were seated in chairs facing a table, or in chairs facing one another.

In the first part of the program, the psychologist presented verbal or nonverbal stimuli, to which the child generally responded incorrectly if at all. The psychologist would then prompt the child to respond with the correct behavior, after which he would then supply reinforcement. On succeeding trials, the prompting was faded out. Negative reinforcement in the form of loud yells and sometimes a slap were used primarily to suppress the child's inattention and self-stimulation, both of which were very high during the first week or two.

The original positive reinforcer was food. All of the child's meals were fed to him in small portions by the psychologist as reinforcement for correct responses during training. Each bite of food was accompanied by verbal approval and caressing the child. The ratio of primary (food) and secondary (approval) reinforcement was manipulated systematically until finally both children were receiving only social approval. With Rick, the seven-year-old boy, this was accomplished in twelve days; with Pam, the nine-year-old girl, it took almost ten months before the food could be removed completely.

Within two months from the beginning of the program, the children's echolalia had been extinguished, they had learned the alphabet in upper- and lower-case, they had learned to read one simple book, and they could verbalize descriptions of objects and actions seen in magazines and books. Results such as these are an impressive demonstration of the efficacy of an approach which has recorded successes in an area where success is extremely rare.

REFERENCES

Bateson, G., Jackson, D. N., Haley, J., and Weakland, J. Toward a theory of schizophrenia. *Behavioral Science*, 1956, *1*, 251–64.

Berkowitz, R. *The disturbed child*. New York: New York University Press, 1960.

Cunningham, M. A. and Dixon, C. A study of the language of an autistic child. *Journal of Child Psychology and Psychiatry*, 1961, *2*, 193–202.

Eisenson, J. Disorders of language in children. *Journal of Pediatrics*, 1963, *62*, 20–24.

Goldfarb, W., Braunstein, P., and Lorge, I. A study of speech patterns in a group of schizophrenic children. *American Journal of Orthopsychiatry*, 1956, *26*, 544–55.

Goldfarb, W., Goldfarb, N., and Scholl, H. The speech of mothers of schizophrenic children. *American Journal of Psychiatry*, 1966, *122*, 1220–27.

Hewett, P. M. Teaching speech to an autistic child through operant conditioning. *American Journal of Orthopsychiatry*, 1965, *35*, 927–36.

Kanner, L. Autistic disturbances of affective contact. *Nervous Child*, 1943, *2*, 217–50.

Kanner, L. and Eisenberg, L. Early infantile autism. *American Journal of Orthopsychiatry*, 1956, *26*, 556–64.

Klein, D. F. and Pollack, M. Schizophrenic children and maternal speech facility. *American Journal of Psychiatry*, 1966, *123*, 232.

Lovaas, O. I. A program for the establishment of speech in psychotic children. In J. K. Wing (Ed.), *Early childhood autism*. London: Pergamon Press, 1966.

Lovaas, O. I., Freitag, G., and Kinder, M. I. Establishment of social reinforcers in two schizophrenic children on the basis of food. *Journal of Experimental Child Psychology*, 1966, *4*, 109–25.

McCarthy, D. A. *The language development of the pre-school child*. Minneapolis: University of Minnesota Press, 1930.

McNeill, D. Developmental psycholinguistics. In F. Smith and G. A. Miller (Eds.), *The genesis of language*. Cambridge, Mass.: The M.I.T. Press, 1966.

Ostwald, P. F. *Soundmaking*. Springfield, Ill.: Charles C Thomas, 1963.

Pronovost, W. The speech behavior and language comprehension of autistic children. *Journal of Chronic Diseases*, 1961, *13*, 228–33.

Sampson, O. C. A study of speech development in children of 18–30 months. *British Journal of Educational Psychology*, 1945, *26*, 144–201.

Wolff, S. and Chess, S. An analysis of the language of fourteen schizophrenic children. *Journal of Child Psychology and Psychiatry*, 1965, *6*, 29–41.

Wood, N. E. Language development and language disorders: A compendium of lectures. *Monographs of the Society for Research in Child Development*, 1960.

CHAPTER 7

LANGUAGE BEHAVIOR
IN NEUROSIS

The discussion of language behavior in neurosis tends to suffer complication as a consequence of several considerations which apply uniquely to linguistic phenomena in neurotic individuals. For one thing, the term "neurotic" lends itself to such vague and generalized usage that it is often impossible to determine from the context whether an author is using the term as a synonym for something as ambiguous and ill-defined as a state of emotional disturbance or as specific as the diagnostic categorization designated by (obsessive-compulsive, e.g.) neurotic. Also, in contrast with other psychopathological syndromes, certain types of linguistic or paralinguistic phenomena (aphonia, dysphonia, mutism) have been assigned a major rather than minor position in the symptomatology of a particular neurotic group, i.e., conversion reactions. Finally, the term neurotic has been applied with complete disregard for denotative specificity to a wide variety of psychogenic conditions presumed to play a role in the "functional" pathology of stuttering.

The literature in this area is rather skimpy. It consists of a few impressionistic sketches of "the neurotic speaker" and some aspects of his communicative behavior, a small group of studies that attempt to relate anxiety measures to vocal qualities, a number of clinical reports on symptoms as aphonia and dysphonia, and several large-grained descriptive studies of neurotic language behavior that are addressed primarily to stylistic features of form and content. We shall briefly examine some reports of the various types mentioned above.

"NEUROTIC SPEAKERS"

Barbara (1960) offers the following description of a "normal or healthy" speaker:

> The healthy speaker has a firm inner feeling of strength and freedom, security and self-confidence, in most situations—including that of speak-

ing. He usually experiences his voice as his own and as originating from within himself. He feels a choice of his own words or groups of words, though there may be some indecision as to word pronunciation. However, once he makes his decision and voluntarily chooses his words, he readily accepts responsibility for his choice, and has, as a result, little difficulty in consummating the speaking itself. (p. 476)[1]

In contrast, Barbara (1962) characterizes the "neurotic" speaker as weak, conflicted, insecure; as egocentric, and possessed of distorted values; as a poor listener; and as prone to "blab-blab" and parrot-like emission. He tends to feel his voice as alien, and his words and ideas as dependent mainly upon circumstances. Any attempt on his part to speak, whether threatening or not, is apt to be the occasion for apprehension or panic. He is strongly dependent upon his audience; and in his concern for the kind of impression he is making, he is invariably preoccupied with what to say and how to say it.

Barbara further delineates the neurotic speaker according to a three-fold typology that includes these interesting patterns:

1. THE MAN OF A FEW WORDS (THE RESIGNED SPEAKER)

Unable to face himself most times in a realistic sense, one of the resigned person's active neurotic solutions is to remove himself from the conflicting situation by assuming the attitude of being the "onlooker or non-participating spectator." He represses or denies many of his real feelings and desires by placing inhibitions and checks in the path of their expression. He may, at the same time, minimize or flatly deny his real assets or potentialities. His aversion toward making realistic sacrifices in order to achieve his life goals causes him to give up the struggle many times and to resign himself to a more "peaceful" position. He rationalizes his resignation by saying, in effect, that "it just isn't worth the effort" or "life is too short to get disturbed about." He may accept his vocation, a partner in marriage or friends which permit him to be somewhat alone, where he can remain to some degree self-sufficient and apart. In this self-imposed confinement, he avoids healthy competitiveness and restricts his real desires and wishes to a minimum. (1960, pp. 480–81)

2. THE MASTER'S VOICE (THE EXPANSIVE SPEAKER)

In the speaking situation, the expansive person feels he should be and is the *last word*. In any discussion, he fears mutual exchange of ideas, is usually stubborn, resistant and highly reluctant to face issues squarely and honestly. He makes use of one-sided, two-valued orientations, refusing to see any other person's viewpoint, is highly egocentric and contemptuous of others who differ with him, or don't see his side of the argument

---

[1] From D. A. Barbara, *Psychological and psychiatric aspects of speech and hearing,* 1960. Courtesy of Charles C Thomas, publisher, Springfield, Ill.

completely and *absolutely*. When trapped or confronted with the truth, he may resort to becoming insulted and indignantly make such god-like statements as: "I've said what I have to say and that is final." Because of his dreaded fear of being in any position but that of superiority, he is driven to becloud issues and distort their true meanings to suit his own ends. . . . (1960, p. 482)

3. THE VOICE OF THE TIMID (THE SELF-EFFACING SPEAKER)

How does the person with predominantly self-effacing attitudes feel and react in the speaking situation? More or less, the shrinking process and self-minimizing effects which seem to pervade in most areas of his life are also prevalent in the area of verbal communications. I like to refer to this form of verbalization as "dwarf-like." A self-effacing person feels and experiences his world and environment as potentially danger-ous, threatening and filled with *giants* of all sorts. He responds to fearful situations by becoming basically helpless, anxious, apprehensive, and fearful of an impending attack to [sic] his personality structure. His counterattack is rarely one of assertion or directness, but one character-ized by shrinking, making "himself psychically smaller," pleading help-lessness, placing himself at the mercy of others, leaning over backwards, seeking dependency, feeling abused, and desperately attempting to ar-rive at a comprehensive solution by living vicariously through others and achieving "protection and surrendering love." (1960, pp. 486–87)[2]

These vignettes, which are rather reminiscent of the Characters of Theophrastus, are not without some interest as impressionistic accounts. Their potential usefulness is sharply limited, however, by a number of considerations. Apart from their extreme generality and vagueness, the profiles present a mixture of observation and inference, and it would be difficult if not impossible to separate the two for analytical purposes. An even more extreme example of this tendency to fuse behavioral ob-servations and dynamic inferences is supplied by Heaver (1960) in the introduction to an article on spastic dysphonia in the same anthology. According to Heaver:

Whenever the mental mechanism of repression and suppression fail [sic] in their intra-psychic conspiracy to hide the seething rage within, the neurotic is pinioned by the slings and arrows of resultant anxiety and fear of self-exposure. Tormented and consumed by the demands of inner hostile impulses, the neurotically sick person seeks surcease from dread feelings of impending disaster which these forbidden thoughts generate. (p. 250)[3]

---

[2] *Ibid.*
[3] *Ibid.*

Such statements are difficult, if not impossible, to evaluate, since their meaning seems to be largely a matter of connotation rather than denotation.

DESCRIPTIVE STUDIES OF NEUROTIC LANGUAGE

Balken and Masserman (1940) made verbatim recordings of stories given to 20 Thematic Apperception Test cards by an initial group of 50 neurotic patients. From this group, a selection was made of 15 patients of "uniformly high intelligence" (I.Q. 118–138), who were then subdivided into three groups of 5 patients "so that each group fitted most closely the respective clinical characteristics of conversion-hysteria, anxiety state, and obsessive-compulsive neurosis." (p. 76) The verbal productions of these patients were analyzed according to the criteria described below in Table 10. On the basis of the results obtained on these 10 criteria, Balken and Masserman offered the following "characteristic differentiations" among the three neurotic groups, together with interpretations as to their meaning.

> In *conversion hysteria* the characteristics of the phantasies are: productions of medium length, a plethora of leisurely descriptive material with little forceful action (low verb-adjective quotient), little vagueness, ambivalence or qualification of statement (high pro-con quotient as contrasted with low certainty-uncertainty and qualification-certainty quotients and with low alternative and "special expressions" ratings), and a minimum use of the first person or of identifications with the narrator. It is of great theoretical interest that these formal characteristics of the phantasies are consistent with the most striking psychodynamic mechanisms of the conversion hysteric; namely, the diminution of overt anxiety by the device of "converting" the repressed erotic or aggressive urge into organic dysfunctions which afford vicarious libidinal gratification and yet are sufficiently self-punitive to resolve in some degree the accompanying neurotic guilt. With his intrapsychic tensions thus autoplastically relieved, the conversion hysteric apparently can then indulge in rich, slow-moving, leisurely phantasies which need exhibit but little action or indecision and which are so lightly charged with projected anxiety that there are almost no direct references to the patient's own difficulties in the stories. Significant also is the fact that there is a corresponding minimum of interpersonal tension in the test situation, as shown by the freedom the patient feels in asking relatively casual questions of the examiner.
>
> In contrast, the phantasies in an *anxiety state* are brief; the action is most dramatic (highest verb-adjective quotient) and often compulsive; alternatives of conation are most frequently sought; special expressions connoting vagueness, hesitation, and trepidation are freely used; and direct identifications of the narrator with characters in his phantasy fre-

TABLE 10

CRITERIA FOR ANALYSIS OF THE LANGUAGE OF PHANTASY

(After Balken and Masserman, 1940)

Criterion*	Significance
1. The average number of words per phantasy.	A measure of the length, if not the richness, of the productions.
2. The number of predicative, participial and attributive adjectives.†	The relative wealth of static description in the phantasy.
3. The relative number of active, passive and intransitive verbs.‡	A high incidence of verbs denotes a kinetic release in the phantasy of anxious tensions in the narrator.
4. The relative frequency of (A) "Pro" statements, subdivided into: (a) Possibility: "this is possible," "conceivable," "it stands a chance," etc. (b) Probability: "thinks likely," "to be expected," "appears to be," etc. (c) Certainty: "positive," "sure," "no question," "inevitable," etc. —as contrasted with (B) "Con" statements, such as: (d) Impossiblity: "incredible," "unimaginable," "unthinkable," etc. (e) Improbability: "not likely," "I don't think," "chances are against," etc. (f) Uncertainty: "afraid to say," "wonder whether," "I don't know," etc. (g) Qualifications: expressions indicating limitation, modification or reservation concerning an assertion.	"Pro" statements indicate relative ability of the subject to make straight-forward statements with relatively little overt doubt and self-criticism. "Con" statements reveal obsessive ambivalences, doubts and defensive denials made by the subject with reference to the material appearing in his own phantasies.
5. Incidence of expressions of conative alternatives, equivalences or vacillations.	Related to the difficulties and ambitendencies encountered by the subject in his attempt to represent and resolve his conative conflicts in his phantasies.

TABLE 10—(Continued)

Criterion*	Significance
6. Zwang expressions, either felt as "I have to," "I must," or projected as "he is forced," "she finds it necessary."	Compulsive tendencies in the subject's thinking.
7. Number of questions asked of the examiner during the test.	Variable; cf. discussion in text.
8. Special expressions, such as (a) Vagueness: "sort of," "kind of," (b) Reasoning: "because," (c) Derivation: "as a result," (d) Means: "this is how," etc., (e) The special interjection "well."	Cf. discussion in text.
9. Number of occurrences of (a) The first personal pronoun, and (b) Direct reference to the narrator: "it seems to me," "the way I see it," "I would say," etc.	Measures of the egocentricity or re-introjection of the subject's imagery.
10. Identification of a character in the phantasy with the narrator: "this might be I," "just like my own story," etc.	Manifest instances of more direct and conscious projections of the subject into his phantasies.

*Among the criteria discarded for the purposes of the present study because they were found to have insufficient determinative value or because they involved too great a degree of subjectivity in interpretation and scoring were the following: (a) the classification of the phantasy as narration, essay or description; (b) the number of separate "ideas" or "elements" in the production; (c) the frequency of repetition of thoughts, phrase patterns, plot or other configurations as a measure of "perseveration"; (d) the use of metaphors, metonymy or synechdoche; (e) the differentiation of "concrete" and "abstract" statements as an indication of "schizoid thinking"; and (f) the scoring of voice, gesture, and facial expressions (e.g., laughter, tears, gestures of annoyance, derision, hopelessness, etc.).

†The adjective count included participial adjectives preceded by the article the or a or by the preposition of, but nouns used as adjectives, adjectives used as nouns (e.g., the wealthy, the idle), quantitative and ordinal numerals and "numeral pronouns" (next, many, and several) and the adjectives certain, various, and different were not counted.

‡Verbs in all forms, including infinitives and participles, were counted. Participles used without nouns and preceded by an article—the or a—or by the preposition of and auxiliary verb (e.g., have, shall, etc.) were not counted.

quently occur. These characteristics of the language of the phantasies are in agreement with the circumstances that in neurotically anxious subjects the intrapsychic tensions have been relieved neither by autoplastic conversion nor by an obsessive-compulsive ritual, and therefore seek expression in vivid, dramatic, incompletely projected phantasies. These productions, however, are themselves cut short by the immediacy of the affective symbolism employed, so that the phantasied situations are left as unresolved as the underlying emotional conflicts of the subject. . . .

In *obsessive-compulsive* neuroses a somewhat similar language syndrome appears, with the highly characteristic modification that the necessity (highest score on "compulsions") the patient feels to rationalize and elaborate the many ambivalences and uncertainties reflected in his phantasies (highest qualification-certainty quotient; extensive use of "special expressions" and lowest pro-con and certainty-uncertainty quotients) greatly increases the average length of his productions. Theoretically these features are again in accord with the psychodynamic pattern of the obsessive-compulsive neuroses, in which latent anxiety frequently breaks through the typical defenses of vacillation, doubt, obsessive rationalizations, and meticulous ritualism of thought and action. It is not surprising, therefore, that the obsessive-compulsive phantasies show a high verb-adjective quotient, a high self-identification factor, and in other ways . . . manifest the dynamically close relationship of this neurosis with an anxiety state. (pp. 76–82)

The authors caution against the interpretation of their results as exhibiting anything more than "incidental diagnostic validity," inasmuch as their selection of patients was dictated by an interest in "prevailing psychic dynamisms" rather than simple diagnostic labels.

Lorenz and Cobb (1954) tabulated word-count data for a variety of patient populations (manics, paranoid schizophrenics, hysterics, obsessive-compulsives and a normal group). Table 11 lists the grammatical categories and word frequencies computed on the basis of 1,000-word samples of consecutive speech. In the absence of statistical treatment, these results can only be viewed as indicative of possible trends. With that qualification in mind, we can see that both neurotic groups showed a lower than normal use of connectives and a greater emphasis on verbs; hysterics used fewer prepositions, while obsessive-compulsives used a greater number of adverbs; hysterics favored the use of the second person singular and the present tense, obsessive-compulsives used both the present and past tenses freely.

It should be pointed out that the frequency with which the personal pronoun "I" occurred in the psychotic and neurotic language samples generated considerable interest in the possibility that such self-references might prove to be pathognomonic for specific psychopathological states.

TABLE 11

GRAMMATICAL DISTRIBUTION AND WORD FREQUENCY ON THE BASIS OF
TEN 1,000-WORD SAMPLINGS FOR EACH GROUP

(After Lorenz and Cobb, 1954)

	Normals %	Hysterics	Obsessive-Compulsives
Substantives	16.7	11.0	10.9
Adjectives	12.2	11.6	10.3
Adverbs	12.5	14.2	15.3
Main Verbs	13.0	16.8	17.1
Auxilary Verbs	3.8	6.5	5.7
Pronouns	13.8	21.9	18.9
Prepositions	10.4	6.2	8.0
Conjunctions	8.9	6.9	6.8
Articles	6.4	4.6	4.8
Interjections	2.4	1.1	1.8
No. of words used once	200	154	159
No. of diff. words/1000	341	289	284

Reprinted with permission, from *A.M.A. Archives of Neurology and Psychiatry.*

Research with the computer program designated the General Inquirer (Maher, McKean, and McLaughlin, 1966) has failed, however, to provide support for this hypothesis.

Stylistic features of hysteric and obsessive-compulsive neurotics were examined in some detail by Lorenz (1955). The study, which is descriptive rather than quantitative, makes use of excerpts from the recorded speech of eight patients "clinically and psychologically evaluated" as hysteric and obsessive-compulsive respectively.

The following is a sample of hysteric language:

> *Patient C:* It scared me pea green . . . I find myself thinking absolutely rigid, stiff as a board . . . let me cogitate, I'm afraid I'm projecting . . . that gibbering about myself is an imposition, silly. This business of being terribly conscious of your talking. Torturing myself with name calling . . . I was terrified, it horrified me . . . thinking in *non sequiturs,* such a queer situation anyway. I can't feel differences, messy gray area where you can't jell. (p. 355)

Characteristic of the patients in this group is the pervasive use of colorful and dramatic language to project a vivid image of the speaker. Events are described in terms of their impact on the patient—and the dramatic effect of the narrative is enhanced by the use of emotionally charged expressions. A sense of immediacy in relating past events is conveyed by the story-teller's device of the past progressive tense in preference over the simple past, e.g., "She was threatening me," rather than "She threatened me." It is as though the patient relived her experiences in the retelling. Lorenz gives a summation:

> . . . the language of the hysteric subordinates objective content to subjective impression and reaction. The focus shifts fluidly from the percept to the perceiver; the attitudes of the speaker emerge more strongly than the content. The expressive and emotive use of language— to evoke, manipulate, appeal, display—is prominent. The speaker attempts to draw the listener into a relationship as a biased spectator and supporter. A sense of immediacy and involvement in the present is conspicuous. Thematic material centers about feelings and wishes. The discursive functions of language are frequently ignored, and volubility is substituted for articulateness. There is a ready absorption of current language habits from the social environment, and a great deal of exaggerated emphasis; but a static quality eventually arises from the cumulative effect of the latter. (pp. 356–57)

In sharp contrast with the vivid, impressionistic language of the hysteric is the circumstantial, colorless, and intellectualized approach of the obsessive-compulsive. Lorenz offers this excerpt:

> *Patient E:* I don't know if there's anything new or not . . . I don't feel capable of deciding such matters but . . . at first I didn't care because I figured eventually I'd get better . . . it always used to bother me . . . if I could interest myself in collecting stamps, for instance, I never did have a hobby I could stick to. I had just started when I came here. I decided . . . I seem to be worse here—there I felt better. (p. 357)

Where the hysteric paints verbal pictures in broad strokes and sweeping flourishes, the obsessive-compulsive is a miniaturist. The emphasis is upon relationships rather than objects, upon evaluation and judgment rather than description. The obsessive-compulsive seems to substitute the scrutiny of feelings for the active experiencing of emotion. Consequently, his choice of words tends to convey the attitude of a somewhat detached and impassionate spectator toward the events in which he is a participant. The author concludes:

> There are a number of structural devices which emerge characteristically in the talk of the obsessive-compulsive. These are: the frequency of prefatory statements and introductory remarks, the frequency of modifying clauses introduced by *that* or *which,* the frequent use of the disjunctives *or, if,* and *but,* the frequency of localization in time and place, and the repetition of words and phrases. All of these detract from the easy progression of ideas and introduce a monotonous, repetitive quality.
>
> Thus in the language of the obsessive-compulsive, the emphasis is on the specific and circumscribed, with an underplaying of subjectively qualifying attributes. There is a concern with relationship in terms of

quantity, comparison, degree, and assertion and negation. The person works over the immediacy of awareness to create distance between himself and the mental event; and self-awareness emerges in terms of observation and scrutiny rather than in terms of the direct apprehension of inner states. Although the range of "feeling" experience varies in different obsessive-compulsive persons, there is a common denominator in that tensions between opposites are stated rather than differentiated affective states. From a structural viewpoint, the language pattern is replete with such stylistic devices as prefatory statements, repetitions, and modifying clauses. (p. 359)

The reader will no doubt have observed that many of the characteristics noted above can be considered typical of the speech patterns of the better educated and intelligent person, raising the quite elementary question of whether Lorenz' differences might not be more parsimoniously explained on the basis of systematic differences in intelligence between her hysteric and obsessive-compulsive patients. Conversion reaction patients tend to be slightly lower than other neurotic types on such factors as intelligence, educational level, and socio-economic status. If patients were matched on these variables, the differences reported by Lorenz might be washed out.

Nevertheless, despite the small number of subjects involved and the lack of quantification or controls, this study provides some worthwhile leads to further investigation of neurotic language behavior. The readiness of the author to seek consistencies at a level of analysis higher than mere lexical frequency counts is a move away from the sterility of sterile atomism.

VOICE QUALITY DEFICIENCIES AND ANXIETY

Anxiety is a concept of focal importance for the understanding of psychopathological conditions, particularly the neuroses. Hence, one might expect to find keen interest among psychiatrists and psychologists in the effects of anxiety upon language behavior in both lexical and nonlexical aspects. Such is not the case. Recognizing the formidable difficulties faced by the research worker in the investigation of anxiety, it is still rather odd to find this terrain almost completely unmapped. It might be of interest, therefore, to spend some time with the few studies that bear in any way upon this significant topic.

Moore (1939) compared 43 college students with speaking voices that were rated superior with 119 students whose voices were classified as breathy, harsh, nasal whiny, or metallic. These 119 subjects were called from a population of 453 students enrolled in the first year speech courses at Colorado State College and Kent State University. All of the students were given the Bernreuter Personality Inventory, and each student rated himself twice during the term on a "speech personality rating sheet." In addition, he was evaluated by 10 advanced speech students immediately following an oral presentation. Special attention was given to students who were deficient in articulation, phonation, and adjustment.

According to the results, speakers with breathy voices scored high on neurotic tendency and introversion on the Bernreuter, speakers with harsh, metallic voices tend to be dominant and emotionally stable, and the speaker with nasal whine scores low in dominance and high in emotional instability.

Duncan (1945) found positive correlations between low social adjustment, as measured by the Bell adjustment Inventory, and judgments of vocal inefficiency in the use of quality, pitch, and force.

In a further study, Duncan (1947) compared the scores obtained on the Bell Adjustment Inventory of 23 patients whose voices had been classified as "hoarse" or "harsh and constricted" with those of a control group free of vocal quality deficiencies. Although the author reported that 10 of the patients attained significantly lower scores than the control subjects in home adjustment, she fails to provide any quantitative evidence in support of the comparison.

Diehl, White, and Burk (1959) reviewed these studies and stated that, although the results appear to support the hypothesis of a relationship between vocal quality and personality adjustment, the numerous methodological defects of the studies precluded any firm conclusions about the relationship. They undertook to investigate a more specific problem: the possible relationship between voice quality and anxiety. Their instrument for measuring anxiety was the Taylor Manifest Anxiety Scale (MAS).

This scale is a paper-and-pencil questionnaire which consists of 225 items. Fifty of these items contribute to an "anxiety" score, while the rest are filler items (Taylor, 1953). Items were originally selected from the Minnesota Multiphasic Inventory (MMPI) which in the judgment of the clinician-raters were descriptive of manifest anxiety. Such items as "I sweat very easily even on cool days" and "My sleep is restless and disturbed" elicited high agreement among judges.

Subjects for this study included 169 males and 10 females with a mean age of twenty-five years, all of whom were seminary students. Recordings were made of individual readings by the subjects of a Biblical passage (Matthew 5) with instructions to deliver the selection as though they were in the pulpit on Sunday morning. The MAS was taken by all subjects either individually or in groups following the recording session.

All recordings were judged for "normal" or "defective" voice quality in the first of two auditions. According to the authors, "Voice quality was labeled 'defective' if in the opinion of each judge it deviated sufficiently from 'normal' to warrant clinical attention." (p. 283) Attempts were made to control for regional effects on vocal quality, and in all cases where the judges were unable to reach unanimity the subject was dropped from the study. MAS scores were not known by the judges at the time of the listening session.

A second series of judgments was made on subjects labeled "defective." Three basic voice quality types—harsh, nasal, and hoarse-breathy, a category which combined the separate characteristics of hoarse and breathy described by Fairbanks (1940)—were used by the judges in categorizing the subjects in the "defective" group.

From the initial population of subjects, 62 were identified as defective in voice quality. These subjects were divided into the following groups: harsh, 19; nasal, 18; and hoarse-breathy 25. The investigators had perfect inter-rater reliability, as evidenced by the fact that none of the subjects with a voice quality deficiency was eliminated from the study for lack of agreement among the judges.

Analysis of variance of mean anxiety scores for the four groups—normal, harsh, nasal, hoarse-breathy—revealed differences among the groups that were statistically significant, as summarized in Table 12. In interpreting their results, Diehl *et al.* have this to say:

> The evidence from Moore's study (in which he found positive correlations between breathiness and neurotic tendencies and introversion, and

TABLE 12

RESULTS OF *t* TESTS BETWEEN MEAN ANXIETY SCORES* ON THE TAYLOR
SCALE OF MANIFEST ANXIETY. GROUPS COMPARED: NORMAL (1),
HOARSE-BREATHY (2), HARSH (3), and NASAL (4).

(After Diehl, *et al.*, 1959)

Groups	N	Mean	S.E. diff.	t
1	113	12.64	1.74	3.31†
2	25	18.40		
1	113	12.64	1.63	.07
3	19	12.53		
1	113	12.64	1.95	.90
4	18	14.39		
2	25	18.40	2.19	2.68‡
3	19	12.53		
2	25	18.40	2.44	1.64
4	18	14.39		
3	19	12.53	2.36	.79
4	18	14.39		

*The 50th percentile on the Taylor = 13.
†Significant at the 0.1% level.
‡Significant at the 2% level.

between harshness and dominance and emotional stability) is supported by the present results. On the basis of Moore's data it is reasonable to predict more anxiety for a hoarse-breathy group than for a normal or harsh group. Since such a prediction is substantiated by the results reported here, a positive relationship between hoarseness-breathiness and anxiety, and a lack of relationship between harshness and anxiety seem more defensible than previously. (p. 285)

The importance of this study and the findings reported will be more apparent perhaps after we have examined the clinical and research reports on hysterical voice symptoms in the next section.

HYSTERICAL APHONIA AND DYSPHONIA

Textbooks in clinical psychology and psychiatry cite "loss of voice" as one of the most common symptoms of hysterical origin. In actual fact, the loss is hardly ever total, even in cases of so-called hysterical *mutism* which, as we shall see later, are more apt to occur under the stress conditions of modern combat than in ordinary circumstances of civilian life. (We shall refer to some evidence that strongly underlines the advisability of differentiating combat stress reactions or service-connected neuropsychiatric disabilities from hysterical disorders.) It is more accurate to distinguish hysterical *aphonia* (an inability to speak above a whisper) and hysterical *dysphonia* (hoarseness) as conversion (hysteria) reactions. Of the two, aphonia is more common; but, as Greene (1964) suggests, ease in diagnosis may account for the difference in reported incidence.

The literature dealing with the relevance of psychological factors to the pathogenesis of aphonia and dysphonia is scanty and of indifferent quality. Excluding case histories and impressionistic reports, what remains is virtually a handful of studies in which some attempt was made to conduct a rigorous investigation. In one of the latter, a study by Purtell and his associates (1951), the authors point out that only two previous writers (Briquet, 1859; Savill, 1909) presented *any* quantitative clinical data on hysteria.

The subjects in the Purtell study included 50 women who were patients in a civilian hospital. The age of onset was less than thirty-five years in all patients. According to the authors, "The disorder was seen only in women. It was concluded that, if patients with compensation, pension, insurance and service or veterans' problems were excluded, hysteria is seen rarely or not at all in men." (p. 909) One of the obvious differences between the women patients and the men patients (which included 20 soldiers on active duty, 1 Coast Guardsman on active duty, 13 veterans, and 4 civilians with compensation prospects) was one of attitude and manner. The women were friendly, loquacious, and affable, while the men were defensive, suspicious, and close-mouthed in describing their symptoms.

Also, the illness was never monosymptomatic in the female patients. No patient reported fewer than 11 symptoms and the mean number of symptoms was 23. This compared with the essentially monosymptomatic features of the men patients' complaints. While not denying the validity of analyses of "war aphonia" by Smurthwaite (1919) and Sokolowsky and Junkermann (1944), Purtell and his colleagues suggest that hysteria (conversion reaction) is almost exclusively a sex-specific neurotic syndrome. Further, they noted that 45 per cent of their female subjects reported symptoms of aphonia, as compared with only 13 per cent among the controls.

These findings parallel those reported by Guze and Brown (1962). Of the 12 patients they studied clinically, 11 were female. Of even greater significance is the fact that 4 of the 5 patients with aphonia were found to have a "defined psychiatric disorder."

It will be recalled that the majority of the subjects in the study by Diehl, White, and Burk (1959) were males and that a significant relationship was found between judgments of hoarseness-breathiness and anxiety as measured by the Taylor Manifest Anxiety Scale. An obvious question to ask is whether the subjects described as exhibiting hoarseness-breathiness in the Diehl study might not be diagnosed clinically as cases of dysphonia—if not all subjects, then a majority of them. If the criteria used by Diehl and his colleagues in evaluating their subjects are quite similar to those on which clinical judgments of dysphonia are based, it strongly suggests that dysphonia and aphonia might represent the male and female reactions respectively to anxiety in individuals predisposed toward "hysteria." At least this is a question for which an empirical answer can be sought.

CONCLUDING REMARKS

There are obvious difficulties in trying to conduct research with psychotic and neurotic patients. Conflicts with hospital routine, scheduling problems, interference with the therapeutic process, and the obvious moral and ethical constraints upon the nature of permissible exploration are only a few of the obstacles that the investigator must be prepared to face. These factors may help to explain why the study of language behavior in the neuroses is in such a rudimentary stage of development.

If progress toward scientific sophistication is measured by the extent to which a discipline acquires some manipulatory control over the variables it seeks to investigate, then the investigation of neurotic language behavior faces a long uphill course. Before we can even discuss the possibility of experimentation, we must first concentrate on isolating and identifying relevant variables.

Very few of the studies reviewed in this chapter meet even the minimal criteria for an adequate descriptive study. Diagnostic bases for the selection of patients are hardly ever specified; neither quantitative data nor statistical comparison of results are common; few studies employ a control group; there is a general failure on the part of investigators to avail themselves of the products of related areas of research; and surprisingly little explicit recognition of the crucial lack of systematic theorizing in this field. All of these deficiencies must somehow be rectified before we can anticipate any further progress toward the understanding of linguistic behavior in the neuroses.

REFERENCES

Balken, E. R. and Masserman, J. H. The language of phantasy: III. The language of the phantasies of patients with conversion hysteria, anxiety state, and obsessive-compulsive neuroses. *Journal of Psychology,* 1940, *10,* 75–86.

Barbara, D. A. Neurosis in speaking. In D. Barbara (Ed.), *Psychological and psychiatric aspects of speech and hearing.* Springfield, Ill.: Charles C Thomas, 1960.

Barbara, D. A. Emotional factors in communicating. In J. L. Robins (Ed.), Distorted communication in the psychoneurotic. *American Journal of Psychoanalysis,* 1962, *22,* 84–104.

Briquet, P. *Traité clinique et therapeutique de l'hysterie.* Paris: J. B. Ballière et Fils, 1859.

Diehl, C. F., White, R., and Burk, K. Voice quality and anxiety. *Journal of Speech and Hearing Research,* 1959, *2,* 282–85.

Duncan, M. H. An experimental study of the relationships between voice and personality among students of speech. *Speech Monographs,* 1945, *12,* 47–61.

Duncan, M. H. Personality adjustment techniques in voice therapy, *Journal of Speech Disorders,* 1947, *12,* 161–67.

Fairbanks, G. *Voice and articulation drill book.* New York: Harper, 1940.

Glauber, I. P. Speech characteristics of psychoneurotic patients. *Journal of Speech Disorders,* 1944, *9,* 18–30.

Greene, M. *The voice and its disorders.* London: Pitman Medical Publishing Company, Limited, 1964.

Guze, S. B. and Bromn, O. L. Psychiatric disease and functional dysphonia and aphonia. *Archives of Otolaryngology,* 1962, *76,* 84–87.

Heaver, L. Spastic dysphonia. In D. A. Barbara (Ed.), *Psychological and psychiatric aspects of speech and hearing.* Springfield, Ill.: Charles C Thomas, 1960.

Lorenz, M. Expressive behavior and language patterns. *Psychiatry, 1955, 18,* 353–66.

Lorenz, M. and Cobb, S. Language patterns in psychotic and psychoneurotic subjects. *A.M.A. Archives of Neurology and Psychiatry,* 1954, *72,* 665–73.

Maher, B. A., McKean, K. O., and McLaughlin, B. Studies in psychotic language. In P. Stone (Ed.), *The general inquirer: A computer approach to content analysis.* Cambridge, Mass.: The M.I.T. Press, 1966.

Moore, W. E. Personality traits and voice quality deficiencies. *Journal of Speech Disorders,* 1939, *4,* 33–36.

Moses, P. J. *The voice of neurosis.* New York: Grune and Stratton, 1954.

Purtell, J. J., Robins, E., and Cohen, M. E. Observations on the clinical aspects of hysteria: A quantitative study of 50 hysteria patients and 156 control subjects. *Journal of the American Medical Association,* 1951, *146,* 902–9.

Savill, T. D. *Lectures on hysteria and allied vaso-motor conditions.* London: H. J. Glaisher, 1909.

Smurthwaite, H. War neuroses of the larynx and speech mechanism. *Journal of Laryngology,* 1919, *34,* 13.

Sokolowsky, R. R. and Junkermann, E. B. War aphonias. *Journal of Speech Disorders,* 1944, *9,* 193–208.

Taylor, J. A. A personality scale of manifest anxiety. *Journal of Abnormal and Social Psychology,* 1953, *48,* 285–90.

CHAPTER 8

LANGUAGE BEHAVIOR
AND VERBAL CONDITIONING
IN THE PSYCHOPATH

Personality abnormalities vary considerably in severity of symptoms and degree of maladjustment to society. But as Bromberg (1948) points out, "the group that supplies the most comprehensive and unmistakable illustrations of maladjustment to social life comprises those persons referred to as psychopathic personalities." (p. 54) Although he may be a "best example" of societal maladjustment, the psychopath is also one of the least understood of the maladjusted personalities.

The concept of psychopathic personality has been wrapped in controversy since its inception. Psychologists, psychiatrists, and criminologists have shown great divergence in their approaches toward defining and characterizing the psychopath. Wilhelm Reich first identified the psychopath as an "impulsive character." Franz Alexander added the conception of the psychopath as a "neurotic character." Many other terms besides psychopathic personality have been used by various authors. Some authorities have labeled these individuals "sociopaths," while Karpman (in Abrahamsen, 1960) stated that psychopathic deviancy is a very specific mental disease to which he gave the name "anethopathy." Clinard (1958) has the following to say:

> Although many believe that the concept of a psychopath is real and that such a personality type sufficiently explains numerous antisocial acts, the term is used so imprecisely and with such a variety of meanings by people who are not clear as to the development processes of a psychopath that its entire usefulness can be seriously questioned. In fact, the authors of one study have reported that they found some 202 different terms applied in one form or another to the psychopath. (p. 208)[1]

---

[1] Reprinted by permission of Holt, Rinehart and Winston, Inc.

116

Pescor (1948) puts it even more succinctly: "There is no general agreement as to what psychopaths are, how they get that way, or what to do with them."

According to Wallinger (1956), the term psychopath—which the author terms a "wastebasket category"—was in fact dropped from the diagnostic nomenclature of the American Psychiatric Association as a result of the 1952 revision. In spite of this seemingly hopeless entanglement of meanings, work continues to be done toward clarification of the concept of the psychopathic personality.

TOWARD A DEFINITION

It seems feasible, for the first objective, to attempt a generalized picture of what the psychopathic personality entails. Lipton (1950) pictures the psychopath as "an individual who is ill equipped from birth to meet the demands of his environment. He may be looked upon as in a defective state with a constitutional lack of responsiveness to the social demands of honesty, truthfulness, decency, and consideration for others. This is coupled with an inability to profit by experience." Coleman (1956) says, "This category applies to individuals who are not classifiable as mentally defective, neurotic, or psychotic, but who manifest a marked lack of ethical or moral development and an inability to follow socially approved codes of behavior." (p. 337)

Probably the most complete definition has been constructed by Cleckley (1949). According to him, a psychopath is a person who may be described as follows:

1. He is free from the signs or symptoms generally associated with psychoses, neuroses, or mental deficiency. He knows the consequences of his anti-social behavior, but he gives the impression that he has little real inner feeling for what he verbalizes so rationally.
2. He is habitually unable to adjust his social relations satisfactorily.
3. The psychopath is undeterred by punishment; in fact, he desires it.
4. His conduct is often lacking in motivation, or if a motive can be inferred, it is inadequate as an explanation for the behavior.
5. He expresses normal affective responses but demonstrates a total lack of concern and callous indifference toward others.
6. He demonstrates poor judgment and an inability to learn by experience, which is seen in "pathological lying," repeated crime, delinquencies, and other antisocial acts. "Patients repeat apparently purposeless thefts, forgeries, bigamies, swindlings, distaste-

ful or indecent acts in public, scores of times." (Cleckley, 1949, p. 415)

One main concern which disturbs some writers, and one that should be mentioned here, revolves around a conception that the psychopath may be neurotic. Pescor (1948), for instance, writes that most psychiatrists concede that psychopaths are not neurotic although some may develop a neurosis or even a psychosis at a later date. Some psychopaths, he says, add to the confusion by malingering insanity in order to escape punishment for their violations of the law. Yet other writers, such as Abrahamsen (1960), definitely maintain that the psychopath does display a neurotic "character disorder." Some will argue that many psychopaths commit crimes as a consequence of a strong feeling of guilt which they attempt to expiate through hoped-for punishment. To distinguish this type of "neurotic" from the ordinary one, the term "neurotic character" has been proposed as a substitute for the psychopathic personality, but this has not really solved anything. Suffice it to say that the differences of opinions are still open to question, and neither point of view can be completely ruled out at this point. Pescor attempted to resolve this difference by suggesting that "the psychopath vents his emotional tension on his environment, whereas the neurotic turns his emotional tension on himself. The one injures society, the other injures himself." (p. 7)

McCord and McCord (1956), who also argue that there is a difference between the neurotic and psychopath, give as a reason for the confusion the fact that the psychopath is often confused with the "acting out" neurotic because their symptoms are so similar; that is, the behavioral symptoms of aggressiveness and asociality are common.

PSYCHOPATHIC TYPES

Many authors have seen value and merit in placing psychopaths in different categories. Realizing some of the formidable difficulties involved in understanding psychopathic behavior, it would seem advantageous to present a diagnostic classification of the psychopathic personality. For the most part, the following categories are those proposed by Bromberg (1948).

Paranoid Psychopath—These individuals are characterized by the persistent feeling of being constantly discriminated against by everyone. They are tense in their manner and continually on the alert for adverse reaction toward themselves, and much of their energy is aimed at righting fancied wrongs or improving the unhappy situation in which they constantly imagine themselves. A distinction must be made between the psychotic individual whose judgment is so distorted by the delusions of persecutions as to be mentally ill and the psychopath whose feelings of being prevailed upon does not pass beyond a paranoid attitude. In both cases the criminal acts in which they become involved are usually of an assaultive nature. However, the paranoid psychopath in whom persecutory attitudes are not channeled into delusions often becomes involved in crimes such as blackmail and extortion which entail verbal rather than physical aggression. The psychology of the paranoid individual is marked primarily by a feeling of grandiosity and secondly by a tendency to react aggressively toward others. They are basically quarrelsome and litigious but do not carry it to the point of actual delusions of persecutions.

Schizoid Psychopath—The schizoid personality encompasses many levels of psychopathology, varying from complete psychosis to attitudes of aloofness and introversion. Although the characteristics of schizophrenic psychosis are present, these individuals generally remain in contact with reality. They are the type of individuals who run away from situations, the shut-ins, and the day-dreamers. Contrary to what might be a natural conclusion, schizoid personalities do commit aggressive crimes. In contradistinction to other types of psychopathic offenders, schizoid personalities who commit crimes are likely to be more seriously affected in terms of intellectual and emotional disintegration. In murder, for example, the mental disorders can be traced to inner conflicts in the offender, which lead to delusional formations and become externalized on the victim. The victim becomes a symbolic representative of the murderer's self.

Aggressive Psychopath—This group of individuals is given to episodes of explosive anger, irritability, destructiveness and the like. Their emotional equipment is insensitive, and their ethical standards are blunted to a degree which justifies their being included under the diagnosis of psychopathic personality. They are "enemies of society," displaying an attitude of social aggression beyond what is considered normal in our competitive world.

Psychopathic Swindler—These persons display marked asocial or amoral trends. Their antisocial activities begin at an early age, They lie, steal, cheat, and break promises over and over again without the slightest compunction. Extremely selfish, they tend to think the world revolves around them and their desires. They are unresponsive to kindness. They are unwilling to accept blame and totally irresponsible.

Sexual Psychopath—The sexual psychopath suffers from serious distortion of his sexual impulses. This produces the need for immediate gratification of these impulses. Struggling with the restrictions of society, he finally discards his inhibitions and succumbs to his urges. Many of this type may be well adjusted in all except the sexual sphere. They may have good educations, hold excellent jobs, and command the respect of their communities until their sex habits are disclosed. On the other hand, there are some, "like the sadists who commit sex murders, mutilate their victims and perpetrate other atrocious crimes, who are more dangerous to the public than a mad dog." (Pescor, 1948, p. 7)

One further point should be given a brief comment. Although it has not been included in the major divisions above, the "cyclothmic personality" should not be completely overlooked. These individuals are given to periods of depression alternating with periods of hyperactivity and elation, but not seriously enough to be recognized as manic-depressive psychotics.

SYMPTOMS

On the whole, the psychopath is very likable on first acquaintance. Although seemingly intelligent, he lacks the depth, sincerity, and wisdom present in the truly intelligent person. They are often found living in a series of present moments without real consideration for past or future and with callous disregard for the happiness of others. Coleman (1956) summarized the wide range of symptoms of this individual and it may be helpful to list them here.

1. Inability to understand and accept ethical values, except on a verbal level, or to pursue socially accepted goals.
2. Marked discrepancy between level of intelligence and conscience development.
3. Egocentric impulsiveness, irresponsibility, lack of restraint, and poor judgment. Prone to thrill-seeking, deviant sexual patterns, and other unconventional behavior. Callous disregard for needs and rights of others.
4. Inability to profit from mistakes and ordinary life experiences except by learning to exploit people and to escape punishment.
5. Inability to forego immediate pleasures for future gains and long-range goals. Hedonistic, lives in the present without consideration of past or future. Unable to withstand tedium and prone to nomad-like activities and frequent changing of jobs. External realities used for immediate personal gratification.
6. Ability to put up a good front to impress and exploit others. Often a charming, likeable personality with a disarming manner and ability to win the liking and friendship of others. Often good sense of humor and generally optimistic outlook. Prone to social climbing.
7. Defective interpersonal and general social relationships. Individual usually cynical, unsympathetic, ungrateful, and remorseless in his dealings with others. Usually shows a history of difficulties with educational and/or law-enforcement authorities. No close friends.

8. Rejection of constituted authority and discipline. Individual behaves as if social regulations did not apply to him and refuses, except on a verbal level, to take any responsibility for his actions. Often shows considerable repressed hostility toward constituted authority or society in general, which may manifest itself in impulsive, hostile criminal acts. Many times drifts into criminal activities but is not typically a calculating professional criminal.
9. Quick ability to rationalize and project the blame for his socially disapproved behavior. Lack of insight into his own behavior. Lies readily even though he knows he may eventually be found out by friends and acquaintances.
10. Irritating, disappointing, and distressing to others. Is frequently a great burden upon family and friends and creates a great deal of unhappiness for others. Often promises to change but rarely does so permanently—incorrigible. (p. 338)[2]

It is interesting to note that these symptoms, Abrahamsen (1944) maintains, are most generally found in young people. More precisely, he contends the peak age for the psychopath is about twenty years of age, with the age distribution varying from about fifteen to thirty-five or forty. He explains that it has been found that the psychopath frequently shows intelligent superiority which, to an extent, has a bearing on a possible early sexual maturity. Emotional instability, he says, is normal in the formative period of life. In a psychopathic person the emotional instability is more pronounced. He reaches this instability earlier than the normal person and he remains in such a condition long after the normal person has reached his state of normal mental and social stability. This is the reason why the psychopathic individual is emotionally immature, impulsive, and aggressive, resembling a spoiled, incorrigible child. His instability begins in childhood, reaches a peak in young adulthood, then dies down in the late twenties and early thirties.

GROSS CHARACTERISTICS OF PSYCHOPATHIC LANGUAGE

As in the case of the specific syndromes we have already reviewed, there have been a number of attempts to discover relationships between nonverbal behavior patterns and characteristics of language behavior in the psychopath. We shall examine one of these studies in some detail, then refer to the experimental literature which has accumulated within the past several years with regard to verbal learning and verbal conditioning processes among psychopaths.

---

[2] Reprinted from *Abnormal Psychology and Modern Life* by James C. Coleman. Copyright© 1964 by Scott, Foresman and Company, Chicago.

A study by Eichler (1965) was conducted at the Patuxent Institution for Defective Delinquents. He used 25 inmates out of 56. The group's mean age was 27.16 years and the mean I.Q. 106.08 by the Wechsler Adult Intelligence Scale. Among the group's members there was no history of crime in the family, and no history of hospitalization for psychosis.

The author hypothesized that the speech habits of an individual reflect the characteristic coping mechanisms which he develops to handle anxiety. Previous findings (Weintraub and Aronson, 1962) showed that typical speech habits reflecting defense mechanisms could be measured objectively, and that the speech pattern used by impulsive patients mirrored their typical behavior pattern.

The procedure used involved a ten-minute talk about any subject or subjects. The patient spoke into a tape recorder and no questions were allowed once the experiment began.

The Weintraub and Aronson scoring method was used. Speech was divided into twelve categories:

1. The quantity of speech—all completed words.
2. Long pauses and silences (more than five seconds).
3. The rate of speech— $\dfrac{\text{total words}}{\text{nonsilence minutes}}$
4. "Nonpersonal" references—A "personal" clause is one whose subject refers to a specific person or persons known to the speaker, including references to the volunteer himself.
5. A shift to the past tense.
6. Negators—not, no, nothing, never, etc.
7. Qualifiers—suppose, more or less, what one might call, etc.
8. Retractor—any word, phrase, or clause which detracts from the statement preceding it. "John is an honest person. Of course he has been involved in some shady deals!"
9. Explaining or justifying—because, due to, as a result of, etc.
10. Direct reference either to the experimenter or the physical surroundings.
11. Expressions of feeling—this does not take into account the tone of voice, facial expression, etc. which are lost in transcription.
12. Evaluators which are value judgments.

Anything less than 200 words was not used and there was a minimum of 600 words for negators and 800 words for shift to past tense.

According to Eichler's results, sociopaths were higher than normals on *negation, retraction, evaluation*. As compared with impulsives, sociopaths were higher on *nonpersonal references*.

The known behavior of the impulsive compares with his verbal responses as follows:

1. Cannot tolerate feelings of anxiety *(expressions of feelings)*
2. Attempts to deny feelings *(negators)*
3. Manipulates human environment *(direct reference)*
4. Arouses guilt *(evaluators)*
5. Tries to undo behavior *(retractors)*

The greater use of *negators* by the psychopaths seems broadly consistent with clinical interpretations of their tendency to protect themselves from awareness of conflict and guilt. Their more frequent use of *qualifiers* is rather less clear; possibly it might correlate with their (often) apparent goal-lessness. With respect to *evaluation,* it seems possible that guilt feelings might lead an individual to impose value judgments habitually upon external factors; hence, the psychopath is seen once again as protecting himself from awareness.

The category *retractors* appears to be an important speech pattern. By an excessive use of retracting statements, the pyschopathic individual is stating an incongruous belief. The difficulty arises from his inability to perceive the contradiction in such statements as those which correlate honesty with "shady deals." He believes the first statement (about honesty) enough to place himself in that position and thus justify his own "shady" behavior. It is almost in the nature of a syllogism which would read:

> All men are honest.
> I am a man.
> Therefore, I am honest.

If one were unaware of the illogic in such a comparison, he would believe himself to be honest regardless of particular dishonest actions. The psychopath frequently acts as though he had internalized this conception and therefore cannot understand the reasons why he becomes the target of blame and accusations.

Regarding *nonpersonal reference,* Weintraub and Aronson feel that the psychopath thereby proves himself to be *not* impulsive. As the authors put it, "The impulsive act is often an explosive outburst of feeling." The psychopath takes time to plan, he delays his actions. The impulsive patient exceeds the psychopath in direct reference words.

VERBAL LEARNING AND RETENTION

The characteristic inability of the psychopath to profit from experience (Cleckley, 1955) suggests either a basic learning deficiency or perhaps an insensitivity to social rewards and/or punishments. Fairweather

(1954) and Kadlub (1956), using a rote serial learning task, found no differences between psychopaths and normals under appropriate conditions of either concrete or social reward. Their results argue against the assertion that psychopathy is invariably accompanied by a basic deficiency in learning capacity or that psychopaths are insensitive to appropriate social rewards. The criterion for classifying subjects as psychopaths was, in both studies, a clinical diagnosis of "psychopathic personality." All subjects were institutionalized criminals.

Hetherington and Klinger (1964) cite evidence of poor avoidance learning in psychopaths (Lykken, 1957) in support of the position that psychopaths are insensitive to punishment. The basic assumption, developed by Mowrer (1960), is that learning to make an avoidance response and learning to inhibit a punished response are both two-stage processes, the first stage of which is the classical conditioning of an emotional response, fear, to an originally neutral conditioned stimulus. Hetherington and Klinger hypothesized that psychopathy is inversely related to an underlying dimension of fear conditionability, which is applicable to normal individuals as well. As subjects, they used female college students, classified on the Psychopathic Deviation scale of the MMPI as being above the mean (high Pd) or below the mean (low Pd). They predicted that high Pd subjects would be less affected by verbal punishment (critical, discouraging statements following each trial) than would low Pd subjects, and that the two groups would not differ under the verbal reward or no reward conditions. These predictions were substantially confirmed for a rote serial learning task. The perfomance of the low Pd subjects (trials to criterion) was significantly lowered by the verbal punishment; the scores of the other five experimental groups were virtually identical.

A single study by Sherman (1957), using a retroactive interference design, provides empirical support for the clinical observation that psychopaths have excellent memories. (Lindner, 1944; Pennington, 1954). The superior retention scores of psychopathic criminals, when compared with "model prisoners," was attributed to the relative absence of anxiety in the psychopathic group.

These studies must be considered merely suggestive of possible avenues of research in this area. Their generality, as well as their importance for psychopathic theory, is limited by the absence of a reliable, objective measure of psychopathy. What is the relation, for example, between "the men most difficult to manage" at a state penitentiary, and college students with high Pd scores on the MMPI? Can we expect the same theory to explain the behavior of both groups? The absence of suitable control groups, particularly in studies using prisoners, is another methodological difficulty facing this research. Noninstitutionalized psychopaths are not easily detected, let alone induced into the psychological laboratory.

The theoretical difficulties faced by these studies concern primarily the problem of translating the language of clinical description into the operationally defined constructs of experimental psychology. The behavior seems to "lose something" in the translation, in addition to possibly being distorted. The experiment of Hetherington and Klinger (1964) provides one example of this problem. The clinical observation is the frequent failure of punishment to modify the antisocial behavior of the psychopath. The confirming laboratory result is the failure of critical and discouraging remarks by the experimenter, between trials, to disrupt the performance of "high Pd" subjects on a rote verbal learning task. The performance of the "low Pd" subjects is explained as follows: Since punishment follows the subject's verbal responses, a conditioned fear reaction develops, leading to partial suppression of those responses. The result is an increase in the number of trials to criterion in the serial learning task. Since psychopaths, on the other hand, are presumably deficient in affective reactivity to social disapproval (Cleckley, 1955), the high Pd subjects show less inhibition of the punished responses. This line of reasoning stems from an attempt to apply uncritically, to human subjects, a principle derived from animal conditioning studies; namely, that punishment depresses all responding. It ignores the subject's awareness of the response-punishment relation: that the punishment is the result of failure to respond, or of errors, is the most likely interpretation. This consideration makes the poor performance of the low Pd subjects the result in need of explanation. If the theoretical background of the study had been a little different, the authors might have concluded that low Pd subjects show a "neurotic" reaction to criticism, and that—in college students at least—"a little Pd" might be a good thing.

VERBAL CONDITIONING

Recently Quay and Hunt (1965) have reported a replication and extension of a previous study (Johns and Quay, 1962), in which psychopathic criminals were compared with neurotic offenders in a verbal conditioning paradigm. The two groups were selected on the basis of their scores on the neurotic and psychopathic subscales of the Delinquency Scale (DS), which was developed in earlier studies (Quay and Peterson, 1958; Peterson, Quay, and Cameron, 1959; Peterson, Quay, and Tiffany, 1961). The conditioning technique used was that reported by Taffel (1955), in which each subject is required to make up a sentence using a given verb and his choice of six personal pronouns. After 20 preliminary trials, during which no reinforcement is given, experimental subjects are told "good" in a "flat, unemotional tone" at the end of sentences in which they use the pronouns "I" or "We." This procedure is followed for an additional 60 trials. The measure of conditioning is the increase in the use of the first person pronouns in the last block of 20 trials when compared with the first (unreinforced) block.

In both studies, the experimental neurotics showed significant increases, whereas the experimental psychopaths and two unreinforced control groups did not. The investigators interpreted this result as providing support for Cleckley's (1955) concept of Semantic Dementia in psychopaths.

The original study was open to a number of methodological criticisms, (Persons and Persons, 1965), some of which were met by the replication. What is of more concern, however, is the theoretical assumption which dictated the choice of the verbal conditioning paradigm. The authors maintain that Kadlub's failure to find differences between psychopathic and normal criminals in serial learning for social rewards was due to the psychopaths receiving self-administered rewards for being "correct." To eliminate such self-administered rewards, Johns and Quay selected a verbal conditioning procedure, under the assumption that verbal conditioning occurs without awareness of the correct response.

Recent evidence (Spielberger, 1962; 1965) indicates that verbal conditioning does not occur without awareness of the response-reinforcement contingency. In fact if the traditional learning-performance distinction of cognitive theory is maintained, so-called verbal "conditioning" is largely a matter of concept learning. Once the subject discovers which responses produce reinforcement, his performance depends upon his motive state and the appropriateness of the reinforcement. The conclusion to be drawn from the Johns and Quay study, then, is that the experimental neurotics, to the degree that they became aware of what the experimenter wanted *and* were willing to give him what he wanted, increased their use of the first-person pronouns. The fact that the experimental psychopaths did not "condition" could mean either that they did not become aware of the response-reinforcement relation or that they were indifferent to the reinforcement. The latter possibility provides another example of the problem of "translation" mentioned previously. The reaction of the psychopathic individual to social reinforcement, as mediated semantically through praise and blame, insults and threats, is an important part of the diagnostic and theoretical configuration of psychopathy. It is doubtfully represented by the "social reinforcement" of the present studies. The word "good," pronounced in a "flat, unemotional tone" by a youthful graduate student, is hardly calculated to produce paroxysms of joy in hardened criminals.

CONCLUSION

Most of the empirical studies reviewed above have attempted to validate, in the laboratory, clinically derived hypotheses concerning psychopathic personality. While such attempts are important and useful for the development of psychopathic theory, they entail the constant risk of oversimplification. The behavior patterns—verbal and nonverbal—which form the basic data that a theory of psychopathy must encompass are not easily translated into the unidimensional response measures of experimental psychology. In addition, a fuller understanding of the language behavior of the psychopath, and of his responses to the language behavior of others, will probably require more extensive knowledge of the role of awareness in detemining complex human behavior than we currently possess. We are fortunate in being able to record slow but steady progress toward the attainment of both objectives.

REFERENCES

Abrahamsen, D. *Crime and the human mind.* New York: Columbia University Press, 1944.

Abrahamsen, D. *The psychology of crime.* New York: Columbia University Press, 1960.

Bromberg, W. *Crime and the mind.* Philadelphia: J. B. Lippincott, 1948.

Cleckley, H. Psychopathic personality. In *Encyclopedia of criminology.* New York: Philosophical Library, 1949.

Cleckley, H. *The mask of sanity.* St. Louis: Mosby, 1955.

Clinard, M. *Sociology of deviant behavior.* New York: Rinehart, 1958.

Coleman, J. C. *Abnormal psychology and modern life.* Chicago: Scott, Foresman, 1956, 1964.

Eichler, M. The application of verbal behavior analysis to the study of psychological defense mechanisms: Speech patterns associated with sociopathic behavior. *Journal of Nervous and Mental Disease,* 1965, *141,* 658–63.

Fairweather, G. W. The effect of selected incentive conditions on the performance of psychopathic, neurotic, and normal criminals in a serial rote learning situation. *Dissertation Abstracts,* 1954, *14,* 394–95.

Hetherington, E. M. and Klinger, E. Psychopathy and punishment. *Journal of Abnormal and Social Psychology,* 1964, *69,* 113–15.

Johns, J. H. and Quay, H. C. The effect of social reward on verbal conditioning in psychopathic and neurotic military offenders. *Journal of Consulting Psychology,* 1962, *26,* 217–20.

Kadlub, K. J. The effects of two types of reinforcement on the performance of psychopathic and normal criminals. Unpublished doctoral dissertation. University of Illinois, 1956.

Lindner, R. M. *Rebel without a cause.* New York: Grune and Stratton, 1944.

Lipton, H. The psychopath. *Journal of Crime, Law and Criminality,* 1950, *60,* 584–600.

Lykken, D. T. A study of anxiety in the sociopathic personality. *Journal of Abnormal and Social Psychology,* 1957, *55,* 6–10.

McCord, W. and McCord, J. *Psychopathy and delinquency.* New York: Grune and Stratton, 1956.

Mowrer, O. H. *Learning theory and behavior.* New York: Wiley, 1960.

Pennington, L. A. Criminal and psychopathic behavior. In L. A. Pennington and I. A. Berg (Eds.), *An introduction to clinical psychology.* New York: Ronald Press, 1954.

Persons, R. W. and Persons, C. E. Some experimental support for psychopathic theory: A critique. *Psychological Reports,* 1965, *16,* 745–49.

Pescor, M. J. Abnormal personality types among offenders. *Federal Probation,* 1948, *12,* 3–8.

Peterson, D. R., Quay, H. C., and Cameron, G. R. Personality and background factors in juvenile delinquency as inferred from questionnaire responses. *Journal of Consulting Psychology,* 1959, *23,* 395–99.

Peterson, D. R., Quay, H. C., and Tiffany, T. L. Personality factors related to juvenile delinquency. *Child Development,* 1961, *32,* 355–72.

Quay, H. C. and Hunt, W. A. Psychopathy, neuroticism, and verbal conditioning: A replication and extension. *Journal of Consulting Psychology,* 1965, *29,* 283.

Quay, H. C. and Peterson, D. R. A brief scale for juvenile delinquency. *Journal of Clinical Psychology,* 1958, *14,* 139.

Sherman, L. J. Retention in psychopathic, neurotic, and normal subjects. *Journal of Personality,* 1957, *25,* 721–29.

Spielberger, C. D. The role of awareness in verbal conditioning. In C. W. Eriksen (Ed.), *Behavior and awareness.* Durham, N. C.: Duke University Press, 1962.

Spielberger, C. D. Theoretical and epistemological issues in verbal conditioning. In Rosenberg (Ed.), *Directors in psycholinguistics.* New York: Macmillan, 1965.

Taffel, C. Anxiety and the conditioning of verbal behavior. *Journal of Abnormal and Social Psychology,* 1955, *51,* 496–501.

Wallinger, J. The psychopath: A confused concept. *Federal Probation,* 1956, *20,* 51–54.

Weintraub, W. and Aronson, H. The application of verbal behavior analysis to the study of psychological defense mechanisms. *Journal of Nervous and Mental Disease,* 1962, *134,* 169–81.

White, R. W. *The abnormal personality.* New York: Ronald Press, 1964.

CHAPTER 9

LANGUAGE BEHAVIOR
IN AFFECTIVE DISORDERS

The term *manic-depressive psychosis* was introduced by Kraepelin (1896) to designate a series of attacks of elation and depression with intervals of relative normality and a generally favorable prognosis. Under the heading of affective disorders we currently include the manic-depressive reactions and psychotic-depressive reactions. Involutional reactions with a depressive coloring were formerly grouped with the affective disorders, but current psychiatric classification procedures treat these as a separate category of psychotic disorders.

Three principal types of manic-depressive reactions are distinguished: (1) manic reactions, (2) depressive reactions, and (3) circular and mixed reactions. The latter category is characterized by patients who alternate between manic and depressive reactions or who exhibit a simultaneous combination of the two types of symptoms. According to Coleman (1956), the incidence of manic-depressive reactions is as shown in Figure 6.

Manic-depressives account for about 6 to 8 per cent of all first admission to mental hospitals, with women showing a predominance of 3 to 2 in the sex ratio. Although manic-depressive reactions have been reported in patients ranging in age from fourteen to sixty-five (Rennie and Fowler, 1942), the median age at the time of first admission is approximately forty.

Focal to the clinical picture in manic-depressive reactions is the prevailing mood of the patient—elation or depression. "The severely depressed individual views the world with extreme pessimism and is deeply convinced that he and others are evil. The euphoric individual is unrealis-

FIGURE 6

COMPARATIVE INCIDENCE OF MANIC-DEPRESSIVE TYPES

(After Coleman, 1956)

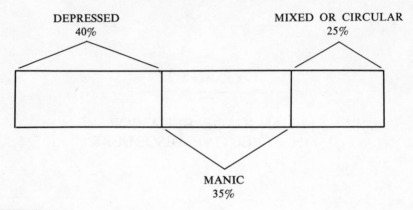

tically optimistic, feels that he and others are wonderful, and elatedly anticipates a rosy future." (Rosen and Gregory, 1965, p. 283)

Against the background provided by this conspicuous deviation from normal mood there may occur a variety of secondary disturbances of cognitive functioning, perception, and overt behavior which are consistent with the predominant emotional tone. In manic reactions there is often a delusional overvaluation of intelligence, sexual attractiveness, power, wealth, etc., and the possible accompaniment of hallucinatory experiences. Depressive patients typically develop delusions of sin and guilt, of self-accusation, worthlessness, and hopelessness. Older depressed patients may also develop bizarre hypochondriacal delusions or delusions of nihilism. The principal types of hallucinatory reactions found in patients with affective disorders are summarized by Rennie and Fowler as follows:

. . . conversed with God; heard sentences—"daughter is dead"; saw iceberg floating, bottle carbolic in ceiling; voices in gramophone, people talking through stomach; saw star on Christmas day; saw and heard dead mother; voices tell her not to eat, to walk backward; sees something white —a vision; saw path of fire running up and down; saw and heard God and angels; saw snake coming to her; trees glitter like gold; saw dead father; animal faces in food; saw and heard animals; heard voices; voices —"they've got me now"; sees dead people and skulls (patient very superstitious); brother's and dead people's voices; God's voice, sees Devil and Hell's flames; saw God; sees husband and coffin; hand pointing to cross; sees her babies in heaven; voice says: "Do not stay with husband";

sees snakes and Negroes; two men digging a grave; saw fire and fire engine repeatedly. (p. 805)[1]

Manic-depressive reactions may vary in duration from a few hours to many years. The shorter the attack, the greater is the likelihood that the patient will be free of marked personality disorganization. Rosen and Gregory state that untreated depressions last an average of one and a half years as compared with 4 to 6 months for untreated manic attacks. Although many patient show spontaneous recovery from manic and depressive episodes, there is a high rate of readmission to mental hospitals. Age is an important variable: older patients show a tendency toward longer attacks, briefer periods of remission, and increasing personality deterioration, particularly manic patients.

LINGUISTIC PROFILES FOR THE AFFECTIVE DISORDERS

Language behavior has received less attention in the affective disorders than in other psychotic syndromes. The general clinical impression seems to be that the language of the manic patient, for example, reflects a flight of ideas and consequently a speeding up of his verbal productivity. Says Sherman (1938):

> The manic is easily distracted and therefore cannot convey his ideas clearly. There is no actual distortion of language except for the type of reaction which represents ideas of grandeur. And this is probably not a true language distortion. (p. 637)

Eisenson (1963) provides us with a general characterization of the language behavior in the manic patient:

> The speech of the manic is symptomatic of his behavior in general and of his disordered thinking. He is likely to talk incessantly and rapidly, incorporating many marginal or tangential ideas into his stream of speech. The rapid tempo often results in slurring and in the production of word fragments. When these are run together they may suggest either neologisms or "word salads." The style of the manic's utterances tends to be telegraphic; many connecting words, participles, relative pronouns, and prepositions are likely to be omitted. Because the flow of ideas is not checked, the content of the patient's speech is highly diversified and is frequently far in excess of the listener's rate of absorption. The manic's speech is at first fascinating, but ultimately wearying. Little if any attention is paid to the auditor; the manic speaks to express his own emotional and mental state. The presence of an auditor serves as a stimulant for

---

[1] Reprinted by permission, from *American Journal of Psychiatry*, 1942, *98*, 801–14.

speaking rather than as a stimulant for communicative utterance. (p. 374)[2]

The role of the flight of ideas is illustrated in this example of the verbalizations of a manic patient (Sherman, 1938):

> Yesterday I went downtown to buy $50,000 worth of real estate but they wouldn't believe me when I said that I would earn enough in the next month to pay them for it. You know my father is a big man in the city. You wear nice clothes and how much does the watch cost? Have you a sister? I have three and they are all very fine girls—girls, curls, furls, isn't that funny? (p. 637)

Perhaps the only indication of distortion in the above example is the clang association "girls, curls, furls," and is indicative of the tendency in manic patients to interpolate irrelevant material only when some external stimulus provokes a flight of associations.

A more extended sample of manic speech is given in the following excerpt from Cameron and Margaret (1951). Some of the general features of manic behavior are also borne out in this case study.

> A thirty-five-year-old biochemist was brought to the clinic by his frightened wife. To his psychiatrist the patient explained, "I discovered that I had been drifting, broke the bonds and suddenly found myself doing things and doing them by telegraph. I was dead tired, and decided to go on a vacation; but even there it wasn't long before I was sending more telegrams. I got into high gear and started to buzz. Then a gentle hint from a friend took effect and I decided to come here and see if the changes in my personality were real." He entered the ward in high spirits, went about greeting the patients, insisted that the place was "swell," and made quick puns on the names of doctors to whom he was introduced. Meanwhile his wife said she was "scared to death." "His friends used to call him 'Crazy Charley,' " she said, "but I haven't seen this streak in him for years."
>
> When his wife had left, the patient soon demonstrated what he meant by "high gear." He bounded down the hall, threw his medication on the floor, leaped up on a window ledge and dared any one to get him down. When he was put in a room alone where he could be free, he promptly dismantled the bed, pounded on the walls, yelled and sang. He made a sudden sally into the hall and did a kind of hula-hula dance before he could be returned to his room. His shouting continued throughout the night, and betrayed in its content the ambivalent attitudes which the patient maintained toward his hospitalization: "What the hell kind of a place is this? A swell place? I'm not staying here. I'm having a hell

---

[2] Reprinted by permission of Appleton–Century–Crofts, New York; © 1963 Meredith Publishing Company.

of a good time. Oh, I'm so happy. I have to get going. My gray suit please, my gray coat please, my gray socks, all gray on their way, going to be gay. I'm going out as fast as I came in, only faster. I'm happier than I have ever been in my life. I'm 100 per cent better than normal." (p. 332)[3]

In contrast to the euphoria, excitement, hyperactivity, and logorrhea of the manic, the depressed patient exhibits dejection, psychomotor retardation, and severe restriction in intellectual productivity. In addition, the patient may perseverate on a single, fixed idea; obsessive thoughts, particularly of suicide or death, may predominate. Like the manic patient, the depressive's language behavior is symptomatic of his disturbance. Says Eisenson:

> The patient speaks slowly, often verbalizing the same thoughts over and over again. This is frequently a loss of insight or judgment as to the significance of the thoughts that are presented; the consequential and the inconsequential, from the listener's point of view, are offered as if they were of equal importance. Diversification of utterance is extremely low, so that the auditor becomes quickly bored and seeks an escape. His efforts to change the direction of discourse are generally futile. The depressive patient speaks to express himself, rather than to elicit responses from his auditor. (p. 376)[4]

In acute depression, the patient may become completely mute and inaccessible to verbal communication of any kind.

SPOKEN LANGUAGE IN THE AFFECTIVE DISORDERS

A study was conducted in 1938 by Stanley Newman, a language specialist, and Vera Mather, a psychiatrist, which easily merits that much abused appellation "classic." In its conception and methodology, this study was far in advance of contemporary investigations of psychotic language. At a time when other researchers in this area were busy making word counts and tabulating verb-adjective quotients, Newman and Mather were making a serious effort to analyze language behavior in affective patients in terms of both linguistic and paralinguistic variables.

To begin with, their study was addressed to phonograph recordings of spoken language, including both spontaneous speech and verbal material elicited by questions from the psychiatrist. In addition, the list of descriptive criteria used in the eventual analysis of speech was built up

---

[3] Reprinted by permission of Houghton Mifflin Company, Boston.

[4] Reprinted by permission of Appleton–Century–Crofts, New York; © 1963 Meredith Publishing Company.

over the course of many replayings of the records. Newman and Mather's final list is given in full below:

I. Articulatory movements:

Lax, vigorous. (Although one may receive a general impression of the character of articulatory movements throughout a person's speech, the pronunciation of the stop consonants *t, d, k, g* provides the clearest indication. These consonants are produced by a closure of the tongue against the palate, followed by a release. In the speech of some persons, however, the closure is only partial or loosely made, and the release is lax; *d* or *t,* for example, will sound like a single-trilled *r.* In the speech of others, the closure is tight and the release is crisp and vigorous; here the *d* or *t* may be accompanied by a slight click.)

II. Pitch:

A. Range of pitch:

Wide, narrow. (In English the greatest changes of pitch are ordinarily found at the end of sentences: the pitch falls at the end of declarative statements and rises at the end of interrogations. But rises and falls that extend over a wide pitch range in the speech of one person will be flattened in the speech of another. Some people speak with so narrow a pitch range that the sentences often end without any perceptible rise or fall; this phenomenon will be referred to as the "hovering" tone.)

B. Pitch changes:

1. General character: gliding, step-wise.
2. Frequency.
3. Variety of patterns: diversified, stereotyped.

III. Emphatic accent:

A. Type:

Rhetorical, constrastive. (Two phonetically distinct types of accent are used for emphasis in English. The rhetorical type can be identified, for example, in "I saw a tall man," when the word "tall" is protracted in length; a slightly raised pitch and a strong force of articulation may also accompany this accent, which expresses the speaker's surprise or wonder concerning the reference of the accented word. In the contrastive type of accent, the intonation which normally comes at the end of the sentence is displaced to the emphasized word, the emphasis being most commonly employed to contrast this word with another one, expressed or implied: in "I saw a tall man" [i.e., not a short one], the word "tall" takes the falling tone which otherwise would appear on "man." Generally a strong force of articulation also marks the constrastively accented word.)

B. Frequency.
C. Types of references receiving emphatic accents.

IV. Tempo:
    A. Individual words: Drawled, choppy.
    B. Stream of speech:
        1. General speed: slow, fast.
        2. Changes of speed:
            a. Frequency of change.
            b. Manner of change: gradual, sudden.
    C. Pauses:
        1. Type: prosodic (pauses between phrases), hesitating (pauses within phrases).
        2. Frequency.
V. Resonance:
    A. Placement:
    Oral, pharyngeal, nasal. (The oral cavity is the primary resonator in speech. But many people when speaking extend and enlarge the pharyngeal cavity, which acts as a resonance chamber for the voice and gives it a "throaty" quality. Nasality results when the voice resonates in the nasal passage and escapes, either partially of wholly, through the nose.)
    B. Glottal activity:
        1. Type: Glottal closures, glottal rasps. (Complete glottal closures occur in some dialect forms of English. Otherwise they are seldom found outside of gross speech disturbances. Much more common are the glottal rasps, produced by an incomplete closure of the glottis; the entire glottis is made to vibrate, with some vertical as well as lateral motion. When rasping occurs, a throaty trill infects the speech.)
        2. Position in statements: at beginning, at end.
    C. Changes in volume:
        1. Frequency of change.
        2. Manner of change: gradual, sudden.
    D. Timbre: Hoarse, shrill, breathy.
VI. Vocabulary and Phrasing:
    A. Level of style: Colloquial, formal, pompous.
    B. Words referring to concepts of degree:
        1. Type: Extreme, neutral. (Concepts of degree can be conceived as distributed on a continuum going from extreme minus to extreme plus. Words referring to either extreme, such as "wonderful" or "terrible, terrible" in V. R.'s record [Case IV.], are to be distinguished from the relatively neutral and colorless words, such as "nice" in W. N.'s record [Case I.])
        2. Frequency.
    C. Tag phrases (e.g., "you see," "I dunno," "you know").
    D. Repetition of phrases, of phrase patterns.
VII. Syntax:
    A. General features of syntactic structure.

    1. Coherence: Tight, loose.
    2. Progression: Continuous, broken.
    3. Elaboration:
       a. Degree of syntactic elaboration: rich, meagre.
       b. Variety of techniques used for elaboration.
  B. Statements:
    1. Type: Statements consisting of a word, of a phrase, of a total predication.
    2. Length.
VIII. Response:
  A. Rapidity in initiating response.
  B. Length of response, in terms of number of statements.
  C. Relation of response to question: Rapport with question throughout response; rapport with question only at beginning of response; response avoiding question; response unrelated to question.
  D. Interrelation of statements in response: Statements clustering about a single theme; statements progressing from primary to secondary themes; statements jumping from one theme to another.
  E. Character of references in response:
    1. References to interlocutor.
    2. Proper names, titles, dates, numbers.
    3. Apologies, corrections, interrogations.
IX. Accessory vocal activity: Sighing, yawning, coughing, clearing the throat, laughing, weeping.
X. Special features:
  A. Comparison of reading with spontaneous speech.
  B. Peculiarities associated with particular contents.
  C. Recurrent themes.   (pp. 914–17)

The forty subjects for this study were drawn from four groups which were characterized by the author as: *classical depression, states of dissatisfaction, self-pity and gloom, manic syndromes,* and *mixed affective states*. Brief descriptions of the groups were given.

1. CLASSICAL DEPRESSION

The patients included in this group all experienced circumscribed illnesses characterized predominately by sadness of mood and retardation. Some showed agitation, tension and self-accusatory ideas. Insomnia, anorexia and constipation were usual. Some had experienced similar illnesses previously with recovery. A smaller number had had episodes of euphoria and acceleration. (p. 917)

2. STATES OF DISSATISFACTION, SELF-PITY AND GLOOM

In this group were included patients experiencing more or less chronic states of dissatisfaction, self-pity and gloom. The illness usually was not circumscribed, and the mood showed more responsiveness to changes in the situation than is seen in classical depressions. Somantic symptoms were less pronounced. In some cases there had been previous episodes suggesting "classical" depressions of several months' duration, but at the time of examination the patient was rather in a rut of self-concern, discontent and self-pity. (p. 923)

3. MANIC SYNDROMES

In this group were included those syndromes characterized predominately by acceleration with euphoria or irritability. Many showed grandiose trends. The illnesses were circumscribed. Many of the patients had had previous similar attacks or had experienced depressive episodes. (p. 926)

4. MIXED AFFECTIVE STATES

The patients included in this group presented mixed pictures but with a predominance of disturbances of affect.

Newman and Mather reported their findings in the form of a tabular summary which is given in Table 13, which is a duplicate of Table 1 and repeated here because of its importance in this discussion. However, such a summary can scarcely begin to do justice to the thoroughness and meticulousness of their analysis. For purposes of illustration, we may cite only one example, their description of the speech in the patients belonging to the group identified as classical depression:

A marked laxity of articulatory movements characterized the speech of these patients. With its sparing use of pitch and accent, their voice had a dead, listless quality: changes of pitch covered a narrow tonal range and were predominantly step-wise rather than gliding; hovering tones often appeared at the end of sentences, where speakers of English usually employ the broadest pitch changes; intonations tended to recur in the same stereotyped patterns; and emphatic accents were either rare or absent entirely. Their speech gave an impression of being slow and halting, because of the frequent appearance of hesitation pauses interrupting the flow of their phrases. In its resonance, their voice was pharyngeal and sometimes nasal; glottal rasping was present, and this, added to the pharyngeal resonance, gave their speech a "throaty" quality. They made little effort to use precise words or elaborate phrases: they spoke in an informal and colloquial style; words referring to concepts of degree had a neutral and colorless character, and they were infrequently used. The sentences of these patients were often loose and fragmentary in construction; syntactic elaboration was meagre, and the syntactic devices tended to be of the simple additive type; such as coordination and parallelism. Responses were slowly initiated, and they were brief, consisting of only one or a few statements; the statements themselves were short, often being nothing more than a phrase. The brevity of their responses gave the patients little opportunity to wander from the point of the question. (pp. 917–18)

TABLE 13

ANALYSIS OF SPEECH CHARACTERISTICS OF FORTY PATIENTS WITH
AFFECTIVE DISORDERS
(After Newman and Mather, 1938)

	Classical Depressions	States of Dissatisfaction, Self-pity, and Gloom	Manic Syndromes
Articulatory movements	Lax	Fairly crisp	Vigorous
Pitch range	Narrow	Wide	Wide
Pitch changes	Step-wise; infrequent	Gliding; frequent	Gliding; frequent
Emphatic accents	Absent or rare	Infrequent	Frequent
Speech tempo	Slow	Average	. . . .
Pauses	Hesitating; frequent	Frequent	Prosodic; frequent
Resonance	Pharyngeal, nasal	Pharyngeal, nasal	Oral, pharyngeal
Glottal rasping	Present	Present	Absent
Level of style	Colloquial	Colloquial	Elevated
Degree concepts	Neutral; infrequent	Neutral; infrequent	Extreme; frequent
Syntactic elaboration	Meagre	. . . .	Rich
Syntactic techniques	Limited	. . . .	Diversified
Initiation of response	Slow	Quick	Quick
Length of response	Short	Varied in length	Long
Statements in response	Developing single theme	Developing single theme	Passing from one topic to another
Rapport with question	Throughout response	Throughout response	At beginning of response

Reprinted from *American Journal of Psychiatry*, 1938, *94*, 913-42.

From such descriptions we receive a full, comprehensive, and detailed picture of language behavior in all salient aspects.

INTERPRETATIONS AND CONCLUSIONS

A fairly well delineated portrait of the manic patient emerges from the study of his language behavior. The content of his utterances is circumstantial and anecdotal—like a diary account of the day's events and activities. There is little personal qualification or evaluation; the speaker is "outside" the things he narrates, a spectator rather than a participant. His speech is discursive and verbose, neither directed toward some specific objective nor used in the service of rational argument. Marginal ideas continually intrude and transient stimuli are a constant source of distraction.

Certainly one of the most striking characteristics of the manic's language behavior is this tendency for the content of his utterances to be determined by associates. The automatic filtering process which in the normal person selects and rejects verbal material and orders semantic content according to a complex encoding process is greatly diminished in the manic patient. For him it is as though each stimulus and each response serves to summon up another. What results is that concatenation of thought and language aberrations we call "flight of ideas." Arieti (1959) states:

> Actually, this type of verbal behavior has a goal—that of maintaining this superficial effervescent euphoria and of escaping from intruding thoughts which may bring about depression. In not-too-pronounced cases the patient realizes that he unduly allows details to interfere with the original goal of his conversation and tries to go back to it, but again he is lost in many details. (p. 427)[5]

Lorenz (1953) and Lorenz and Cobb (1952) report a relative increase in the use of pronouns and verbs, a relative decrease in the use of adjectives and prepositions, and a high verb-adjective quotient (i.e., the proportion of adjectives is decreased) in the speech of manic patients. They conclude: "If the assumption of a correlation between emotional states and verb-adjective quotient is correct, the manic patient's speech gives objective evidence of a heightened degree of anxiety." (p. 428)

Such conclusions sound eminently plausible and appear congruent with those arrived at through a study of other aspects of manic behavior, but they are at least open to question. Newman and Mather (1938) caution against the danger of confusing formal identity and functional identity: "It cannot be assumed that any given characteristic has the same interpretation in the speech of all persons." (p. 939) If this admonition holds true for individual elements of language behavior, it must have even greater significance for such artificial constructions as the verb-adjective ratio. In any event, the interpretations that have been made of the meaning of the verb-adjective ratio in the context of the original studies (e.g., Buseman, 1925) are highly debatable.

It seems reasonably clear from the few studies available on language behavior in the affective disorders that there is little evidence of gross

---

[5] Reprinted by permission of Basic Books, Inc., New York.

pathology or disorganization at the level of structural elements. Most of the phenomena in these patients can be explained on the basis of psychomotor acceleration or retardation. The defect, as Arieti (1959) has suggested, occurs at higher integrative levels of language formulation.

REFERENCES

Arieti, S. Manic-depressive psychosis. In S. Arieti (Ed.), *American handbook of psychiatry*, Vol. 1. New York: Basic Books, 1959.

Busemann, A. *Die Sprache der Jugend als Ausdruck der Entwicklungsrhythmik*. Jena: Fisher, 1925.

Cameron, N. and Margaret, A. *Behavior pathology*. Boston: Houghton Mifflin, 1951.

Coleman, J. C. *Abnormal psychology and modern life*. Chicago: Scott, Foresman, 1956, 1964.

Eisenson, J., Auer, J. J., and Irwin, J. V. *The psychology of communication*. New York: Appleton-Century-Crofts, 1963.

Kraepelin, E. *Psychiatrie: ein Lehrbuch für Studierende und Ärtzte*. Leipzig: Barth, 1896.

Lorenz, M. Language as expressive behavior. *A.M.A. Archives of Neurology and Psychiatry*, 1953, *70*, 277–85.

Lorenz, M. and Cobb, S. Language behavior in manic patients. *A.M.A. Archives of Neurology and Psychiatry*, 1952, *69*, 763–70.

Newman, S. Behavior patterns in linguistic structure. In *Language, culture and personality*. Menasha, Wis.: Sapir Memorial Publication Fund, 1941.

Newman, S. and Mather, V. G. Analysis of spoken language of patients with affective disorders. *American Journal of Psychiatry*, 1938, *94*, 913–42.

Rennie, T. A. C. and Fowler, J. B. Prognosis in manic-depressive psychoses. *American Journal of Psychiatry*, 1942, *98*, 801–14.

Rosen, E. and Gregory, I. *Abnormal psychology*. Philadelphia: W. B. Saunders, 1965.

Sherman, M. Verbalization and language symbols in personality adjustment. *American Journal of Psychiatry*, 1938, *95*, 621–40.

CHAPTER 10

LANGUAGE BEHAVIOR
IN SCHIZOPHRENIA

A major difficulty that inheres in any attempt to analyze the behavioral phenomena of schizophrenia is the problem of dealing with such a broad range of complex behaviors as though they were similar. We must begin by recognizing that the term schizophrenia refers to a group of disorders with some common features and some wide behavioral differences, rather than to a single disease entity with a well-defined series of symptoms. There is even some justification for questioning whether the numerous and variegated psychopathological manifestations currently labeled schizophrenia should not be considered distinct syndromes.

It must also be noted that, in addition to inter-individual variation in symptomatology, schizophrenic reactions show intra-individual variation over the course of time. If one were to conceive of "mental health" as a continuum, schizophrenia would have to be depicted in terms of a range rather than a point on a scale.

Among the most frequent behavioral manifestations of schizophrenia, we might list the following:

1. Withdrawal from, and retraction of interest in, the environment.
2. Disturbances of thought expressed in blocking, symbolization, incoherence, perseveration, and condensation.
3. Increased daydreaming and autistic behavior in general.
4. Alteration of overt behavior with a tendency toward excess. This may be either in a marked increase of motor activity, or a marked decrease in the direction of immobility. Motor behavior tends to be characterized by perserveration and stereotypy.
5. Distortion or inappropriateness of affect, especially in regard to the underlying thinking of the individual and the meaning of the

situation. The divergence between feeling and thinking is perhaps the most general characteristic of schizophrenic behavior.

Four principal varieties of schizophrenia have been distinguished on the basis of certain predominant features, although a broad range of combinations is possible and there may be a succession of different pictures in the same patient in the course of the disturbance. The four major categories are hebephrenic, catatonic, paranoid, and simple deteriorating type. The hebephrenic type is characterized by silliness, fluctuation, incoherence, and fragmentation of thinking and performance. The catatonic type is characterized by general tenseness and rigidity with the chief characteristics lying in the field of psychomotor disturbances. The paranoid type is characterized by delusional experiences of a highly fantastic nature, inconsistent, illogical, bizarre, with a good deal of mysticism, persecutory and grandiose notions, and various hallucinations. The simple deteriorating type is characterized by a gradual loss of interests and ambitions, a slow withdrawal from family contacts, a persistent sliding into general listlessness and apathy.

Kanner (1943) makes a distinction between the adult schizophrenic and the child schizophrenic, indicating that the older a child is at the onset of the disturbance the more closely do the clinical features resemble the adult patterns. In smaller children there is less content and less variability. Potter (1933) indicates that if the central nervous system is the functional medium by which thinking, feeling, and acting are expressed, then it is to be expected that deviations of thinking, feeling, and acting are apt to be different in children than adults because the central nervous system is in a developmental stage. The level of intellectual development and the life experiences of the child are limited in comparison with those of the adult. Language developed to a degree of complexity is a product of mature intelligence. Children are not capable of complicated abstractions nor do they possess the facility to verbalize fully their feelings. The delusional formations seen in childhood are relatively simple and their symbolization is particularly naïve. Potter finds that the outstanding symptoms in childhood schizophrenia are found in a consistent lack of emotional rapport.

Within the broad scope of schizophrenic behavior, linguistic phenomena were among the first features to attract attention because of their striking and often bizarre qualities. As Gottschalk, Gleser, Magliocco, and D'Zmura (1961) have described:

> ... the content of the patient's communications has been found difficult to understand or quite unintelligible. The language has been seen as ambiguous, with a tendency to diffusion or generalization. The words, themselves, have been noted to be used inexactly, and frequently there is frank incoherence or disjunction. Elliptical statements may occur. The

sentences may have frequent self-contradictions and euphemisms, and they may contain many self-references and impersonal construction. (p. 101)

Written productions as well as the spoken utterances of schizophrenics have engaged the attention of investigators. The first specimens given below, representing extracts from documents written by schizophrenic patients, were reported by Maher (1966). Italicized words are those identified as neologisms.

1. "I am St. Michael the Archangel and the Red Horse of the Apocalypse. Some may say I have delusions of grandeur, but like Jesus Christ, I glorify myself for my Father's sake. For additional proof, I refer you to metaphysicians and Jehovah's Witnesses. I am in disguise and one might say a blessing in disguise. . . . I am for Goals for Americans, Strategy of Peace, Medical Care for the Aged, the Common Market, Peaceful Co-existence, and Self-Preservation not survival of the fittest, and also for freedom of religion."

2. "If things turn by rotation of agriculture or levels in regards and 'timed' to everything; I am re-fering to a previous document when I made some remarks that were facts also tested and there is another that concerns my daughter she has a *lobed* bottom right ear, her name being Mary Lou. . . . Much of abstraction has been left unsaid and undone in this product/milk syrup, and others due to economics, differentials, subsidies, bankruptcy, tools, buildings, bonds, national stocks, foundation craps, weather, trades, government in levels of breakages and fuses in electronic too all formerly 'stated' not necessarily *factuated*."

3. "The players and boundaries have been of different colors in terms of black and white and I do not intend that the futuramas of supersonic fixtures will ever be in my life again because I believe that all known factors that would have its effect on me even the chemical reaction of ameno [sic] acids as they are in the process of *combustronability* are known to me." (p. 395)

The next selections, reported by Lorenz (1961), are extracts from recorded interviews with schizophrenic patients.

1. "Am I a good cook? It depends in whose house I'm cooking. . . . No, I haven't had any dreams. They took the Ladies Home Journal out of my room and I haven't had any dreams. . . . Do you know the census population of the made world? I seem to have become so to speak the property of other people."

2. "I started with a sense that justice was next to the nebulous thing which no one can describe, but which dissolves all other relationships in its vapor, so that one notices other influences only insofar as they may help this nebulous aim, but without feeling of judgment otherwise."

3. "My teeth are killing me by expert dentistry of Dr. Brown the dentist and must be pulled as soon as possible as I will not live as I am

duped by expert dentistry. . . . After John Black has recovered sufficiently to do things in special neutral form of life the honest bring-back-to-life doctors agents must take John Black out through making up design meaning straight neutral underworld shadow tunnel. . . . (pp. 95–96)

Certain problems are involved in the reporting of language specimens which even persons devoid of professional training would have little difficulty recognizing as severely deviant. Lorenz (1961) cautions against the tendency to generalize from limited samples of schizophrenic language usage to *a* schizophrenic language: "When we have a name for something, we tend automatically to assume the existence of a corresponding reality. Language, as used by schizophrenic patients, becomes identified by the term 'schizophrenic language.' This term suggests an entity with distinct features, a language differing from ordinary language." (p. 95)

Says Forrest (1965), with regard to the failure of investigators to establish a "schizophrenic dictionary" for use by the friends and relatives of patients. "Their question—Is there a schizophrenic language?—is as fruitless as the older quest for a poetic language. If one may search in vain for *a* schizophrenic language, one may on the other hand easily find schizophrenic language." (p. 1)

LANGUAGE AND THOUGHT IN SCHIZOPHRENIA

As we noted in the first chapter ("Historical and Systematic Perspectives"), much of the early and even relatively recent history of language study in schizophrenia was addressed to the search for formal characteristics of schizophrenic language. Tabulations of word count frequency, type/token and verb/adjective ratios, and detailed analyses of theme and content such as we have already described constituted the bulk of systematic inquiry. Said Maher (1966):

> Many investigations have been directed toward the discovery of formal differences between schizophrenic language and other kinds of language without regard to the testing of hypotheses. Other studies have attempted to find similarities between schizophrenic language and that of other specific groups in the hope of adding to the probability that schizophrenia may be subsumed under some more general category or process.
>
> Generally speaking, we may regard these studies of formal characteristics as having two possible values. First, they attempt to discover simple differences per se, and as such they might provide empirical bases for the development of hypotheses about the processes involved in schizophrenic language. However, their second value lies in their relevance for existing hypotheses. (p. 398)

We shall devote some discussion to this aspect of schizophrenic language study.

Arieti (1955) has suggested that the language of the schizophrenic may be studied in two ways: the dynamic and formal. The dynamic approach studies language from a predominantly motivational point of view, that is the schizophrenic is motivated to change his speech for a purpose —possibly a defense to defend himself from society in an effort to survive. The motivation is maintained by a chain of psychogenic causes and effects which originate early in the development of each individual. Arieti takes the position that the schizophrenic is motivated for one purpose—the removal of anxiety. In disconnecting himself from society, he feels safer and less disturbed. In rejecting society, he creates his own individuality and language. In this attempt to be unique, the schizophrenic resorts to archaic ways of expressing feelings and thoughts which were long ago discarded in the course of evolution. The schizophrenic goes through what Arieti terms "teleologic regression." The schizophrenic uses material (words and symbols) from the environment but remolds them by his own archaic psychological processes. His attempt to be unique thus fails to a certain extent because he resorts to methods which are not individualistic but may be classified and analyzed in structural categories. Thus what was a dynamic, historical process becomes crystallized in formal mechanisms. Any attempt to study the formal mechanisms of schizophrenia must be conscious of these dynamic qualities, of this fleeting mutability.

Arieti feels that the pathology of language as it appears in schizophrenia has three major headings:

1. Impairment of the ability to abstract.
2. Impairment of the ability to symbolize.
3. Impairment of the ability to socialize or to integrate into society.

These three impairments overlap and are possibly different expressions of the same phenomenon. All three should be considered and integrated for an overall view.

Goldstein (1944) indicates that expressions of abnormal concreteness are characteristic of the behavior of the schizophrenic. Goldstein defines the concrete attitude as *passive* and the abstract attitude as *active*. The concrete attitude is realistic, given over and bound to the immediate experience of a given thing or situation in its particular uniqueness— thinking and acting are directed by the immediate claims made by one particular aspect of the object or situation in the environment. The abstract attitude, in being active, transgresses the immediately given specific aspect or sense impression and abstracts from particular properties. It is oriented by the conceptual viewpoint. The abstract attitude is basic for the ability to assume voluntary mental set, to shift voluntarily from one aspect of a situation to another, to keep in mind simultaneously various aspects, to grasp essentials of a given whole, to break up a whole into parts, to generalize, to abstract common properties, to plan ahead, to think symbolically, and to detach the ego from the outer world.

"Concrete," as used to characterize behavior and activity, indicates we are governed to an abnormal degree by external stimuli and the images, ideas, and thoughts which act upon us at the moment. The schizophrenic experiences only those objects to which he can react in a concrete way. He does not consider the object as part of an ordered world separated from himself as the normal person does.

The strange words of the schizophrenic become understandable when considered in relation to the concrete situation which the patient experiences at the moment and wants to express in words. There is an absence of generic terms which signifies categories or classes, or, if used, do not refer to generalizations. For example, color-sorting tests were given in which a patient would name various shades of green rather than indicate they were all green. The colors did not represent the category but an individual property of an object. Goldstein suggests an origin in a disturbed function of the frontal lobes and the subcortical ganglia; also suggesting the possibility that the concreteness of the schizophrenic might be considered as a way out of the organism's unbearable conflict—a protection against the danger of severe catastrophe.

Kasanin (1944) suggests that the development of thought in a child occurs in three stages:

1. Physiognomic thinking—animation of objects and projection of his ego in them.
2. Concrete thinking—realistic and literal—reference to particular objects (uneducated or undeveloped thinking is of this type).
3. Abstract thinking—occurs after adolescence with education (property of the educated, adult person).

In using blocks of different sizes, shapes, and colors (developed by Ach), it was determined that the schizophrenic thinks largely in more concrete realistic matter of fact terms in which things have a personal rather than symbolic value. The schizophrenic is unable to grasp certain general principles. The schizophrenic refuses to use the normal person's classification when it is explained to him. The schizophrenic puts heterogenous blocks together, insisting that they are "all policemen," etc. The schizophrenic appears to classify according to physiognomic aspects of the material, and there is endless hesitancy and vacillation, taking all possibilities into simultaneous consideration. Kasanin postulates a reduction in the capacity of the schizophrenic to think abstractly and admits that there is uncertainty as to exactly when conceptual thinking develops.

Von Domarus (1944) indicates that the normal person (logician) accepts identity only upon the basis of identical subjects, whereas the schizophrenic (paralogician) accepts identity based upon identical predicates. In the example, "Socrates is a man—all men are mortal—Socrates is mortal," the schizophrenic would come to the conclusion: "Socrates is a man—I am a man—I am Socrates." Von Domarus gives as an additional example a schizophrenic patient in the insane asylum of the University of Bonn who believed that Jesus, cigar boxes, and sex were identical. Upon investigation as to the reason for this, it was found the connection was that of their having the identical element of being encircled: Jesus is a saint with a halo encircling his head, a package of cigars is encircled by a tax band and a woman is encircled by the sex glance of a man. Encirclement is the quality expressing essence to the schizophrenic. Von Domarus suggests that the laws of logic of a schizophrenic are those employed by primitive people or higher animals. Arieti feels that such things as the identification between the symbol and the object symbolized, the confusion between the part and the whole or the whole for the part, the bizarre composition of different objects such as are seen in schizophrenic drawings and neologisms can all be interpreted as applications of Von Domarus' principle.

In the impairment of ability to symbolize (Arieti, 1955) four categories of increasing complexity are listed:

1. Signs—presence of certain things.
2. Images—visual, auditory, etc.—perceptions of external objects or objects themselves.
3. Paleosymbols—symbols created by the individual when he selects a part or a predicate to represent the objects he wants to symbolize.
4. Common or social symbols—paleosymbols accepted socially, eliciting the same reaction in another person.

According to Arieti, the schizophrenic abandons the common symbols and reverts to signs, images, and paleosymbols. When the schizophrenic loses the use of social symbols he also desocializes himself—thereby living in isolation. As the schizophrenic becomes more desocialized, the understanding of his language becomes more difficult, reaching a peak in the "word salad." The "word salad" consists of speech made out of words that seem unrelated to one another, such as "the house burnt the cow horrendously always."

Arieti maintains that the schizophrenic's impairment of language, since it is functional, is not permanent. In the absence of anxiety, he has the potential to regain it.

CRITIQUE

The views of Von Domarus/Arieti have not been allowed to go unchallenged. Nor has the abstract/concrete dichotomy (Goldstein) escaped criticism. Said Brown (1958):

> Research workers believe in the psychological unity of children, in the mind of primitive man, in the animal mind. They believe in disease entities called schizophrenia and aphasia. And so they are disposed to unify each category through the use of a common descriptive term. All of these categories are fallen away from the healthy, civilized, human adult. Each category lacks one attribute of the category to which the researcher himself belongs. There is a beautiful simplicity in the notion that all departures from ourselves are basically the same kind of departure. *Abstract* is the word that has been chosen to name the special quality of mind and *concrete* the word for all other minds. The words have been used so as to maintain this master preconception rather than with referential consistency. The result is that *concrete* and *abstract* name all sorts of behaviors having no clear common properties. These unwitting shifts in reference are responsible for the general agreement that all kinds of subhuman mind are concrete as opposed to the abstract mind of the healthy, civilized adult. (p. 297)[1]

Brown reviewed several experimental studies which reported performances for schizophrenic subjects that were more concrete than the performances of normal subjects. These included the De la Garza and Worchel (1956) findings that schizophrenics were less oriented in time and space than normals, and Moran's (1953) report that schizophrenics were less able to deal with abstract analogies and less likely to give abstract definitions for words than normals. Brown observes:

> It is the general rule with these studies to find a statistically significant group difference but also to find that the two distributions have a large area of overlap. This means that these characteristics are not reliably diagnostic. Some of the performances of the schizophrenic clearly involve a preference for narrow categories (e.g., a failure to define a term by its superordinate) but many do not and it is often difficult to figure out the general definition of concreteness under which the performance is subsumed. Furthermore, there are some schizophrenic performances which must be judged abstract by our definition. Morgan, for instance, found that schizophrenics would accept an abnormally large number of synonyms for words. They gave to words an exceptionally wide range of meanings. (p. 294–95)[2]

Cameron (1963) has also been critical of the kinds of evidence advanced to support the regression hypothesis. He maintains that schizo-

---

[1] Reprinted by permission of the Macmillan Company, New York.
[2] Reprinted by permission of the Macmillan Company, New York.

phrenic thought does not simply involve concreteness, that there are difficulties which are peculiarly schizophrenic with tests such as the Vigotsky Blocks. For example, a schizophrenic patient may group the examiner's arm with the red blocks because the blood in the examiner's arms is also red.

Maher (1966) has raised objections with respect to the variations introduced by Arieti in the original formulations of Von Domarus. First, he denies that the formal laws of logic are representative of how normal people think in commonplace situations. Second, he contends that Arieti's substitution of "paleologician" for "paralogician" (i.e., the schizophrenic) adds the connotation of regression to paralogic—a connotation that Von Domarus did not intend. In any case, Maher suggests that the elaborate set of assumptions involved in this kind of theorizing is hardly justified when it is possible to explain instances of paleologic much more parsimoniously on the basis of simple generalization. According to Maher:

> When we say that patient accepts two dissimilar things as being identical, we mean that he behaves toward both of them in the same way—that he does not discriminate between them either in his verbal responses or in his other behavior in relation to them. Insofar as he is responding to the attribute that the predicate describes, his behavior is appropriate. It is when he is responding to attributes not covered by the predicate that his lack of discrimination become pathological. Even here, the behavior is only pathological when it is applied to one of the subjects; it may be quite appropriate when applied to the other. Let us consider a hypothetical example.
>
> A patient reasons as follows: "General Eisenhower is a veteran. My therapist is a veteran. Therefore my therapist is General Eisenhower." He then addresses his therapist as "General," salutes him whenever they meet, stands to attention in his office, and so forth. All of this is inappropriate behavior in relation to the therapist. Should he happen to meet General Eisenhower, the same behavior would be appropriate. Thus the behavioral consequences of paleological reasoning are exactly the same as the behavioral consequences of extended stimulus generalization. Behavior which is appropriate to one set of stimulus conditions is elicited by a stimulus of minimal (but some) similarity. What makes this generalization pathological is that it is being elicited by a degree of similarity that would be too small to elicit it in the normal subject.
>
> Looked at in this way, the problem of paleological reasoning is not that it is assuming identity on the basis of similar predicates. The problem is that the patient assumes identity on the basis of the similarity of very *limited* predicates. Where the range of attributes covered by a predicate is comparatively broad, the absence of discrimination between the subjects of those predicates is not at all unusual.
>
> Consider now a normal example. A person who has been ill-treated by someone with a foreign accent avoids the next person he meets who has

a foreign accent. We should say that this is an example of simple avoidance learning generalizing to the stimulus of the foreign accent. Regarding the same events as the outcome of "reasoning," we might argue that the person was thinking paleologically in the following way: "The man who injured me had a foreign accent. This man has a foreign accent. Therefore this is the man who injured me." The avoidance behavior would then be seen as the outcome of a serious error in logic! (pp. 426–27)

The author goes on to point out that when verbal intelligence is controlled and emotionally provocative stimuli are avoided, hospitalized schizophrenics and normal subjects give comparable performances on logical reasoning tests.

THE HYPOTHESIS OF OVERINCLUSION

Cameron (1938; 1963) asserts that a special characteristic of schizophrenic language is its extremely loose organization . . . the substitution of an approximate but related term or phrase for the more precise definitive term is characteristic. Schizophrenic thinking tends to stick to everything it touches. Its loose structure permits the presence at the same time of potentially contradictory elements. This is possible simply because the actual contadiction which would arise in the process of the functional organization of concept-formation does not come to pass. The schizophrenic's understanding of word meanings will be different from that of the control subjects in that it will be characterized to a greater extent by substitution of approximate but imprecise terms.

According to Cameron, the schizophrenic doesn't have the ability to "select and eliminate" words. Schizophrenics will be less able than the control subjects to maintain adequate boundaries in their concepts and will tend toward "overinclusion" in their understanding of word meanings. The schizophrenic's ability to integrate words into meaningful sentences will be impaired, relative to the performance of the control subjects.

Cameron feels that the schizophrenics cannot verbalize a conceptual relationship among a group of words. They have lost this "categorical attitude." Schizophrenics will be less able than control subjects to form verbal concepts with words they can define equally well. The conceptual level of verbal concepts formed by schizophrenics will be less "abstract" than that of the control subjects. Schizophrenic subjects will be less adequate than the control subjects in the ability to reason symbolically with words they can define. The schizophrenic's associations to words that he can define will show less meaningful relationship to the stimulus word than will the control subjects' association.

The fact remains that the schizophrenic's score on a standard vocabulary test does not appear to drop significantly. The impact of schizophrenia results in an impairment of the individual's understanding of word meanings.

In summary, the following differences became evident: (1) The schizophrenic is significantly less precise in his understanding of word meanings. This is most evident in his relative failure to differentiate between word meanings. (2) The schizophrenic is less able to use his words as conceptual instruments, e.g., his ability to form verbal concepts and to reason in analogies tests appears impaired. (3) The schizophrenic's ability to integrate words into meaningful communications appears impaired, though he may "define" the same words in the same way that the control subject does.

SOCIAL REINFORCEMENT AND VERBAL CONDITIONING IN SCHIZOPHRENIA

Buss and Lang (1965), in their exhaustive and painstaking review of research on the causal factors that produce deviant behavior in schizophrenics in response to what for normals would be positive or negative reinforcement, identify two hypotheses to account for such discrepant performance. The first is the suggestion that the schizophrenic is overly sensitive to affective and/or punishing stimuli. The second asserts that schizophrenics are not responsive to the usual incentives employed in experimental studies as a consequence of their withdrawal from interpersonal situations.

In its basic form, the hypothesis of insufficient motivation in schizophrenia can be traced back to the related views of several clinical theorists (Cameron, 1947; Fromm-Reichman, 1950; Jenkins, 1952; Arieti, 1955; and Bateson, Jackson, Haley, and Weakland, 1956). These theorists speculated that the schizophrenic has sustained so much rejection, censure, or failure in his early relationships with people that he seeks to avoid or withdraw from all interpersonal situation. In S-R terms, contact with others has acquired secondary negative reinforcing properties for the schizophrenic as a consequence of its association with reproof or punishment.

The family studies of Lidz, Fleck, and Cornelison (1965) emphasize the stressful nature of intrafamilial communication patterns within the schizophrenogenic family setting and its impact upon the developmental experiences of the future patient. Their contention rests upon the clinical observation that the parents of schizophrenic children often confront their children with consistently uncomfortable interpersonal situations. Secondly, through their behavior in such interactions, the parents provide inadequate role models for the child's future behavior. The child in such situations finds interaction with his parents aversive, yet their proximity insures that the child will learn to imitate at least some of their inappropriate behavior.

As a rule, clinical descriptions of schizophrenics almost always mention apathy and isolation as major components of this behavioral disorder. In addition, the tendency to withdraw from interpersonal contact is already an established clinical feature that is used to differentiate this disorder from other psychiatric syndromes. Withdrawal as well as psychological deficit[3] has been explained in terms of the schizophrenics' hypersensitivity to rejection. Given this base, the insufficient motivation hypothesis incorporated the notion that social disinterest is a sufficient condition to account for deficit (Buss and Lang, 1965). Consequently, the schizophrenic is seen as being unmotivated to perform well in various experimental paradigms while normal subjects will often try to please the experimenter and continue their attempts to master often meaningless and boring tasks (Orne, 1962).

Evidence to support the notion that schizophrenics are neither motivated to please the experimenter nor to achieve the laboratory criterion of success comes from a study by Slechts, Gwynn, and Peoples (1963). It was shown that casual social reinforcers, such as nods of the head or saying "mmm-hm" after particular verbal behaviors, were followed by a significantly greater number of the criterion responses for normals as compared to schizophrenics.

If the lack of motivation hypothesis is correct, it should follow that given appropriate rewards and/or punishments, the performance of schizophrenic patients should become more like that of normals in various experimental tasks. The research, however, that attempts to answer this presumably logical deduction has been conducted for the most part by behavioral scientists who are more interested in understanding the nature of the differential response to particular classes of verbal reinforcers on the part of schizophrenics than in the causes of psychological deficit. This last group of experimenters is best described perhaps as only secondarily interested in discovering the origins of such differential sensitivity to reward and punishment (Maher, 1966; Buss and Lang, 1965; and Garmezy, 1966).

PRAISE HYPOSENSITIVITY AND CENSURE HYPERSENSITIVITY

The pioneering work of Rodnick and Garmezy (1957) in the area of censure and schizophrenia suggested that censure was disruptive to the schizophrenic and, as a consequence, his performance suffered. In a series

---

[3] The term *psychological deficit* was introduced into the literature by Hunt and Cofer (1944) to describe the lack of performance shown by psychiatric subjects, in contrast with normals, on various laboratory or experimental tasks.

of experiments, Rodnick and Garmezy demonstrated the existence of a relationship between social censure and such diverse experimental tasks as concept formation, auditory and verbal discrimination, verbal learning, retention, and size estimation.

Almost a decade later, Garmezy (1966) refined his original censure hypothesis in the light of much new experimental evidence. After criticizing and rejecting the insufficient motivation hypothesis and the notion that the schizophrenic is a "social motive defective," Garmezy raised a number of specific questions directed toward discovering whether schizophrenics are selectively reactive to various types of reinforcement. He stated that there is substantial evidence that punishment evokes powerful aversive reactions in schizophrenics, but that the consequences of such aversiveness as measured in performance may differ, depending on the specific experimental design. In this regard, Garmezy's latest solution to the controversy over whether verbal punishment causes increments or decrements in schizophrenic performance is straightforward:

> If the response alternative that permits avoidance of the censuring signal is a task congruent response, behavior facilitation should follow; if the response alternative is non-congruent, performance decrements should ensue. (p. 139)

After a painstaking review of all of the available data from praise and reproof studies completed with schizophrenics, Silverman (1963) concluded: (1) the avoidance and escape habits of schizophrenics are capable of modification in adaptive fashion; (2) a relatively weakened approach disposition is characteristic of the schizophrenic when presented with what for normals are positive incentives; (3) when noxious reinforcement[4] is administered to schizophrenics on a response contingent basis (i.e., when it identifies a response by which censure can be avoided) it has proven to have a consistently more facilitative effect on performance in experimental tasks than does positive reinforcement; and (4) that it also appears the longer the interval between the subject's response and presentation of the noxious reinforcement, the less effective is the reinforcement upon his behavior. When noxious reinforcement is presented at the end of a task, there is not only an absence of performance facilitation, but rather there is performance deterioration.

Johannsen (1964) in his review paper concerning motivation in schizophrenic performance established that the majority of the studies examining this problem supported the notion that verbal reward was in-

---

[4] The term *noxious reinforcement* was used by Silverman to refer to (1) physically unpleasant stimuli (e.g., white noise, electric shock) which are used experimentally to influence behavior, and (2) verbal and other symbolic stimuli which are used as reinforcers and which are generally considered psychologically "painful" in the sense that they are personally threatening or injurious to self-esteem.

effective in improving schizophrenic performance or incapable of sustaining a high degree of proficiency. This generalization was based on research covering a wide range of psychological tasks: motor tasks, card sorting, reaction time studies, letter cancellation, discrimination learning, paired associate learning, and verbal conditioning.

Johannsen has explained discrepant results (i.e., verbal reward causing more performance facilitation than verbal punishment and/or censure resulting in performance decrement) by noting that when censure is either implied by the very presence of an experimenter, or when there is no obvious response contingent reinforcement contingency, deficit will result. Personal qualities of the examiner have also been named as a factor in facilitating the effects of verbal reward with schizophrenics (Johannsen and Cambell, 1964). Given the consistency of the above findings, it is not surprising to find a consistent summary statement in the literature that schizophrenics appear to have an extraordinary need to avoid censure and at the same time are hyposensitive to the effects of verbal reward. It is also commonly held by many experimenters that where improvement follows censure, the schizophrenic's desire to avoid further punishment is somehow activated (Silverman, 1963; Johannsen, 1964; and Garmezy, 1966.)

From all the evidence cited above, it becomes clear that the original censure hypothesis (i.e., censure always results in deficit) is no longer tenable. What has replaced it is a new formulation that emphasizes the differential responsiveness of schizophrenics to verbal praise and reproof stimuli. One area of the experimental literature where this most recent edition of the censure hypothesis has been given frequent testing includes studies of verbal conditioning in schizophrenia. Therefore, it would seem appropriate to review some of these studies in order to assess the implications of their findings for the hypothesis that predicts differential responsiveness on the part of the schizophrenic to different verbal stimuli.

VERBAL CONDITIONING IN SCHIZOPHRENIA

Cohen and Cohen (1960) found that the praise reinforcement "good" in a verbal conditioning paradigm had generally negligible reinforcement effects for schizophrenic subjects while neurotic groups produced significant acquisition curves. These results for the schizophrenic in the Cohen and Cohen study were in sharp contrast to the findings of Cohen *et al.* (1954), where praise reinforcement in a Taffel-type (1955) task revealed that an experimental group of general medical patients had successive increments in the reinforced response. In both of the above studies, the subjects were presented with 80 3 x 5 inch cards, each of which had the same six pronouns (I, We, He, They, She, You) typed on them and paired with a different verb in the past tense. Subjects were asked to make up a sentence beginning with any one of the pronouns and containing the verb indicated on the card. The experimenter responded by saying "good" in a flat, unemotional tone at the end of every sentence which the subject began with I or We.

In a comprehensive study that investigated the reinforcing values of specific verbal stimuli on different diagnostic groups, Leventhal (1958) found equivalent terminal verbal conditioning levels for normals and acute schizophrenics under verbal punishment ("not so good"), but that schizophrenic performance under the verbal reward condition ("good") did not improve in contrast to that of normals. A more recent study employing a Taffel-type task by Kilberg (1962) revealed that verbal reward ("good") led to significantly greater verbal learning for normals than for the schizophrenic subjects he tested. In the later study, however, it was also found that the normal subjects were significantly more aware of the reinforcement contingencies, whereas in the Leventhal study subjects who displayed awareness of the purpose of the experiment during the post-experimental question period were eliminated from the analysis of the results.

In contrast to the majority of the evidence that suggests verbal reward is ineffectual, or at least not as effective a reinforcer in conditioning schizophrenics as verbal punishment, there have been a few experimental studies that can be interpreted as exceptions. Before employing a Taffel-type task, Johannsen and Campbell (1964) had the social responsiveness of chronic female schizophrenics rated by hospital staff on four 5-point rating scales which were said to measure the following dimensions: outgoingness, friendliness, isolation, and alertness. Analysis of the results revealed that only highly responsive female schizophrenics did condition for one of two experimenters. These findings were interpreted as suggesting that chronic female schizophrenics who retain a moderate degree of social responsiveness are capable of being verbally conditioned, but that personal qualities of the examiner may be a factor in facilitating the effects of verbal reward.

Finally, Ells (1967) studied the effects of operant level of pronouns and awareness upon the verbal conditioning of chronic schizophrenics. It was found that only the medium operant level pronouns ($\times$ medium operant $=$ 29 per cent use) could be conditioned by "good" with these hospitalized subjects. Furthermore, an investigation of individual schizophrenic performance revealed only one-fourth of these schizophrenics in the study had significant improvements from their operant levels. Since 96 per cent of these subjects were aware of "good," inattention to social reinforcement was considered to be a minor factor contributing to conditioning failures. A strong positive relationship between awareness of the response reinforcement contingency and conditioning was found with these chronic schizophrenics. The latter finding was suggested as being the crucial factor accounting for the deficit in schizophrenic nonresponsiveness to "good" in Taffel-type sentence construction verbal conditioning tasks.

It is perhaps important to note that of the above experiments that lend some support to the notion that schizophrenics can be conditioned by positive verbal reward, only one study, Johannsen and Campbell, employed both verbal praise and reproof and even in this study positive results with verbal reward were found for only one of the two experimenters. Likewise, in the Ells study, mentioned above, only a select minority of the total number of subjects tested were conditioned by the verbal reward "good."

Although there is substantial evidence to support the modified censure hypothesis it is not the only possible means used to explain the results in studies of verbal conditioning in schizophrenia where differential responding to verbal praise and reproof was established. One of the most potent challenges to the censure hypothesis has come from a group of related studies carried out by Janet Taylor Spence and associates regarding the meaning of blank trials in problem-solving or verbal-conditioning studies.

ON THE MEANING OF BLANK TRIALS

Several recent studies by Spence *et al.* (1963, 1964, 1966a, 1966b) and Levine *et al.* (1964) have supported the hypothesis that if subjects are given no prior explanation of the reinforcement procedures in problem-solving or verbal conditioning studies, the effects of the blank trials (i.e., trials where no reinforcement is given, the nothing trials of a right-nothing condition) on performance, as well as those of the outcome events are probably most important in accounting for the experimental results. On the basis of evidence from a pair of different studies (Spence, 1964; Levine *et al.*), Spence proposed that in the absence of instructions about the meaning of blank trials, the "nothing" trial tends to be treated as if it meant "right." Consequently, this tendency to misinterpret the meaning of blank trials can be used to explain the performance equivalence of the R-W (Right-Wrong) and W-b (Wrong-blank) verbal reinforcement conditions in various experimental paradigms. A similar explanation is possible for R-b (Right-blank) subjects as the strong initial tendency to regard blank as "right" often conflicts with the demands of the experimental context to treat it as wrong and thereby successful task performance is retarded.

Spence *et al.* (1963) designed a study comparing the discrimination learning of schizophrenics, nonschizophrenic patients, and college students when all three groups were informed what "nothing" meant on blank trials. She found there were no differences in performance between groups given the two different verbal reinforcement procedures (R-b versus W-b). In a more comprehensive study, Spence (1966b) studied the effects of verbal reinforcement on a problem-solving task. Three different instructural conditions: a group given problem-solving instructions and explanation of the reinforcers to be used (PS-I), a group given only problem-solving instructions (PS-NI), and a verbal conditioning group given neither problem-solving instructions nor explanation of the reinforcers (VC) and three combinations of reinforcement (R-b, W-b and W-R groups were employed in the experiment). The subjects were V.A. medical patients and all were presented with the same Taffel-type (1955) sentence construction task. Performance improved with amount of previous information (p < .001) and was better in all instructional conditions under the Wrong-blank than Right-blank (p < .01). Right-Wrong performance was similar to Wrong-blank in the problem-solving conditions but superior to Wrong-blank in the VC groups. Post-experimental interviews confirmed the hypothesis that the relative ineffectiveness of blank in the R-b reinforcement combination may come about because of a pre-established tendency to treat it as meaning "right."

In summary, a majority of studies with schizophrenic subjects which have employed both response contingent praise and censure including those verbal conditioning studies viewed here (Leventhal, 1958; Cohen and Cohen, 1960; Kilberg, 1962) have found that the schizophrenics' performance is facilitated by the latter but not former type of reinforcement. A minority of studies (Johannsen and Campbell, 1964; Ells, 1967) suggests that verbal reward can be an effective reinforcer for certain subgroups of schizophrenics and/or under special circumstances. However, these findings are further limited because the Ells study only tested subjects under conditions of verbal praise and the Johannsen and Cambell experiment which did utilize both verbal reward and punishment revealed that verbal praise was an effective reinforcer for female subjects tested by only one of two experimenters.

For the most part these results have been explained in terms of the schizophrenics' presumed hyposensitivity to verbal reward, his hypersensitivity to verbal punishment and consequent avoidance patterns. Yet, alternative hypotheses have been suggested. Ells maintains that the critical factor accounting for the deficit in schizophrenic nonresponsiveness to "good" is their lack of awareness of the response reinforcement contingency. In addition the latest finding of Spence (1966c) regarding the effect of blank trials in a sentence construction task suggests that subjects' inclination to misinterpret the meaning of blank in R-b treatment conditions may have much to do with the nonequivalence of subject performance in R-b versus W-b verbal reinforcement conditions of various experimental paradigms.

It is obvious from a review of the most pertinent research concerning verbal conditioning in schizophrenia that all the evidence is not in. Although a majority of investigators have found that schizophrenics are hyposensitive to verbal praise and hypersensitive to verbal censure when compared with normals, there have been exceptions. Ells found that chronic schizophrenics who knew about the nature of the response-reinforcement contingency were responsive to verbal praise. In addition, the latest findings of Janet Taylor Spence reviewed here suggest that certain ambiguities reported by experimental subjects concerning the meaning of "nothing" trials may have a lot to do with the differential acquisition of appropriate behaviors in various experimental paradigms. Spence's contention assumes importance if we remember that a large number of the studies that have supported the revised censure hypothesis have relied on evidence obtained when the results of right-nothing and wrong-nothing treatment conditions are compared.

THE PROCESS/REACTIVE DISTINCTION

Mabry (1955) reported an attempt to distinguish between "scattered" and "nonscattered" schizophrenics, a distinction which roughly corresponds to the process/reactive or organized/regressed continuum. She found that the total number of words proved to be significantly less for the nonscattered subjects than for either scattered subjects or normals. This distinction between regressed and organized (or process and reactive) also proved important in a study in Blumenthal (1964). He reported greater speech disruption as measured by nonfluencies, in regressed schizophrenics under interpersonal stress.

Clinicians are forced by the organized/regressed distinction to recognize that schizophrenia is a collection of disorders rather than a single entity. Psychiatric taxonomists have, to the present, used language *content* almost exclusively in creating their classifications of schizophrenia. That this approach is unquestionably too narrow is amply illustrated by considering the variable of information-processing ability. Pearl (1963) studied the information-processing ability of schizophrenics by using Shannon's guessing-game technique as a measure of language-processing ability. Shannon's method assumes that persons have an implicit knowledge of language statistics when required to guess the next letter of a meaningful language sequence. Pearl controlled for vocabulary level using the vocabulary subtest of the WAIS. When the experimenter eliminated subjects whose verbal ability was high, and used only schizophrenics of low vocabulary skill, two groups of schizophrenics were distinguished: those poor in language-processing ability and those somewhat less than average for the normal population. It turns out that those who were poor in language-processing could be classified as process schizophrenics, while those who were somewhat less than average could be classified as reactive schizophrenics.

In the interests of illustrating a point, Pearl's study has been turned around. Actually, he identified the reactive and process schizophrenics first; and following their identification, he then administered Shannon's guessing-game technique. However, this kind of exposition of Pearl's experiment emphasizes the contention that, if schizophrenics were categorized on important linguistic variables other than content, new relationships as powerful as the reactive/process distinction would suggest themselves.

In addition to language-processing ability, the conditionability of statements and order of approximation are variables which should be considered. Salzinger and Portnoy (1964) were able to condition the self-referred affect statements of reactive schizophrenics, but were unable to condition the same statements of process schizophrenics. Lewinsohn and Elwood (1961) used various orders of approximation (from 1 to 8) as an independent variable. Each statement presented to a subject involved a different order of approximation. The subject's task was to recall as many words from each statement as he could. Reactive schizophrenics recalled words in the same manner and to the same degree as normal controls. Chronic schizophrenics, on the other hand, showed considerable impairment in ability to recall words.

One of the major uncontrolled variables in the word-association studies, and in many of the studies preceding these, is the effect of hospitalization upon verbal behavior. Many of the studies quoted employ long-term chronic schizophrenic patients who have lived for many years in an impoverished environment, i.e., a mental hospital. As a result, many of the speech characteristics identified by such studies are possibly artifacts of hospitalization, rather than characteristics of schizophrenic language. Wynne (1963), recognizing that institutionalization has potential effects upon verbal ability, used eight verbal measures to compare two groups: short-term schizophrenics and long-term schizophrenics. The short-term schizophrenics proved superior to long-term patients on six of the eight measures. Wynne concluded that the most important variable related to the decline of verbal abilities in both schizophrenics and a control group of patients with a physical disease was length of stay in the hospital. This variable must be given adequate representation in future studies of verbal behavior of schizophrenics.

CONCLUDING REMARKS

The enormous scope of this subject matter and the voluminous literature on schizophrenic language behavior practically insure that some important areas of research will be slighted in a review of this brevity. We can do no more than acknowledge the value and importance of the work of investigators whose contributions have not been dealt with in this chapter: Bannister's (1960, 1962) research on the serial invalidation hypothesis; the distinguished series of investigations by Chapman and his associates (1960, 1961, 1964) on multimeaning responses in the verbal performance of schizophrenics; the theoretical formulations by Mednick (1958, 1959) concerning the role of gradients of stimulus generalization as a model for schizophrenic thought disorder; and the experimental work performed by Spence and Lair (1964), Woods (1961), and others in exploration of Mednick's hypotheses. What makes the contributions of these scientists of special significance is the fact that they are indicative of a trend toward the increasingly fruitful application of experimental procedures and methods to the meaningful problems of clinical psychology and psychiatry.

In closing this chapter we may note that Kraepelin (1907) included in his concept of *derailment* such phenomena as changes of pitch, rate, rhythm, loudness, and timbre of spoken language, sniffling, snorting, smacking of lips, etc., many of which we have identified elsewhere as paralinguistic phenomena. The precise nature of the contribution of such cues to the total diagnostic assessment has heretofore been largely a matter of guesswork and estimation. At clinical staff meetings, as the present writer can affirm from direct experience, it is by no means unusual to hear statements to the effect that a particular patient "sounded schizophrenic." When asked to define the "schizophrenic sound," the clinician may react in one of several ways. He may dismiss the question and the questioner; he may tell the questioner that it is difficult to describe exactly what the "schizophrenic sound" is, but that any experienced psychologist or psychiatrist knows what he means; or he may honestly admit that he is unable to delineate the expression more accurately. It is in this respect that the potential significance of acoustic analysis and sound spectography becomes apparent for psychiatry. By means of techniques such as these, we may eventually be able to operationalize the "schizophrenic sounds" to the extent that we can add another reliable instrument to our diagnostic collection.

REFERENCES

Arieti, S. *Interpretation of schizophrenia.* New York: Brunner, 1955.

Bannister, D. Conceptual structure in thought-disordered schizophrenics. *Journal of Mental Science,* 1960, *106,* 1230–49.

Bannister, D. The nature and measurement of schizophrenic thought disorder. *Journal of Mental Science,* 1962, *108,* 825–42.

Bateson, G., Jackson, D., Haley, J., and Weakland, J. Toward a theory of schizophrenia. *Behavioral Science*, 1956, *1*, 251–64.

Blumenthal, R. The effects of level of health, premorbid history, and interpersonal stress upon the speech disruption of chronic schizophrenics. *Journal of Nervous and Mental Disease*, 1964, *139*, 313–23.

Brown, R. *Words and things*. New York: The Free Press, 1958.

Buss, A. H. and Lang, P. J. Psychological deficit in schizophrenia: I. Affect, reinforcement, and concept attainment. *Journal of Abnormal Psychology*, 1965, *70*, 2–24.

Cameron, N. Reasoning, regression, and communication in schizophrenia. *Psychological Monographs*, 1938, No. 221.

Cameron, N. Experimental analysis of schizophrenic thinking. In J. S. Kasanin (Ed.), *Language and thought in schizophrenia*. Berkeley: University of California Press, 1944.

Cameron, N. *The psychology of behavior disorders*. Boston: Houghton Mifflin, 1947.

Cameron, N. *Personality development and psychopathology*. Boston: Houghton Mifflin, 1963.

Chapman, L. J. Confusion of figurative and literal usages of words by schizophrenics and brain-damaged patients. *Journal of Abnormal and Social Psychology*, 1960, *60*, 412–16.

Chapman, L. J. A reinterpretation of some pathological disturbances in conceptual breadth. *Journal of Abnormal and Social Psychology*, 1961, *62*, 514–19.

Chapman, L. J., Chapman, J. P., and Miller, G. A theory of verbal behavior in schizophrenia. In B. A. Maher (Ed.), *Progress in experimental personality research*, Vol. I. New York: Academic Press, 1964.

Cohen, B. D. and Cohen, E. Verbal reinforcement in schizophrenia. *Journal of Abnormal and Social Psychology*, 1960, *60*, 443–46.

Cohen, B. D., Kalish, H., Thurston, R., and Cohen E. Experimental manipulation of verbal behavior. *Journal of Experimental Psychology*, 1954, *47*, 106–10.

De La Garza, C. D. and Worchel P. Time and space orientation in schizophrenia. *Journal of Abnormal and Social Psychology*, 1956, *52*, 191–95.

Eisenson, J., Auer, J. J., and Irwin, J. V. *The psychology of communication*. New York: Appleton–Century–Crofts, 1963.

Ells, E. M. Effects of operant level, interview with experimenter, and awareness upon the verbal conditioning of chronic schizophrenics. *Journal of Abnormal Psychology*, 1967, *72*, 208–12.

Forrest, D. V. Poiesis and the language of schizophrenia. *Psychiatry*, 1965, *28*, 1–18.

Fromm-Reichman, F. *Principles of intensive psychotherapy*. Chicago: University of Chicago Press, 1950.

Garmezy, N. The prediction of performance in schizophrenia. In P. H. Hoch and J. Zubin (Eds.), *Psychopathology of communication*. New York: Grune and Stratton, 1966.

Goldstein, K. Methodological approach to the study of schizophrenic thought. In J. S. Kasanin (Ed.), *Language and thought in schizophrenia.* Berkeley: University of California Press, 1944.

Gottschalk, L. A., Gleser, G. C., Magliocco, E. B., and D'Zmura, T. L. Further studies on the speech patterns of schizophrenic patients: Measuring inter-individual differences in relative degree of personal disorganization and social alienation. *Journal of Nervous and Mental Disease,* 1961, *132,* 101–13.

Haley, J. An interactional description of schizophrenia. *Psychiatry,* 1959, *22,* 321–32.

Hunt, J. McV. and Cofer, C. N. Psychological deficit in schizophrenia. In J. McV. Hunt (Ed.), *Personality and the behavior disorders,* Vol. II. New York: Ronald Press, 1944.

Jenkins, R. L. The schizophrenic sequence: Withdrawal, disorganization, psychotic reorganization. *American Journal of Orthopsychiatry,* 1952, *22,* 738–48.

Johannsen, W. J. Motivation in schizophrenic performance: A review. *Psychological Reports,* 1964, *15,* 839–70.

Johannsen, W. J. and Campbell, S. Y. Verbal conditioning in chronic schizophrenia: The effects of reinforcement class and social responsiveness. *Psychological Reports,* 1964, *14,* 567–72.

Kanner, L. Autistic disturbances of affective contact. *Nervous Child,* 1943, *2,* 217–50.

Kasanin, J. S. The disturbance of conceptual thinking in schizophrenia. In J. S. Kasanin (Ed.), *Language and thought in schizophrenia.* Berkeley: University of California Press, 1944.

Kilberg, J. The differential effect of nonverbal and verbal reward in the modification of verbal behavior of schizophrenics and normal subjects. Unpublished doctoral dissertation, Columbia University, 1962.

Kraepelin, E. *Clinical psychiatry.* (Translated by A. R. Diefendorf.) New York: Macmillan, 1907.

Leventhal, A. M. Effects of differential verbal reinforcement on psychiatric and nonpsychiatric hospital patients. Unpublished doctoral dissertation, State University of Iowa, 1958.

Levine, M., Leitenberg, H., and Richter, M. The blank trials laws, the equivalence of positive reinforcement and nonreinforcement. *Psychological Review,* 1964, *71,* 94–103.

Lewisohn, P. M. and Elwood, D. L. The role of contextual restraint in the learning of language samples in schizophrenia. *Journal of Nervous and Mental Disease,* 1961, *133,* 79–81.

Lidz, T., Fleck, S., and Cornelison, A. R. *Schizophrenia and the family.* New York: International Universities Press, 1965.

Lorenz, M. Problems posed by schizophrenic language. *Archives of General Psychiatry,* 1961, *4,* 603–10.

Mabry, M. Language characteristics of scattered and nonscattered schizophrenics compared with normals. *Journal of Psychology,* 1955, *57,* 29–40.

McNeill, D. Developmental psycholinguistics. In F. Smith and G. A. Miller (Eds.), *The genesis of language.* Cambridge, Mass.: The M.I.T. Press, 1966.

Maher, B. A. *Principles of psychopathology.* New York: McGraw-Hill, 1966.

Mednick, S. A. A learning theory approach to research in schizophrenia. *Psychological Bulletin,* 1958, *55,* 316–27.

Mednick, S. A. Learning theory and schizophrenia: A reply to a comment. *Psychological Bulletin,* 1959, *56,* 315–16.

Moran, L. J. Vocabulary knowledge and usage among normals and schizophrenic patients. *Psychological Monographs,* 1953, *67,* No. 20.

Orne, M. On the social psychology of the psychological experiment: with particular reference to demand characteristics and their implications. *American Psychologist,* 1962, *17,* 776–83.

Ostwald, P. F. *Soundmaking.* Springfield, Ill.: Charles C Thomas, 1963.

Pearl, D. Language processing ability of process and reactive schizophrenics. *Journal of Psychology,* 1963, *65,* 419–25.

Potter, H. W. Schizophrenia in children. *American Journal of Psychiatry,* 1933, *12,* 1253.

Ringuette, E. L. and Kennedy, T. An experimental study of the double-bind hypothesis. *Journal of Abnormal Psychology,* 1966, *71,* 136–41.

Rodnick, E. H. and Garmezy, N. An experimental approach to the study of motivation in schizophrenia. In M. R. Jones (Ed.), *Nebraska symposium on motivation.* Lincoln: University of Nebraska Press, 1957.

Salzinger, K. and Portnoy, S. Verbal conditioning in interviews: Application to chronic schizophrenics and relationship to prognosis for acute schizophrenics. *Journal of Psychiatric Research,* 1964, *2,* 1–9.

Silverman, J. Psychological deficit reduction in schizophrenia through response-contingent noxious reinforcement. *Psychological Reports,* 1963, *13,* 187–210.

Slechts, J., Gwynn, W., and Peoples, C. Verbal conditioning of schizophrenics and normals in a situation resembling psychotherapy. *Journal of Consulting Psychology,* 1963, *27,* 223–27.

Spence, J. T. Verbal discrimination performance under different verbal reinforcement combinations. *Journal of Experimental Psychology,* 1964, *67,* 195–97.

Spence, J. T. Effects of verbal reinforcement combination and instructional condition on the performance of a problem solving task. *Journal of Personality and Social Psychology,* 1966, *3,* 163–70. (a)

Spence, J. T. Effects of verbal reinforcement combination on the performance of a four-alternative discrimination task. *Journal of Verbal Learning and Verbal Behavior,* 1966, *5,* 421–28. (b)

Spence, J. T. and Lair, C. V. Associative interference in the verbal learning performance of schizophrenics and normals. *Journal of Abnormal and Social Psychology*, 1964, *68*, 204–9.

Spence, J. T., Lair, C. V., and Goodstein, L. D. Effects of different feedback conditions on verbal discrimination learning in schizophrenics and non-schizophrenic subjects. *Journal of Verbal Learning and Verbal Behavior*, 1963, *2*, 339–45.

Sullivan, H. S. The language of schizophrenia. In J. S. Kasanin (Ed.), *Language and thought in schizophrenia*. Berkeley: University of California Press, 1944.

Taffel, C. Anxiety and the conditioning of verbal behavior. *Journal of Abnormal and Social Psychology*, 1955, *51*, 496–501.

Von Domarus, E. The specific laws of logic in schizophrenia. In J. S. Kasanin (Ed.), *Language and thought in schizophrenia*. Berkeley: University of California, 1944.

Woods, P. J. A test of Mednick's analysis of the thinking disorder in schizophrenia. *Psychological Reports*, 1961, *9*, 441–46.

Wynne, R. D. The influence of hospitalization on the verbal behaviour of chronic schizophrenics. *British Journal of Psychology*, 1963, *109*, 380–89.

PART 3

OTHER TOPICS IN LANGUAGE AND PSYCHOPATHOLOGY

CHAPTER 11

THE DOUBLE BIND CONCEPT

Sullivan (1944) has expressed the belief that language serves the vital function of preserving feelings of security among one's fellow-men. The schizophrenic's peculiarities of language, he proposes, arise from his extreme need to feel secure. The schizophrenic does not believe that speech will help him attain gratification; his speech is used to counteract feelings of insecurity. The problem lies in recurrent severe disturbances in his relationships with people which result in a confusion of the critical faculties concerning the structure of spoken and written language.

Cameron (1944) suggests that the schizophrenic has somehow managed to get himself isolated from the common social environment. The organized adult's language behavior and thinking are outgrowths of repeated social communication which depends on the development of an ability to take the role of other persons, to be able to reproduce their attitudes in one's own responses and so learn to react to one's own behavior as others are reacting to it. The acquisition of this ability is what makes a social person. Cameron feels that schizophrenics are people who have never been able to develop role-taking skills and therefore have not been able to establish themselves firmly in the cultural pattern. In the face of emotional conflicts and disappointments the schizophrenic withdraws into fantasy life, which eventually dominates all of his thinking and excludes social life altogether.

Kasanin (1944) also maintains that the most important cause of disturbance in the language and thought of the schizophrenic is the disarticulation of the schizophrenic from his social context. It is obvious that early in childhood the child or infant goes through some traumatic process which interferes with his relationship to the outside world. The nature of this process involves the peculiar pattern of communicative behavior in the parent-child context to which the name "double bind" has been given.

The double bind hypothesis was first advanced by Gregory Bateson and his associates (1956). Essentially it is a theory which emphasizes the communication or interaction which occurs between parents and child. According to the theory, the parents (usually the mother) continually communicate conflicting or incongruent messages to the child. This occurs because for some reason the mother has a fear of intimate contact with the child, but is unable to accept this fear and denies it by overtly expressing "loving behavior." These two different and conflicting orders of messages are presented to the child at the same time.

The presentation of these incongruent messages poses quite a problem for the child. Since the mother is the primary love object, the child would like to be able to discriminate accurately between the messages he receives from her. However, if he does this, he will be punished by the realization that his mother does not really love him. On the other hand, if he does not discriminate accurately between the messages and accepts his mother's simulated loving behavior as real, he will then approach his mother. When he does this, she will become hostile toward him, causing him to withdraw. After he withdraws, she will punish him verbally for withdrawing from her because it indicated to her that she was not a loving mother. Consequently the child is punished if he accurately discriminates between the messages or if he inaccurately discriminates between the messages. Hence, he finds himself in a double bind.

The only real escape for the child from this situation is to communicate with his mother about the position in which she has put him. However, if he does this, she will probably take his comment as an accusation that she is not a loving mother and will punish him for saying it. In other words, the child is not allowed to talk about the situation in an effort to resolve it.

Because this sequence of events occurs over and over again in the child's home life, his ability to communicate with others about their communication to him is greatly impaired. As a result, he is incompetent in determining what other people really mean when they communicate with him and also incompetent in expressing what he really means when he communicates with others.

Due to this impairment of his ability to relate to others effectively, the child may begin to respond defensively to others with incongruent responses when presented with this double bind situation. In addition, he may manifest withdrawal or other mechanisms of defense which are part of the symptomatology of schizophrenia.

THE LOGICAL BASIS FOR DOUBLE BIND

Bateson (1955) reports that the basic conception of the double bind grew out of his observation of animals in a seminaturalistic setting. As part of a ten-year study of communication he was interested in the ways animals use signals in their interactions. The critical nature of these stimuli is best seen when animals are at play. Such activity requires a surprisingly sophisticated message system which in effect communicates, "These actions, in which we now engage, do not denote what would be denoted by these actions which the actions denote." (Bateson, 1955) A playful bite must not be misperceived as an attack even though it is the same in form as an attack. Two messages, the "bite" and "This is play," are on different levels of communication and both are required in order for play to occur. The first statement denies the assertion of the second, and vice versa, and thus forms an Epimenides type of paradox.

In logic an example of this type of paradox would be the following:

> All statements within this frame
>
> are true
>
> I love you.   I hate you.

Because the first statement is about the second statement, it is, by definition, on a different level of abstraction. And since each statement denies the assertion of another statement, the set of statements constitutes a paradox. It is a contradiction that follows a correct deduction from consistent premises. Bertrand Russell, with this *Theory of Logical Types* (Whitehead and Russell, 1913), was the first to "solve" this type of paradox with the general rule whatever involved all of a collection must not be one of the collection. Therefore the Epimenides type of paradox is an example of a type of reasoning, i.e., an inappropriate use of concepts drawn from two levels.

Russell's approach accounted for antinomies, or paradoxes arising in formal logical systems; and Carnap (1942) proposed a similar theory to account for those hidden inconsistencies which arise out of the structure of language (Paradoxical Definitions). By theorizing that there exists an object language and a meta-language about objects and a meta-language about the meta-language ad infinitum, and by applying Russell's rule, paradoxes of the type "I am lying" can be defined as meaningless self-reflexive statements. This brief discussion of logic is necessary because Watzlawick, Beavin and Jackson (1967) indicate there is something basic

to the paradox that has pragmatic implications for everyone. The fundamental conception of the double bind grows directly out of these logical
considerations.

INITIAL APPLICATIONS

Haley (1955) made some immediate extensions of Bateson's insights to
fantasy, hypnosis, and psychotherapy. At about this same time, the Palo
Alto group began to study schizophrenic communication. They hypothesized that the symptoms of the schizophrenic were due mainly to an inability to assign the correct communicational mode to his own messages,
to messages from others, or to his own thoughts and feelings (Bateson,
Jackson, Haley and Weakland 1956). "Communicational mode" was
not defined, but apparently it refers to levels of communication: the schizophrenic seems to be suffering from inner conflicts of logical typing *a la*
Russell. Bateson *et al.* stated that, if their reading of the symptoms were
correct and the hypothesized schizophrenia were esentially the result of
familial interaction, it ought to be possible to arrive a priori at a formal
description of those sequences of experience which would induce such a
series of symptoms. The result of this deductive interactional approach to
schizophrenia was the first explication of the double bind hypothesis.

In the 1956 paper the stress was on the relationship between the
schizophrenic victim and his anxious mother. The major elements of the
double bind were: (1) two or more people who have (2) repeated experience with a communication pattern consisting of a (3) primary negative injunction and a (4) secondary injunction conflicting with the first
at a more abstract level, plus (5) a tertiary negative injunction prohibiting
escape from the field. The complete set of ingredients is no longer necessary when the victim learns to perceive his universe in "double bind patterns." In their discussion of schizophrenia specifically, Bateson *et al.* add
the concept of an intense relationship, defined as one in which the schizophrenic feels that it is crucially important that he discriminate accurately
what type of message is being communicated in order that he may make
the appropriate responses. Furthermore the individual is unable to comment on the double bind to allow him to correct his misperception. Presumably the motivational state inferred here guarantees the necessary
repeated experience with the double bind, and the inability to comment
is analogous to an inability to leave the field.

Lu (1962) and Ferreira (1960) objected to the dyadic emphasis
of the Bateson *et al.* presentation and advanced the "quadruple bind" and
"split double bind," respectively, to describe pathological communication patterns involving more than two family members. At about the same
time Weakland (1960) attempted a systematic extension of the initial

conception to three-party interactions. The Lu paper is interesting because it reports a double bind patterns that is cultural in origin. The mothers of the schizophrenics in the study apparently attempted to make their children both dependent and independent at the same time; and an analysis of "sick" versus "well" siblings indicated that the schizophrenics were the children who attempted to obey both injunctions. Unfortunately the promised full analysis of Lu's sample of schizophrenics has never appeared in print.

Ferreira's paper contends that the double bind hypothesis has greater generality than as a theory of schizophrenia. He found that the families of delinquent boys tend to be characterized by bipolar messages from the parents to the children. These take the form:

1. A to B: "Thou shall not . . . x (or I will not love you)
2. C to B: "Thou shall not . . . obey, hear, etc. . . . A's message (or I will not love you).

The child finds it impossible to obey both messages and is often pushed out of the field (i.e., the family interaction pattern). The major difference between this formulation and the one set forth by Bateson *et al.* (1956) is the lack of a tertiary negative injunction. It is possible that various "types" of double bind characterize various "types" of disturbed families, and that schizophrenic, neurotic, delinquent, or homosexual behavior is simply an attempt by the victim to adjust to the peculiar demands of this type of environment. Mishler and Waxler (1965) report that there are initial indications of considerable similarity among families which produce a variety of disturbed children.

Weakland (1960) emphasized that both individuals in the interaction were caught up in the double bind and also that more than two individuals could be involved. He went on to postulate that the concealment, denial, and inhibition inherent in the basic contradictory pair of messages make the achievement of an adequate response nearly impossible. This was the first attempt to define some of the processes which prevent meaningful responses to paradoxical communications.

Jackson (1961) developed some of the themes of Haley's (1955) analysis of psychotherapy and formulated the concept of the therapeutic double bind. Basically this is the idea that all forms of psychotherapy set up double binds through the requirements they place on the patient in the situation. Jackson and Haley (1963) explicated the double binds in psychoanalysis and Haley (1963) has extended the analysis to other types of therapy. A "cure" in this formulation comes about when the patient finally realizes the nature of the game the therapist is playing and refuses to play further. Watts (1961) stresses the "gamesmanship" aspects of this type of therapy and then attempts to picture the basic structure of society as a double bind consisting of rules which confer independence and in doing so take it away again. One of the unfortunate aspects of the double bind is that it can be applied fairly easily to almost any aspect of human behavior.

Watzlawick (1963) reviewed the literature on the double bind up to 1961 and commented that very few of the references cited dealt with the essential component of the double bind, i.e., the Theory of Logical Types. He also stressed that the double bind was not equivalent to a failure to discriminate stimuli in an experimental situation. Pavlov's (1927) experiments on experimentally induced neuroses are an analogue because the animal was first trained to discriminate the circle and oval. Behavior broke down when the discrimination was made impossible for the animal, not because of the inability to discriminate but because a previously established contingency pattern was broken.

In a short companion articles, Bateson, Jackson, Haley, and Weakland (1963) reviewed their recently concluded research project and offered a series of observations and conclusions with respect to the double bind. The double bind, they stated, is a necessary but not a sufficient condition in accounting for the etiology of schizophrenic disorders. However, they make it plain that they regard the double bind as an inevitable byproduct of schizophrenic communication.

They emphasize that observable communicative behavior and relationships are the appropriate object of empirical and theoretical analyses involving the concept of double bind. They prefer to conceptualize the "conflicting definitions of the relationship," rather than a simple relationship involving a binder and a victim.

During the past five years, the Palo Alto group has dealt mainly with various aspects of schizophrenia and family therapy and only incidentally with the double bind. Only those papers which seem germane to a definition of the phenomenon are reported in the following sections of this chapter. Mishler and Waxler (1965) provide an excellent review of the recent contributions to schizophrenia and a comparison of various theoretical approaches to family therapy.

DEVELOPMENT OF DOUBLE BIND

A number of recent attempts have been made to define more precisely the double bind. Watzlawick (1965) provided the most comprehensive analysis of the relationship between the double bind and logical paradoxes. He postulates a set of Pragmatic Paradoxes which are simply the Semantic Paradoxes (Paradoxical Definitions) which occur in one form or another in communication. Two of the commonest types of Pragmatic Paradoxes are Paradoxical Injunctions (the core of the interactional double bind) and Paradoxical Predictions.

Paradoxical injunctions are statements which demand conflicting types of behaviors. Most commonly in human communication they are statements like "you ought to love me" or "don't be so obedient" which demand behavior which can only be spontaneous. This is the usual conception of the double bind and presumably can be handled by either commenting on the communication (meta communicating), attempting to bind the binder, or retreating into a paradoxical (schizophrenic) mode of communication which enables a person to communicate that he is not communicating without actually communicating anything (Watzlawick 1965).

The relationship of paradoxical predictions to the double bind is not clear. The paradox in this case is based on the contention that "reason and trust do not mix." This is most clearly seen in the Prisoner's Dilemma Game where trust of the other player and rational self-interest dictate alternative strategies, and the strategy usually adopted is one involving minimal loss. In this case the paradox depends upon the player's analysis of the situation conflicting with his analysis of another's intentions. Unfortunately in human interactions A must make predictions about B because he cannot know B as B knows himself. This raises the melancholy prospect that in at least some cases the victim may bind himself as much or more than he is bound by others in an interaction situation. This conception also allows the prediction that an outside observer who has had some previous contact with the individuals in a communication situation will probably mislabel some straightforward interactions as double binds. The observer's previous experience could result in erroneous predictions about various metalevels of the ongoing communication.

Sluzki, Beavin, Tarnopolsky and Veron (1967) have made a pioneering effort to redefine the double bind in more experimentally meaningful terms. They postulate that there may be many different types of double binds, all based on differing paradoxical injunctions. They redefine the Bateson *et al.* (1956) criteria in terms of disqualifying statements and attempt to indicate some of the common reactions to this "transactional disqualification." This approach is important because it attempts to tie a specific type of double bind to a specific set of behaviors. Unfortunately they present only clinical data and their list of reactions is almost certainly too limited, but this is undoubtedly the only way to analyze the double bind in complex interaction situations. The theoretical literature on the double bind is replete with what are labeled examples of the double bind, but in many cases the bind is by no means as clear to the reader as it is to the writer. Even in the best collection of this material, a tape published by Watzlawick (1964), the nature of the bind is not always immediately apparent. When an entire family pattern is observed, analysis becomes almost incredibly complex (Jones, 1964). Haley (1963) has admitted that the therapist frequently does not become aware of the binding nature of some interactions until considerable time has elapsed.

Bateson, *et al.* (1963) have complained that the double bind is not the core of their work, and have indicated that their major focus of interest was the development of a communicational approach to the study of behavior. The first full version of this theory was presented recently by Watzlawick, Beavin, and Jackson (1967). In this publication they offer a model for the analysis of the behavioral effects (pragmatics) of human communication. Basic postulates include: the impossibility of *not* communicating (since even silence has some sort of communicative significance); the idea that every communication consists of a message and an *injunction* (metacommunication) which constrains behavior; and the notion that the nature of a relationship is contingent upon the patterning of the communicational sequences between the participants.

The fact that human beings can communicate both digitally and analogically[1] is the source of many of the paradoxical features of human relationships. The difficulties involve semantics, on the one hand, and syntactics, on the other hand. That is, digital language does not possess adequate semantic resources in the area of relationships, although it boasts a complex and versatile syntax, Conversely, analogic language has adequate semantics, but lacks a logical and well delineated syntax for dealing with relationships.

Watzlawick and his associates (1967) present a modified and expanded formulation of the double bind which establishes a number of criteria for defining the double bind. First, it is essential that two or more people be involved in the kind of intense relationship (love, loyalty, dependence, etc.) that has a "high degree of physical and/or survival value" for them, individually or collectively. Second, a message is transmitted within this context that poses mutually exclusive interpretations, i.e., if it is an injunction, it must be either obeyed or disobeyed. Third, there are constraints present in the situation which prevent the individual from "leaving the field" by withdrawing or by means of metacommunication. This last stipulation is necessary if double binds are to be defined as paradoxes and not mere contradictions, since in contradiction an alternative is left open to the individual, whereas this is not true of the paradox.

This recent definition of the double bind is both more explicit and easier to work with than those presented in other papers. It should be fairly easy to set up a situation where two people are in a fairly intense

---

[1] *Analogic codification* involves communication via pictures or images of actual objects, people, or situations; *digital codification,* as exemplified by words and numbers, are artificially created and discrete entities which have representational or symbolic properties. Analogic communication can occur in an instantaneous, all-at-once fashion; digital communication, on the other hand, is sequential (Ruesch, 1961).

relationship in a laboratory setting. The experimental procedures developed in social psychology should be useful here. The wide list of situations mentioned should allow a variety of different experiments which simply control the type of situation as an independent variable.

Simply stated, the second element of the double bind mentioned above indicates that any communication which modifies another communication in any way can potentially set up the binding situation. The two types of disqualification mentioned are probably part of a much larger set of binds which would require a set of investigations testing the effect of various ways of setting up mutually exclusive assertions. The conflicting messages could of course be introduced into the situation by a stooge, but it would probably be easier to use a set of standardized messages and structure the situation so that the individual feels it is essential to respond appropriately to the correct meaning of the message. A very important line of research would deal with the ability of individuals to perceive double binds present in a larger set of communications and also would attempt to determine how people normally attempt to deal with paradoxical messages. The effects of varying the supposed source of the communication should also be tested since a communication from a "significant other" should have a different effect than a communication from a less important source. Finally the effect of various operational definitions of the levels of communication must be evaluated.

The final element of the double bind, the restriction on metacommunication or withdrawal, may be difficult to set up in an experimental situation, but the initial instructions or the context of the experiment could probably control this. The Watzlawick, Beavin, and Jackson definition is wide enough to allow a variety of experiments but narrow enough to impose some regularity on the eventual results of such experimentation.

EXPERIMENTATION ON THE DOUBLE BIND

Most of the available material on the double bind is anecdotal in nature and there have been few well designed studies. A review of the literature, however, seems to indicate that this pattern is changing and more researchers are becoming interested in this area of inquiry.

Haley (1964), in a departure from his usual approach to family research, analyzed triads drawn from forty well and forty disturbed families. By simply measuring the order in which individuals talked he was able to significantly differentiate the two types of families. The addition of a fourth family member, however, changed the interaction patterns and washed out the difference (Haley, 1967).

Coser (1960) pointed out the importance of laughter in setting up double binds. Zuk, Boszormeny-Nagy and Heiman (1963) were able to reliably count the number of laughs in a family therapy situation and report a significant inverse relationship between the number of times the parents and their schizophrenic daughter laughed. Zuk (1964) is following up this study and is attempting to systematically relate laughter to the double bind. The Zuk *et al.* and the Haley studies are important not because they buttress the double bind concept but because they represent useful ways of studying interactions in situations where double binds may be present.

Schuham (1967) reports on three doctoral dissertations (Ciotola, 1961; Potash, 1965; Loeff, 1966) which involved the double bind. Ciotola exposed schizophrenics and nonpsychotic psychiatric patients to an impossible auditory discrimination and then tested their reaction times to simple auditory discriminations. The fact that there were no differences found is not surprising since, to satisfy the definition of the double bind, the order of presentation of discrimination tasks would have to be reversed. Also, since it is possible that the double bind may be involved in all types of behavior pathology, the comparison group should have more accurately reflected the general population.

Potash matched undifferentiated male schizophrenics and hospital employees on age, education, and intelligence and tested them in a two-person, three-choice game. It was hypothesized that the schizophrenics would choose more often to withdraw from the game and this was not confirmed. Why this game is an analogy to the double bind is not clear from the Schuham article, but an important part of the conception of the double bind is that the schizophrenic cannot withdraw from the situation except through his pathological communication. A more meaningful measure in this type of situation would have been the changes, if any, in the schizophrenic's behavior as he confronts the situation. Normals should handle it in somewhat different ways.

A very useful design is embodied in the study by Loeff. He presented normals, schizophrenics, and delinquents with a set of metaphors in which the content and verbal affect were in direct conflict. Semantic differential scales, though not rating scales, significantly differentiated normal and combined pathological groups. The schizophrenics were not deficient in their perception of the metacommunication and both pathological groups responded more to the affect than to the content level. As Schuham (1967) points out, both of these findings conflict with the Palo Alto group's conceptualization of schizophrenia. The differential results found with semantic differential and rating scales is interesting and bears directly on the question of how double binds are perceived. Variations on Loeff's design are likely to form a significant segment of future work on the double bind.

Berger (1965) developed a questionnaire consisting of thirty double bind statements and applied it to patients with a record of communicational difficulties, nonschizophrenic hospitalized patients, ward attendants, and college students. The initial form differentiated schizophrenics and college students, and a form containing the twelve most discriminating items differentiated the two groups of hospitalized patients. The five items which best discriminated the schizophrenics from the other groups reflected either an affect/content or a father/mother conflict. The results indicate that it may be possible to develop a discriminating measure based on certain types of double bind statements. Schuham objects to the procedure of requesting subjects to recall experiences on the grounds that such a procedure is unreliable. Berger, however, reports a significant test-retest reliability when the questionnaire is given over a one-week period.

Perhaps the clearest example of the weaknesses of the double bind conception can be found in two studies of letters to schizophrenics. Weakland and Fry (1962) postulated that such letters are typical of the communication patterns normally present between the sender and the recipient and as such are a "permanent and objective piece of data, on one level (?), unitary, condensed and easier to study." They arrived at their conclusions without study of nonschizophrenic letters and in a number of cases their analysis of the sample letters is based more on their intimate knowledge of the patient rather than on what was actually written. Ringuette and Kennedy (1966) obtained forty letters from parents to their schizophrenic and nonschizophrenic offspring, and also asked volunteers to write similar letters. Three of the Palo Alto group rated the letters on a 7-point scale (schizophrenic to nonschizophrenic); first-year interns with experience in the double bind theory applied Weakland and Fry's criteria; experienced informed and uninformed clinicians sorted the letters into schizophrenic and nonschizophrenic categories; and naïve raters used a 7-point like/dislike scale. Only the naïve and the interns with double bind experience were consistent raters, and the Palto Alto judges scored a surprising .19. The "expert" and the "trained" judges were also unable to differentiate the volunteer letters from the rest. The Ringuette and Kennedy study clearly indicates the uselessness of a global definition when one is trying to correctly perceive a phenomenon in a complex set of communications which are presumed to contain that phenomenon. The same processes which lead to the unreliability of clinical diagnosis are probably at work in this situation.

SUMMARY AND REDEFINITION

The work of the Palo Alto group has already served the important purpose of shifting attention from psychic factors to the study of interactional processes through the analysis of communicational behaviors. Their interest, however, centers on the creation of a useful theory and not on the design of useful experiments to test that theory. Any attempt to investigate rigorously the pragmatic effects of communication must redefine the global definitions of phenomena now available into smaller, more carefully limited and operational statements which can be utilized in the design of experiments. In the specific case of the double bind this must involve recognition of the fact that, if the double bind exists, it is only the generic label for a large class of interactions satisfying some set of criteria drawn from logic and that the properties and effects of different "types" of double binds may well have different behavioral effects. The properties of these binds will in part depend upon the way the three aspects of the double bind are operationally defined.

The requirement of an "intense relationship" could, for example, be defined as a situation in which the individual is motivated to perceive correctly and/or respond appropriately to a set of communications. The experimental question then becomes: How can we set up experiments to initiate and maintain this "set?" If, by definition, any statement which refers to another statement is logically on a higher level than the first statement, then the process of setting up conflicting communications on different levels becomes clear. The various dichotomies (abstract/concrete, verbal/nonverbal, etc.) mentioned in the literature become different ways of operationalizing the basic concept and presumably have some validity and probably also differential effects. Finally, an experimental situation can be so structured as to limit metacommunication and leaving the field.

In conclusion, the experimental investigation of the double bind requires some major compromises between the desire of the Palo Alto group to extend a basic concept to large blocks of human behavior and the rather severe limitations and requirements of experimentation. This necessarily involves either the restriction of the concept to a limited range of behaviors or the breaking up of the concept into a number of categories which can be investigated separately.

REFERENCES

Bateson, G. A theory of play and fantasy, *Psychiatric Research Reports,* 1955, *2,* 39–51.

Bateson, G., Jackson, D., Haley, J., and Weakland, J. Toward a theory of schizophrenia. *Behavioral Science,* 1956, *1,* 251–64.

Bateson, G., Jackson, D., Haley, J., and Weakland, J. A note on the double-bind. *Family Process,* 1963, *2,* 154–57.

Berger, A. A test of the double-bind hypothesis of schizophrenia. *Family Process,* 1965, *4,* 198–205.

Cameron, N. Experimental analysis of schizophrenic thinking. In J. S. Kasanin (Ed.), *Language and thought in schizophrenia*. Berkeley: University of California Press, 1944.

Carnap, R. *Introduction to semantics*. Cambridge, Mass.: Harvard University Press, 1942.

Ciotola, P. The effect of two contradictory levels of reward and censure on schizophrenia. Doctoral dissertation, University of Missouri. *University Microfilms*, 1961, *61*, 2278.

Coser, R. Laughter among colleagues. *Psychiatry*, 1960, *23*, 81–95.

Ferreira, A. The double-bind and delinquent behavior. *Archives of General Psychiatry*, 1960, *3*, 359–67.

Friedman, L. An examination of Jay Haley's *Strategies of psychotherapy*. *Psychotherapy: Theory, Research, and Practice*, 1965, *2*, 181–88.

Haley, J. Paradoxes in play, fantasy, and psychotherapy. *Psychiatric Research Reports*, 1955, *2*, 52–58.

Haley, J. *Strategies of psychotherapy*. New York: Grune and Stratton, 1963.

Haley, J. Research on family patterns: an instrumental measure. *Family Process*, 1964, *3*, 41–65.

Haley, J. Speech sequences of normal and abnormal families with two children present. *Family Process*, 1967, *6*, 81–97.

Jackson, D. *The etiology of schizophrenia*. New York: Basic Books, 1960.

Jackson, D. Interactional psychotherapy. In M. Stein (Ed.), *Contemporary psychotherapies*. New York: The Free Press, 1961.

Jackson, D. and Haley, J. Transference revisited. *Journal of Nervous and Mental Disease*, 1963, *137*, 363–71.

Jones, D. M. Binds and unbinds. *Family Process*. 1964, *3*, 323–31.

Kasanin, J. S. The disturbance of conceptual thinking in schizophrenia. In J. S. Kasanin (Ed.), *Language and thought in schizophrenia*. Berkeley: University of California Press, 1944.

Loeff, R. Differential discrimination of conflicting emotional messages by normal, delinquent, and schizophrenic adolescents. Doctoral dissertation, Indiana University. *University Microfilms*, 1966, *66*, 1470.

Lu, Y. Contradictory parental expectations in schizophrenia. *Archives of General Psychiatry*, 1962, *6*, 219–34.

Mishler, E. and Waxler, N. Family interaction processes and schizophrenia. *Merrill-Palmer Quarterly*, 1965, *11*, 269–315.

Pavlov, I. P. *Conditioned reflexes*. New York: Oxford University Press, 1927.

Potash, H. Schizophrenic interaction and the conception of the double-bind. Doctoral dissertation, Michigan State Universty. *University Microfilms*, 1965, *65*, 2052.

Ringuette, E. and Kennedy, T. An experimental study of the double-bind hypothesis. *Journal of Abnormal Psychology*, 1966, *71*, 136–41.

Ruesch, J. *Therapeutic communication*. New York: Norton, 1961.

Schuham, A. The double-bind hypothesis a decade later. *Psychological Bulletin*, 1967, *68*, 409–16.

Sluzki, C., Beavin, J., Tarnopolsky, A., and Veron, E. Transactional disqualifications. *Archives of General Psychiatry*, 1967, *16*, 494–504.

Stein, M. (Ed.), *Contemporary psychotherapies*. New York: The Free Press, 1961.

Sullivan, H. S. The language of schizophrenia. In J. S. Kasanin (Ed.), *Language and thought in schizophrenia*. Berkeley: University of California Press, 1944.

Watts, A. *Psychotherapy east and west*. New York: Mentor Books, 1961.

Watzlawick, P. A review of double-bind theory. *Family Process,* 1963, *2*, 132–53.

Watzlawick, P. *An anthology of human communication*. Palo Alto: Science and Behavior Books, 1964.

Watzlawick, P. Paradoxical prediction. *Psychiatry*, 1965, *28*, 368–74.

Watzlawick, P., Beavin, J., and Jackson, D. *Pragmatics of human communication*. New York: Norton, 1967.

Weakland, J. The double-bind hypothesis of schizophrenia and three-party interaction. In D. Jackson (Ed.), *The etiology of schizophrenia*. New York: Basic Books, 1960.

Weakland, J. and Fry, W. Letters of mothers of schizophrenics. *American Journal of Orthopsychiatry*, 1962, *32*, 604–23.

Whitehead, A. N. and Russell, B. *Principia mathematica*. 3 volumes. Cambridge: Cambridge University Press, 1910–1913.

Zuk, G. A further study of laughter in family therapy. *Family Process*, 1964, *3*, 77–81.

Zuk, G., Roszormeny-Nagy, I., and Heiman, E. Some dynamics of laughter during family therapy. *Family Process*, 1963, *2*, 302–13.

CHAPTER 12

NEW WORD COINAGE IN
THE PSYCHOPATHOLOGICAL CONTEXT

In view of the quantity and variety of research interests in psychotic language behavior, it is rather surprising that neologisms have so long escaped systematic scrutiny. Neologisms were among the linguistic anomalies in schizophrenia that first attracted the attention of earlier investigators like Fleishchhacker (1930), Kleist (1914), Schneider (1930), Storch (1922), and White (1926). In recent years, however, despite a predilection on the part of textbook writers in psychiatry and psychology for quoting bizarre examples of new-word coinage by psychotic patients, there has been little or no discussion of the problems and issues posed by neologisms within the context of psychopathology. While a great deal of information has accumulated on other gross characteristics of psychotic language, this topic continues to be dominated by anecdotes and conjecture.

The term neologism has been applied with a notable lack of consistency to a bewildering diversity of phenomena and to the processes presumed to mediate such phenomena. Neologisms have been viewed from the extremes of nonsense and meaningfulness: Thus, an authority in speech pathology (Robbins, 1963, p. 74) defines the neologism as the "construction of meaningless words," while White (1926, p. 341) refers to the patient whose neologism "compressed within it practically the entire history of her psychic conflict." Neologisms have been interpreted as antitheses of stereotypy and elasticity in conceptualization (Woods, 1938); as mediated by pathological features of thought (Arieti, 1955) or by qualities inherent in language itself (Forrest, 1965); as attempts on the part of the patient to communicate (Weinstein, 1962) and as attempts to *avoid* communicating (Sullivan, 1944); as analogous to the psychic productions of dream states and of young children (Warren, 1934); as the proximal end of a process that eventuates in verbigeration or word-salad speech (Robbins, 1963); as regressive phenomena, as compensatory or copying mechanisms, or as something akin to verbal intrusory errors produced in the speech of normals by toxic or fatigue states (Cameron and Magaret, 1951).

Since information is sparse on the relative incidence of neologisms in psychotic language, their significance for the diagnostic process is at best equivocal. Although they appear to form a more prominent part of the symptom picture in hebephrenic reactions than in other groups, the absence of reliable data leaves this statement, too, open to question. Practically nothing is known as yet about their functional properties or their possible relevance to prognosis and treatment.

The preceding considerations might be construed as offering justification for abandoning the term altogether in favor of a more precise description in individual cases of the diverse phenomena presently subsumed under this designation. Whether or not the facts which are reviewed in the following pages support such a conclusion, it is abundantly clear that, if the neologism is to retain any usefulness or value as a construct, some effort must be made to clarify the confusion surrounding its employment in both the clinic and the laboratory. The present chapter is intended as a first approximation in that direction.

DEFINING NEOLOGISMS

Specialized lexicographic sources (English and English, 1958; Piéron, 1957; Robbins, 1963; Warren, 1934) yield a variety of meanings for the term neologism: (1) a newly coined word; (2) a newly coined phrase; (3) an old word used in a new and different sense; (4) an old phrase used in a new and different sense; and (5) the behavior or act of coining words.

English and English state that "coining new and bizarre words is a common symptom among psychotics" and characterize as *neolalia* "speech containing many words devised by the speaker." (p. 340)

Warren defines the neologism as the "construction of new words, as a characteristic of the insane, of the dream state, and of young children." (p. 177)

Piéron identifies neologisms as "expressions verbales nouvelles, ayant, chez certains aliénés, un caractére pathologique, de même que des expressions scripturales, des *néographismes,* auxquels J. Bobon (1955) a ajouté des expressions graphiques par dessus en peintures symboliques appellées *néomorphismes,* et des expressions gestuelles de signification magique appellées *néomimismes,* les unes et les autres d'origine delirante." (p. 234)

Robbins gives a number of terms for patholinguistic processes related to new-word coinage: *idioglossia,* "invented language" (p. 54); *jargon aphasia,* "an extreme grade of *syntactical aphasia* in which the patient fails to emit the intended word often enough to give one an inkling as to his train of thought. Several words are run together as one, the syllables being articulated but wrongly accented. It is frequently complicated with the appearance of meaningless words (p. 60); *schizophasia,* "production of meaningless words and sounds" (p. 90); *schizophrasia,* "the fantastic, incoherent disconnected speech manifest in dementia praecox and resulting from two irrelevant trains of thought going on simultaneously." (p. 90)

It was Bryan (1933) who originally directed attention to the strong influence of professional context upon psychiatric definitions of the neologism: "To most physicians the word neologisms suggests pathology; to the philologist they are not always abnormalities." (p. 579) In its original etymological derivation, the term neologism implies nothing more than "a new word or new meaning for an established word." (Webster, 1957, p. 984). When a prominent psychiatrist chooses to speak of "a need to 'distantiate' from others," (Meerloo, 1960, p. 469), we applaud his use of a strikingly novel and effective expression. The same expression from a patient would unhesitatingly be set down as a symptom of disturbance.

In a rare moment of skittishness, English and English remark that "coining new and bizarre words is a common symptom among psychotics, but in only slightly different form it infects scientists and scholars. One should particularly be wary of Greek neologisms when they bear the gifts of apparent—but only apparent—precision." (p. 340)

As Pronko (1963) points out, once the user initiates us into the mysteries of its usage, "we can adopt the word and use it among ourselves as linguistic legal tender." (p. 300) He cites the newspaper columnist who provides us with an inexhaustible source of picturesque speech and patter: *reminuisances* are long-winded reminiscences; a *reno-vation* is a divorce; and a *sinema* is a risqué movie. Pronko goes on to mention the competition among writers in Shakespeare's day in the deliberate minting of new words. The writer's principal reward for the successful launching of a neologism was to hear it repeated in widening social circles. Says Pronko: "The poor schizophrenic with his lack of social skills is not at all ego-involved even in making himself understood, let alone having others adopt his brand-new verbal creation." (p. 300)[1]

Such glib characterizations, with their implications for schizophrenics *in general,* become increasingly unacceptable in the light of systematic investigations of psychopathological language. If there is nothing intrinsically pathological in the coinage of new words and expressions, there is no a priori basis for judging the linguistic productions themselves by different standards according to motivation or intent, which are matters for

---

[1] Reprinted by permission of the Williams & Wilkins Co., Baltimore.

inquiry rather than inference. In any event, it seems gratuitously presumptive to deny verbal inventiveness to the schizophrenic sui generis, when a large mass of evidence points to the contrary.

NEOLOGISMS AS PATHOGNOMONIC SIGNS

Neologisms seem to occur with the greatest frequency in the verbal output of schizophrenics. Noyes and Kolb (1963) are quite firm in stating that "The use of neologisms by the mental patient always suggests a schizophrenic psychosis." (pp. 337–38) Other writers (Fish, 1962; Kisker, 1964; Rosen and Gregory, 1965; White, 1964) are substantially in agreement. The diagnostic category most frequently mentioned in relation to neologisms is hebephrenic reactions.

Bryan's (1933) population of neologists was predominantly schizophrenic, but also included one patient with general paresis, one manic-depressive, one patient with cerebral arteriosclerosis, and one patient with acute alcoholic hallucinosis. She did not indicate whether any differences were apparent (e.g., in frequency of output of neologisms) among her patients, but she did make the extremely interesting and provocative observation that all of the patients in the study were, or had been, hallucinated. For many patients, "the voices" had supplied the neologisms.

A search of the literature failed to disclose any sources of hard data on the extremely important question of comparative incidence of neologisms. In the absence of such information, one hesitates to accept consensus statements about the frequency of neologisms in schizophrenic patients and the rarity of neologisms among patients with other types of pyschiatric disorder. An object lesson is provided by the study of Rubert *et al.* (1961) on the relative incidence of olfactory hallucinations. Nineteen out of 24 unselected psychotic patients and 11 out of 12 chronic hallucinating schizophrenic patients reported olfactory hallucinations when asked specifically. The authors conclude that the rarity of olfactory hallucinations is apparent rather than real, and is due to the fact that psychiatrists do not inquire about them, they are less disturbing to the patient than voices or visions, and the sense of smell plays a less important role in human behavior.

Systematic investigation of the comparative incidence of neologisms seems absolutely essential before one can attribute meaning and significance to them as pathognomonic signs of mental illness.

WORDPLAY

Woods (1938) suggests that neologisms may represent blends or condensations of thought or "they may be half-playful formations which, for the most part, spring from a desire to play with words." (p. 292) Kisker

(1964) states that "some patients find a particular satisfaction in rhyming and the play of words." (p. 346) He illustrates these tendencies with a letter from a patient to the physician in which an essentially quite simple idea is intellectualized and elaborated.

"Dear Doctor,
   I hope that last letter of mine didn't offend you in any way. I couldn't help snickering, laughing and sneering as I wrote all that stuff. I was immensely involuntarily amused at my own bumptious presumptiousness [sic] and generally (to me) delicious maliciousness. (p. 346)

In her comparative study of schizophrenic and normal language, White (1949) failed to elicit any neologisms from her schizophrenic patients in response to a series of structured verbal tasks. She did, however, identify eleven nonsense words given by schizophrenics as against none by the normal controls. "To be considered a nonsense word, the word had to be given as a word by the subject, and when he was questioned, to be accepted by him as a word." (p. 64) Some of these nonsense words were: "ladylation," "appleless," "dropletess," "owic," "wester," and "panter." According to the author, such nonsense words could not be considered "true neologisms because they were not spontaneous language but responses to confusing stimuli." (p. 73) She suggests that the absense of neologisms in her sample reflects a less severe stage of illness than that exhibited by the patients observed by Bleuler and Kraepelin. Says White: "Since many of Bleuler's and Kraepelin's signs were not found in our group, we might conclude that neologisms, rhyming, akataphasia, word salads, condensations, and symbolization do not appear in schizophrenia but do occur in 'demented' praecox." (p. 73)

The value and importance of White's criterion for distinguishing nonsense words from true neologisms, i.e., whether the word is "elicited" or "emitted," are further revealed in the aberrant associations given by two schizophrenic patients to the Kent-Rosanoff word association test. Laffal (1965), referring to the data presented in Table 14, points out the preponderance of nonsense words, perseverations, and irrelevant responses over pertinent associations. "It is almost impossible to escape the impression that, although the patients complied with the examiner's request for verbal associations, they worked hard at giving worthless responses." (p. 52)

CLASSIFICATIONS AND CONCEPTIONS

Schneider (1930) is one of the few authors who has made an attempt to construct a classification of neologisms in accordance with hypotheses concerning the processes assumed to mediate new-word coinage. The more conventional categorization of neologisms into condensations, displacements, and distortions is based upon rather gross and easily dis-

TABLE 14

TABLE SHOWING SOME OF THE WORD ASSOCIATIONS OF
TWO DEMENTIA PRAECOX PATIENTS
(AFTER KENT AND ROSANOFF, 1910)

Stimulus Word	Case No. 4752	Case No. 5183
table	meadow	muss
dark	black	gone
music	sweet	caffa
sickness	dead	monk
man	mansion	boy
deep	near	lesson
soft	sooner	ness
eating	formble	pie
mountain	gair	Gus
house	temble	muss
black	benched	court
mutton	ranched	beef
comfort	bumble	ness
hand	semble	koy
short	simber	ness
fruit	narrow	dalb
butterfly	Ben	flack
smooth	gum	mess
command	bramble	cork
chair	low	ness
sweet	temper	Bess
whistle	bensid	toy
woman	hummery	girl
cold	gunst	cork
slow	bemper	mass
wish	tip	vell
river	gumper	mouth
white	Andes	cast
beautiful	gimper	ness
window	hummer	crow
rough	geep	ratter
citizen	humper	zide
foot	zuper	malloy
spider	gumper	straw
needle	himper	cast
red	gumper	Roman
sleep	moop	scack
anger	rumble	gois
carpet	slamper	noise
girl	hinker	call
high	humper	hort
working	gumpip	Kaffir
sour	imper	romerscotters

TABLE 14—*Cont.*

Stimulus Word	Case No. 4752	Case No. 5183
earth	gumper	bell
trouble	humper	tramine
soldier	guipper	gas
cabbage	phar	cor
hard	her	kalbas

cernible features of the neologistic response. Little evidence has been presented thus far to suggest that such features are either stable or significant. In addition, such classifications are apt to exclude more phenomena than they include.

Schneider's work has been reported by Bryan (1933) and we shall make use of her account. Schneider classifies neologisms into five types, which Bryan exemplifies by reference to the neologisms she collected from the patients in her descriptive study:

1. *Verwelchung*, the Frenchifying or Italianizing of a word; we have "thiefus," an American college graduate's expression for a thief, similar in formation but Latinized into a noun.

2. *Abwandlung*, the changing of a verb to a noun suggests to Schneider a trend toward cosmic experience. We have patient Elizabeth MacL. who spoke of the "nearing of a masculine figure"; Margaret C. said she was "real-estated" in explaining that she means that money was paid down in advance for her delivery here; Mary B. speaks of the "bed-rudgers"—and Elizabeth F. compounds words a la Keats (?) and says she has the power to "turn-in," that is "that a woman could turn into a man"—"the power of turning in a piece of cake or pie without going to the store." The last of these does seem to show a trend toward cosmic experience or magic.

3. *Umformung*, is the simple transformation of a word; Lila C. invents the word "camerist" which means those who "go before the camera" and may mean one who takes a picture.

4. *Wort-zusamensetzung*, (word-compound) is common: the "I-maker," the "ribbon-sparkle" (planet) "cherry-pain" and "Frank-mistress."

5. *Neushöpfung*, (literally "new creation") varies from the words carefully spelled out and explained such as "fyscopathic" and "vicyce lightse," "theopathy" and "adamousius" to "poive," "yourkin," and "waxene," etc., that one must spell and explain if one can. There are interesting compound phrases that are too fascinating to separate: "Paid-land," "the Becourse or (Because) Trust Company," "poor-nuorshudder-slide," "Glass-pantsee," "L.M.A.," "Bi. M. A.," "D.A. Invisible," etc. (p. 585)

Another theorist who has dealt with neologisms in some detail is Kleist (1914) whose views have been summarized by Fish (1962).

> A neologism may be a completely new word whose derivation cannot be understood, or it may be a word which has been incorrectly built up but its origins are clearly understandable, logically and grammatically, as due to a misuse of the accepted methods of word formation. Sometimes a neologism is an accepted word which is being used in an unusual way so that an old word acquires a new meaning. Kleist considers that some neologisms are due to speech disorder, so that literal paraphasia may produce neologisms due to sound distortions, and verbal paraphasia may lead to the production of new words or the use of known words in a special way. This means that some neologisms are in fact stock words. When verbal paraphasia takes place in connection with secondary word formation, neologisms occur which are stock secondary word formations. The same disorder gives rise to unusual word derivations or to the construction of unusual word combinations which appear as neologisms. In severe agrammatism all particles and adverbs are omitted and a long string of inadequately related words is produced. This gives rise to the type of neologism which has been called a "word monstrosity." In other patients, the nelogisms appear to be related entirely to some delusional experience and the patient uses a neologism to describe or designate a delusional experience or idea which is outside his normal experience. This type of neologism can be called a "technical neologism" and can be regarded as a personal jargon invented to describe the peculiar schizophrenic experiences. In other patients the neologisms seem to be due to auditory hallucinations and the patient reproduces neologisms used by the phonemes[2], or may feel himself obliged to use certain words to placate the hallucinatory voices or to protect himself from them. Mannerisms and stereotypes may lead to the repeated use of distorted words so that in some cases neologisms are really catatonic symptoms. (p. 25)[3]

Kisker (1964) supplies an example of what Kleist identified as a "flight into intellectualism," as shown by the patient who called a candle a "night illumination object." This process seems to figure prominently in the neologistic constructions of the patient described by Kisker:

> At the time of the initial interview, the patient believed that she was a professor at the University of Smithsonian in England, and that she was the only woman professor among many men. She said that she had attended many other universities in Europe, and had been accepted as an

---

[2] Fish employs the term phoneme here to refer to the "voices" experienced by the patient in his auditory hallucinations. This is quite arbitrary usage on the author's part; the term phoneme already has a different "official" meaning in the science of linguistics, where it refers to the minimal unit of distinctive sound-feature. Thus, Fish provides a handy illustration of his own definition above of the neologism as "an accepted word which is being used in an unusual way so that an old word acquires a new meaning"!

[3] Reprinted by permission of the Williams & Wilkins Co., Baltimore.

authority on the planets and the satellites. She placed great emphasis on the fact that she was the only woman professor, and that she was obliged by the University of Law to have relations with any of the male professors who desired it. She believed there was a war on between the University of Smithsonian and Purdue University for the mastery of her three specialties which are psychiatry, "sexiatry," and "mythiatry."

The following excerpts from an interview with the patient show her frequent use of neologisms: "I am here from a foreign university . . . and you have to have a "plausity' of all acts of amendment to go through for the children's code . . . and it is no mental disturbance or 'puterience' . . . it is an 'amorition' law . . . there is nothing to disturb me . . . it is like their 'privatilinia' . . . and the children have to have this 'accentuative' law so they don't go into the 'mortite' law of the church." (pp. 343–44)

Woods (1938) reports a case description of a pre-senile psychotic whose speech contains a number of neologisms such as "blass blucket." One questions whether phonological blendings of this sort actually merit inclusion among true neologisms. Language lends itself readily to the production of such phenomena under conditions of accelerated rate of speech. If a person says "toy boat," for example, over and over again as rapidly as he can, sooner or later he will produce something that sounds like "toy boyt." It seems worth noting that Woods' patient was described as being under "terrific" speech pressure.

Arieti (1955) remarked of some schizophrenic thought that frequently mental processes occur that are stimulated only by verbalization. Forrest (1965) has spoken of the parallel between the poet and the schizophrenic in terms of the tendency on the part of both "for the use of language to be dictated by qualities inherent in the language, and therefore extrapsychic." (p. 3) As an example of this need to "bring to the words the *authority* of phonetic order," Forrest mentions Kraepelin's patient who, in response to the word "Bett" spoken to him aloud, went through a process of "senseless ringing of the changes on a syllable" in the following manner: "Bett, Bett, Bett, dett, dett, dett, ditt, dutt, dutt, daut, daut, daut, dint, dint, dint, dutt, dett, datt. Wenn ich angefangen habe, fahre ich fort bis zu Ende." (p. 3) Again one hesitates to identify such clang associations as genuine neologisms.

It is also questionable whether expressions produced by compounding (*"Wort-zusamensetzung"*) should be classified as neologisms. Referring to Bleuler's comparison between condensation in the dream, where "quite heterogeneous parts of different images may be fused together into a perceptual whole," and "distortions of speech" in schizophrenia, Forrest (1965) suggests that:

. . . when the fusion of images is described by the schizophrenic, he may or may not feel it appropriate to condense his words as well.

This may occur by hyphenation, with the production of compounded substantives as noted by Lorenz, Kraepelin (for example, *"Wasserpadagogium"*), and Bleuler, whose patient was tormented by "elbow-people." There may also be a fusion of the parts of more than one word into a single word—for example, Bleuler's patient who "owns Algiers" and suffers from "neuralgiers."

This sort of combination occurs normally in the history of language, where it is called a blend or portmanteau word (examples are *smog,* from smoke and fog, and *slithy,* from slimy and lithe). I do not see why patients' coinages should not be dignified by the precise term "portmanteau word," since other terms suggest they are peculiar to schizophrenic speech. (p. 5)

Similar arguments could be made with regard to foreignization (*"Verwelchung"*) and changing one part of speech to another (*"Abwandlung"*). Words like "roomette," a diminutive Pullman compartment, represent the "frenchification" of homegrown English expressions for the purpose of achieving a greater measure of elegance; and poetry abounds in examples of the second: the haunting line by E. E. Cummings, "but if a lark should april me," achieves a memorable effect by using a noun as a verb.

If we exclude from categorization as neologisms those expressions which can be identified as portmanteau words, nonsense words, phonological blendings, foreignization, and examples of changing one part of speech to another, we are left with a classification that includes the following types of neologistic constructions:

1. *New-word creation* (*"Neushöpfung"*): technical or true neologisms.
2. *Verbal paraphasia,* the use of known words in special, idiosyncratic, or bizarre ways.
3. *Severe agrammatism,* which produces, among other kinds of linguistic distortions, the kind of construction identified [by Fish, 1962] as a "word monstrosity."

While obviously still far from satisfactory, such a classification offers some reduction in the number and variety of phenomena subsumed under the term neologism and helps to differentiate neologistic constructions more accurately from stammering, intrusory errors, slips of the tongue, verbal rituals, witticisms, and obscure terminology.

SOME DIRECTIONS FOR FURTHER RESEARCH

It seems fairly obvious from the preceding brief review of the literature that what is needed in this area is a comprehensive, systematic program of investigation, in both depth and breadth, of neologistic phenomena at all levels of analysis: phonological, morphological, semantical, syntactical, and pragmatical. To conduct such a program would call for the development of new concepts, interpretations, tools and instruments, research methods, and approaches; and it would require the contribution of specialized knowledge and skills from specialists in linguistics, psycholinguistics and psychopathology.

To outline a program of this kind in detail is beyond the scope of this paper and the capabilities of the present writer. Nevertheless, it is possible to mention some problems which are identified clearly enough to provide an immediate target for research.

Brown (1958) has stated that most if not all neologisms conform to the phonology and morphology of the patient's native language:

> The disease (schizophrenia) does not seem to disrupt that very fundamental pattern. In addition most neologisms are constructed according to some standard morphological pattern. Their meanings can often be guessed from the constituent morphemes. This would simply be linguistic invention were it not for the fact that the patient seems to think his neologisms are conventional forms requiring no explanation. (pp. 292–93)[4]

It is difficult to regard Brown's contentions as more than an expression of opinion. Most clinicians—with rare exceptions, at any rate—are lacking in the kind of linguistic expertise required to furnish a precise phonemic transcription of their patients' speech, particularly in instances of atypical speech. The inadequacies of the conventional orthographies in representing patterns of spoken language are too well known to require extensive comment. They pose even greater problems in the representation of neologisms. One can only guess at the original sound pattern for which coinages like "poive" and "iava" are allowed to stand as referents. Surely terms like those quoted by Brown ("hydroscenic," "prestigitis," "rodential") display considerable regularity in their construction. But the real question is whether such terms are truly representative of neologisms in psychotic language, or whether they reach the pages of the professional journals and books via a highly selective filtering process.

The question, of course, is an empirical one, which requires the participation of the linguist in the recording and analysis of neologistic constructions in representative samples of psychotic speech and language behavior.

Another problem has to do with the relevance of neologisms to the diagnostic process, specifically in the case of schizophrenic disorders. It will be remembered that White (1949) reported her failure to discover

---

[4] Reprinted by permission of the Macmillan Company, New York.

most of the pathognomonic signs of schizophrenic language mentioned by Bleuler and Kraepelin, including "neologisms, rhyming, akataphasia, word salads, condensations, and symbolization." (p. 73) She attributed this failure to the difference in patient populations (i.e., her group was almost exclusively composed of early and first admissions, as compared with the longer term patients analyzed by Bleuler and Kraepelin), and concluded that such phenomena "do not appear early in schizophrenia but do occur in 'demented' praecox." (p. 73)

Such distinctions as process/reactive and chronic/acute naturally come to mind. Would an investigation of the comparative incidence of neologisms between selected process and reactive patients reveal significant differences? As chronicity increases, does schizophrenic language become more like that of patients with organic brain damage? These questions deserve answers in the form of empirical data.

Finally, a rather straightforward and obvious line of investigation concerns the functional properties of the neologism as a verbal free operant. Reading the literature, one acquires the conviction that patients who show a high rate of output for new words may be responding to the social reinforcement properties of the examiner's questions and expressions of interest. As a logical first step toward the systematic investigation of neologisms, it would be extremely interesting to examine the influence of operant conditioning procedures and schedules of reinforcement upon the production of neologisms in a sample group of psychotic patients. It would also be of considerable interest to learn whether the processes of new-word coinage are susceptible to eventual extinction.

REFERENCES

Arieti, S. *Interpretation of schizophrenia.* New York: Brunner, 1955.

Brown, R. *Words and things.* New York: The Free Press, 1959.

Bryan, E. L. A study of forty cases exhibiting neologisms. *American Journal Of Psychiatry*, 1933, *90*, 579–95.

Cameron, N. and Margaret, A. *Behavior pathology.* Boston: Houghton Mifflin, 1951.

English, H. B. and English, A. C. (Eds.) *A comprehensive dictionary of psychological and psychoanalytical terms.* New York: Longmans, Green, 1958.

Fish, F. J. *Schizophrenia.* Baltimore: The Williams and Wilkins Company, 1962.

Fleishchhacker, H. Störungen des Sprachverständnisses bei Schizophrenen. *Monatsschrift für Psychiatrie und Neurologie*, 1930, *77*, 1.

Forrest, D. V. Poiesis and the language of schizophrenia. *Psychiatry*, 1965, *28*, 1–18.

Kisker, G. W. *The disorganized personality*. New York: McGraw-Hill, 1964.

Kleist, K. Aphasie und Geisteskrankheit. *Münchener Medizinische Wochenschrift*, 1914, *61*, 8.

Laffal, J. *Pathological and normal language*. New York: Atherton Press, 1965.

Meerloo, J. A. M. Some conversational patterns with the neurotic. In D. Barbara (Ed.), *Psychological and psychiatric aspects of speech and hearing*. Springfield, Ill. Charles C Thomas, 1960.

Noyes, A. P. and Kolb, L. C. *Modern clinical psychiatry*, (6th ed.). Philadelphia: W. B. Saunders, 1963.

Piéron, H. *Vocabulaire de la psychologie*. Paris: Presses Universitaires de France, 1957.

Pronko, N. H. *Textbook of abnormal psychology*. Baltimore: The Williams and Wilkins Company, 1963.

Robbins, S. D. *A dictionary of speech pathology and therapy*. Cambridge, Mass.: Sci-Art Publishers, 1963.

Rosen, E. and Gregory, I. *Abnormal psychology*. Philadelphia: W. B. Saunders, 1965.

Rubert, S. L., Hollender, M. H., and Mehrof, E. G. Olfactory hallucinations. *Archives of General Psychiatry*, 1961, *5*, 313–18.

Schneider, C. *Die Psychologie der Schizophrenen*. Leipzig: Georg Thieme, 1930.

Storch, A. *Das Archaisch-Primitive Erleben und Denken der Schizophrenen*. Berlin: Springer, 1922.

Sullivan, H. S. The language of schizophrenia. In J. Kasanin (Ed.), *Language and thought in schizophrenia*. Berkeley: University of California Press, 1944.

Warren, H. C. (Ed.) *Dictionary of psychology*. Boston: Houghton Mifflin, 1934.

Webster's New World Dictionary of the American Language. Cleveland: The World Publishing Company, 1957.

Weinstein, E. A. *Cultural aspects of delusion*. New York: The Free Press, 1962.

White, M. A. A study of schizophrenic language. *Journal of Abnormal and Social Psychology*, 1949, *44*, 61–74.

White, R. W. *The abnormal personality*. New York: Ronald Press, 1964.

White, W. A. The language of schizophrenia. *Archives of Neurology and Psychiatry*, 1926, *16*, 395–413.

Whitehorn, J. and Zipf, G. K. Schizophrenic language. *Archives of Neurology and Psychiatry*, 1943, *49*, 831–51.

Woods, W. L. Language study in schizophrenia. *Journal of Nervous and Mental Disease*, 1938, *87*, 290–316.

CHAPTER 13

PSYCHOPATHOLOGY
AND THE POLYGLOT

The polyglot—the person who possesses linguistic competence in more than a single language—presents a fascinating series of challenges and problems for both the psycholinguist and the psychopathologist. When two or more linguistic codes are available, what are the factors which determine the selection of one over the other in the encoding of psychopathological experiences? In terms of the Sapir-Whorf (linguistic relativity) hypothesis, does the possession of more than a single language code therefore imply the possession of more than one *Weltanschauung*? Are delusional and hallucinatory formations susceptible to influences from competing linguistic systems within the polyglot individual? Does bilingualism contribute in any significant way to emotional instability? These and many more intriguing questions are raised by the phenomenon of multilingualism vis-à-vis psychopathology.

Language disturbances, particularly aphasia, have absorbed the interest of specialists from several disciplines: psychology, psychiatry, neurology, speech pathology, speech therapy, and linguistics. Linguistic and psycholinguistic issues have been discussed in a number of papers and reports (Lambert and Fillenbaum, 1959; Leischner, 1948; Minkowski, 1928; Osgood and Miron, 1963). Despite the obvious constraints imposed by the small numbers of cases dealt with in the literature, the study of bilingualism in aphasia has already achieved some noteworthy successes.

Even fewer studies of psychopathological factors in multilingualism have been reported, and those are entirely descriptive. Nevertheless they represent our total available resources on this extremely interesting and important topic, so we shall consider them in some detail. First, however,

194

it seems worthwhile to devote a brief preliminary discussion to some general aspects of multilingualism.

THE PHENOMENON OF BILINGUALISM[1]

Whether starting from a common origin or emanating from several sources, language has come, through a process of differentiation, to assume today approximately 1,500 different forms. To this large number should be added hundreds of dialects within various languages, some of which are as mutually unintelligible as separate language systems.

Because of movements of populations through migration and conquest, and in more recent historical periods through immigration, colonization, and annexations of territory, groups of people speaking different languages have been thrown together in daily contact and communication. The coexistence of two languages within the same political unit or geographic region has given rise to the phenomenon of bilingualism, whose extent today is probably greater than ever before in human history because of a greater mixture of populations and easier means of communication in the present world.

Contact and convergence between two different languages or cultures results in a sociological situation wherein the same individual learns elements from a linguistic or cultural system other than his native system. Linguists refer to this learning situation as *language contact* and to the particular learning process as *bilingualization*. Linguistic change resulting from such contact is called *interference*. Says Diebold (1961), "in both language and culture contact, there are two aspects to be considered, viz., a sociological learning process, viz., bilingualism and acculturation, and a result of that process: change in one or both of the systems, viz., linguistic interference and cultural borrowing." (p. 98)

Numerous examples of languages in contact suggest that bilingualism is seldom, if ever, mutually balanced between the two groups of speakers. It appears that more speakers from one of the speech groups becomes bilingual than the other. In most bilingual situations the two languages involved do not carry equal social prestige ". . . and this represents the complex psychological and sociological phenomenon of culture conflict. A truly bilingual situation where the two languages are on equal footing is rarely encountered." (Yamamoto, 1964, p. 476) One of the languages is usually more dominant, carries greater social approval, is the representative of the "superior culture." This situation is found especially in countries of immigration and colonization.

---

[1] Although there are theoretical grounds for distinguishing between bilingualism and multilingualism (i.e., the practice of using alternately three or more languages), for the sake of convenience we shall use the terms indiscriminately in this chapter.

Many factors for this language "differential" have been noted by researchers. Arsenian (1945, p. 81) states that "the earlier the acquisition of a second language, the stronger its impression upon the individual and the more effective its use by him." Diebold (1961) comments:

... the two language structures set up limits of variability to interference. My data strongly suggests that sociological factors like the age of learning, the learning situation itself, and intergroup social relations are equally crucial factors. (p. 111)[2]

Arsenian examined bilingualism in relation to a number of factors other than immigrant adjustment and reported the following findings:

1. *Bilingualism and sex.* No consistent or statistically significant differences exist between the extent of the bilingual background of boys and girls in either (of the experimental) groups.
2. *Bilingualism and parental influence.* The influence of parents on the bilingual status of their children is shared equally by father and mother.
3. *Bilingualism and racial groups.* The average bilingual score of foreign-born Italian, Jewish, and mixed groups is higher than the average for these same racial groups born in the United States. (Arsenian, 1945).

It is obvious that the development of bilingualism is a complex operation sensitive to many environmental factors.

TWO HYPOTHESES REGARDING BILINGUAL COGNITIONS

It is the mark of a fluent bilingual individual that he manages to keep his language-generating essentially unilingual. Observations have pointed to some major organizing principle as yet unidentified by research which underlies the psychological separation of the bilingual's two languages. It may be that experiences are coded once, in common, and each of the bilingual's languages draws from this experience; or it may be that events are coded separately in the language in which they are experienced. Says Kolers (1963):

If verbally defined past experiences were tagged, or coded, and stored in common, they would presumably be in some supralinguistic form such as "thoughts" or "ideas" ... A bilingual's languages would then act as independent tape for this common storage, and experiences stored in one language could be retrieved and described directly in the other.... We will call this the shared hypothesis.

Alternatively, if verbally defined past experiences were tagged in a form specific to one language ... a bilingual would have a different store

---

[2] Reprinted by permission of the Linguistic Society of America, Austin, Tex.

of experiences to refer to for each of his two languages, or would be required to tag a given experience multiple, one in each language. It would be impossible to refer directly to . . . in one language an experience or event tagged in the other; such references would require an additional step of translation. We will call this the separate hypothesis. (p. 291)

In a test of these hypotheses, Kolers performed a word-association experiment with three groups of bilingual subjects. Four test sequences were studied, i.e., the stimulus word in English responded to in (a) English, or (b) the native language; and a translation of the word into the native language responded to in (c) English, or (d) the native language. There were five semantic categories of words.

Kolers' principal finding showed that subjects tended to give different associations to a word in their native languages from those they gave in English to its translation. "Further, when the test is made interlingually—the stimulus in one language and the response in the other—again little similarity is found. . . . The present results suggest that an image can only be a concomitant but cannot be an essential property of the cognitive referent of a noun." (p. 297) The results tend to suggest, at least as far as word associations, no fixed images acting as a basis for responses in both languages, and thus lend support to the "separate" hypothesis.

In a later study (1964), Kolers examined another aspect of this question. The study sought to determine whether a language skill developed in one language transferred necessarily to a bilingual's second language. The principal finding was that a cognitive operation practiced on one set of of materials does not necessarily transfer to another set. "While S can make information stored in one encoding system available in another, what he can do with it seems to depend upon specific skills he has developed in each system, and, presumably, upon equally specific skills for transferring between them." (Kolers, 1964, p. 247) This also supports the "separate" hypothesis.

Some experimenters have studied this problem in terms of some of the factors mentioned in the first section. For example, Lambert *et al,* (1958), studied the influence of language-acquisition contexts on bilingualism, using university students with extensive experience in both English and French. Bilinguals were classified as having learned their two languages in either separated or fused contexts. It was hypothesized that experience in separated, as compared with fused language-acquisition contexts, comparatively enhances the effectively separated use of the bilingual's two languages. It was found that:

> Experience in separated contexts comparatively increases the associative independence of translated equivalents in the bilingual's two languages. If the bilingual has learned his two languages in culturally dis-

tinctive contexts, the semantic differences between translated equivalents is comparatively increased. There was no difference found in facility to switch from one language to the other than can be attributed to contextual influences (p. 243).

In discussing the differences of meaning between languages, Roger Brown (1965) states that it is necessary to have some kind of standard grid or coordinate system that describes the reference domain. He presents an example using the dimension of color names in several different cultures. Brown then comments on the relationship of meanings and words in different languages:

> The findings of ethnoscience and comparative semantics suggest that it is a rare thing to find a word in one language that is exactly equivalent in reference to a word in an unrelated language. If each lexicon is regarded as a template imposed on a common reality, these templates do not match up. On the level of grammar, differences of meaning between languages are more striking and probably of greater significance. (p. 317)[3]

Research in the area of semantic shift in bilinguals has made use of this color-naming phenomenon. Susan Ervin (1961a), examined the color-naming of Navaho bilinguals, in comparison with two monolingual groups. It was found that the categories for color used by the bilinguals differed systematically from the monolingual norms. The differences could be predicted on the basis of an assumption of verbal mediation by the response-term which is most rapid. Ervin concluded:

> If an implicit response occurs in the suppressed language, it mediates a response in the overt language. When two responses have often been emitted in the presence of the same external stimulus, they acquire a chained relation to each other, in the sense that one later may elicit the other without the presence of the external stimulus. (p. 234)

This postulated process of chained learning provides some support for the "shared" hypothesis mentioned earlier by establishing the possibility of a number of responses chained to a common stimulus. Of relevance to our later discussion of bilingualism and emotion is Ervin's comment that, "It seems likely that processes similar to those found for colors would occur in semantic shifts in other domains of meaning, such as emotion-terms." (p.241)

TYPES OF BILINGUALISM

Various models have been proposed to account for the ways in which people can store two different sets of language symbols and voluntarily

---

[3] Reprinted by permission of the Macmillan Company, New York.

bring one or the other set into use. According to Weinreich (1953), if two words from different languages are interpreted by the bilingual as having different meanings, even though these words have the same referent, then the two systems are coexistent; if they are considered to have the same meaning, they constitute a compound sign and belong to a *partially merged* system; and if one of them is not considered to have a referent at all, but only to refer to a corresponding word in the other language, the systems are *completely merged,* with one system subordinate to the other.

The above classification does not explain, however, the ways that symbols are brought into use. Penfield and Roberts (1959) describe a "single switch" model in which it is postulated that, when one language is "turned on" (i.e., is in use), the other one is "turned off." As a more reasonable alternative to this model, they propose a "double switch" model in which it is possible for one system to operate in relation to the stimulus (the word being read or heard) while the other system is operating in relation to the response (the word being spoken or written).

Ervin and Osgood (1954) proposed a distinction between *compound* and *coordinate* bilingualism based on the ways in which an individual learns two languages. In the case of compound bilingualism, two sets of linguistic signs, one appropriate to language A and one appropriate to language B, are associated with the same set of meanings. On the encoding side, the same meanings are alternatively associated with two sets of responses, one in language A and one in language B. In the coordinate bilingual system, the set of linguistic signs and responses appropriate to one language comes to be associated with one set of meanings, but the linguistic signs and responses appropriate to the other language become associated with a somewhat different set of meanings.

Another conception deals with the way that information is stored. Kolers (1968) describes a "single tank" system in which all information is centrally stored and with equal accessibility on the part of both languages. The other extreme is a 'two-tank" system in which the symbols of the two languages are stored in separate places. Kolers postulates that the true storage mechanism is best described by neither of these two extremes.

Kolers gave bilingual French-English subjects four passages to read. One of the selections was all in English; one was completely in French; one was half-English and half-French, with English syntax and word order; the last was also half-English and half-French, but with French syntax and word order. Subjects were tested on the length of time they needed to read the passages in order to attain a score of 75 per cent correct on a comprehension test. Very little difference was found in the length of time required to read the passages silently, but when they read aloud more time was needed for the mixed passages.

Dalrymple (1967) used a bilingual form of the Stroop Color-Word Test, in which color words are printed in a different color from the color denoted by the word itself, and subjects are required to respond with the color of the word rather than the meanings of the color word. Dalrymple used French and English bilinguals, and his experimental conditions were as follows: English stimulus words and responses (i.e., subjects were presented with English color words and were instructed to respond in English); English stimuli and French responses; French stimuli and English responses; and French stimuli and French responses. There was also a control condition in which the stimulus words were not color words. He found that subjects required a longer period of time to respond to the experimental presentations than to the control presentations, but found no significant differences in response time among the four experimental conditions. It seems clear that the control/experimental differences can be explained on the basis of the greater difficulty involved in making dissonant responses in the latter case, but the fact that all four variants of the experimental condition yielded similar results seems to pose some of the same questions as those raised by Kolers' findings.

If bilinguals operated on some "single switch" systems, it would seem reasonable to assume that more time would be required for the mixed passages and bilingual S-R situations than for the monolingual ones. The "double switch" type of model on the other hand, would offer a better basis for interpreting Dalrymple's results, because the two systems postulated by this model are viewed as dealing autonomously with stimuli and with responses, respectively. Nevertheless, it does seem that the mixed passages ought to require a longer time to read, inasmuch as it is the stimuli that are mixed in the experimental conditions. It would seem that we are dealing here with a partially merged system (Weinreich, 1953), because in Dalrymple's study both sets of symbols appear to have referents and seem to have, if not identical, at least similar meanings. The experimental results do not provide much information on the type of storage arrangement of the symbols, but rather lend themselves more readily to hypothesizing about the way in which material is released from the storage centers.

BILINGUALISM AND PERSONALITY

Relatively few studies have investigated the relationship between bilingualism and personality. Spoerl (1943) has made one of the earliest and most significant contributions to this small body of research. Her study, although inconclusive in some respects, is virtually unique and has been praised by many writers, including Arsenian (1945), Weinreich (1953), and Yamamoto (1964).

Spoerl studied various aspects of personal adjustment among 101 bilingual college students and 101 monolingual students enrolled as freshmen at American International College in 1939, 1940, and 1941. Sixtynine of her bilingual subjects and 69 monolinguals were categorized as belonging to the Survey Group, while the remaining 32 bilinguals and 32 monolinguals were assigned to the Intensive Study Group.

The 101 bilingual students represented 16 different foreign languages: Armenian, French, Finnish, German, Greek, Italian, Lithuanian, Polish, Portuguese, Russian, Swedish, Syrian, Ukrainian, and Yiddish. [sic: Only 14 languages were listed.]

Spoerl first studied problems of academic and verbal adjustment in the Survey Group. The result of this phase of her study led her to suspect a rather high incidence of maladjustment among the bilingual students. She based this finding on the three principal lines of evidence given below.

EVIDENCE OF EMOTIONAL MALADJUSTMENT

1. *Mortality during the first year*. Twenty-seven per cent of the dropouts from the bilingual group reported "personal maladjustment" as the primary reason of withdrawal, while none of the control students gave this reason.
2. *Interviews with personnel office*. Thirty-seven per cent of the bilinguals sought interviews to discuss problems with the director of this office in addition to the routine interview granted to each entering student.
3. *The findings from the Bell Adjustment Inventory*. The significant items, found by chi-square analysis, were concerned with feelings of disappointment on the part of parents, domination by parents, parental criticism, and envy of the happiness of others.

The members of the Survey Group were matched for mental ability on the Henmon-Nelson Test, for age and for sex, but not for socioeconomic status. Spoerl then turned to the Intensive Study Group, in which the subgroups were matched on all four factors, for a further examination of bilingual problems.

Four instruments for measuring emotional differences were used: The Allport-Vernon Study of Values, the Bogardus Test of Social Distance, the modified Kent-Rosanoff Association Test, and the Morgan-Murphy Thematic Apperception Test.

THE ALLPORT-VERNON STUDY OF VALUES

The bilingual students differed from the control group in only one aspect; i.e., social values. They made either significantly high or significantly low scores.

Spoerl interprets these extreme scores as reactions to social frustration, indicating that the high scorers reacted aggressively; whereas, the low scorers reacted by retreating.

BOGARDUS TEST OF SOCIAL DISTANCE

The entire freshman class at the American International College was given this test in Spoer's study. The unit of measurement was the least social distance acceptable for each national group. The results showed that there was a difference of more than .5 of a point for only seven of the sixteen national groups as rated by bilingual and monolingual students. The seven groups included Greek, Italian, Lithuanian, Polish, Portuguese, Russian, and Syrian. The rank order of least social distance acceptable by the bilinguals and by the monolinguals for the different national groups was as follows: Italian, Polish, Russian, Lithuanian, Greek, Portuguese, and Syrian.

Spoerl comments that, while none of the differences are significant, they are all in the same direction. She notes further that, of the total number of bilingual students in the Survey and Intensive Study Groups, 80 per cent belong to these seven "nonaccepted" groups, whereas only 20 per cent belong to the "accepted" groups. She concludes that the results offer support for one of the most important considerations in the emotional maladjustment of the bilingual student—the fact that his national group was not accepted by the class as a whole or even, to some extent, by himself.

KENT-ROSANOFF ASSOCIATION TEST

An adaptation of this test was given to the entire 1941 freshman class. Stimulus words which Spoerl considered of value included: *Yankee, foreign, society, different, language, understand, respectable, alien,* and *citizen.*

Yankee. There was a significant difference between the responses of the two groups to this word. Bilingual students tended to answer in terms of the Civil War; whereas the controls answered in terms of "Connecticut Yankee."

Spoerl interprets these responses as indicating the bilingual's lack of identification with New England; i.e., his environment. Instead, he responds in terms of grade-school history.

Foreign. There were no significant differences in response to this word. Some control students associated derogatory words with "foreign" such as "odd," "dislike," and "stupid." None of the bilinguals showed this association. In contrast, they gave words such as "abroad," "home," and "neighborly."

Society. Spoerl detected a manifestation of social inferiority in the responses of bilingual students to this word. More bilinguals than controls responded with words such as "snob," "high class," and "big shots."

Different. Spoerl noted only two individual responses to this word—"intellectual," and "so-what," by bilingual students. She interprets "intellectual" as a response indicating it as an acceptable mode of being different. The other response indicates a violent response such as, "So what if I am different."

Language. Three classes of responses to this word were identified: (1) "Emotional"—having to do with accent or nationality. (2) "Languages"—naming a specific tongue. (3) "Act of speech"—word such as "talk" and "speech."

There was a clear distinction between the responses of the two groups in the third category.

Understand. A large percentage of bilinguals responded in terms of understanding; i.e., "chemistry," "language," etc.

Spoerl concludes that a response to the word "understand" is a reaction to a past in which there was a lack of understanding, a past which is very much present, emotionally. Thus, the necessity for understanding is the first response of the bilingual student.

Respectable. Two controls in Spoerl's study responded with "father," while none of the bilinguals did so. Three of the bilinguals answered "teacher"; none of the controls did so. Spoerl's interpretation that the bilinguals refused to identify with their foreign fathers is almost more Freudian than Freud.

Alien. The responses were similar in effect to the responses listed above to the word "foreign."

Citizen. Spoerl equates responses to this word to the responses given to the word "Yankee."

THE MORGAN-MURPHY THEMATIC APPERCEPTION TEST

A quantitative analysis of the results of the test produced no differences between the bilingual and control groups. Therefore, qualitative results were examined. The results approximate the "individual responses" in the Kent-Rosanoff test.

Stories of "spying" by the bilinguals were interpreted as expressing intrafamily conflicts. There was also evidence to support the theory that there was lack of identification among the bilinguals both with the present environment and with that of the parents. Attempts to repress aggression were also evident. The bilinguals resolved mother-daughter and mother-son conflicts by having the children leave home.

SUMMARY

Spoerl points out that some of the maladjustment among bilinguals may stem from social pressure but that the major part of it can be traced to the conflict within the bilingual home. The pertinent question, as Spoerl sees it, is to determine whether the home conflict is a direct result of bilingualism or whether it emanates from the culture conflicts of the "second generation."

Her final conclusion that maladjustment of bilingual students is due to social frustration and family disharmony is qualified by the type of responses made by bilingual students to the words "language" and "understand." The interpretation of these responses did not fit into the pattern of home conflict and social frustration as the sole causes of maladjustment. With this qualification, she implicitly admits that at least a small part of the bilingual's maladjustment does stem from bilingualism itself.

BILINGUALISM AND PSYCHOSIS

Robertson and Shamsie (1959) studied the gibberish produced by a multilingual schizophrenic patient. The patient, a native of India, aged thirty, and diagnosed as a chronic hebephreniac, spoke several languages. His mother-tongue was Gujeratic, spoken by those of the Parsi religion to which the subject belonged. He spoke, read and wrote both Hindi (the national language of India) and English with complete fluency and correctness. He also knew a small number of German and Norwegian words and phrases. Recordings were made of the subject's entire verbal production in response to a series of tests and tasks administered under different conditions on three different occasions. Analysis of the data showed: "The phonological structure of B.'s gibberish was essentially English with general influences also present from his two Indian languages and a specific influence present from German." (p. 7)

The report went further to indicate that the meanings of the findings were somewhat ambiguous. "It is not clear how far the circumstances that B. was multilingual was relevant to the fact that his thought disorder especially took the form of speaking gibberish. It is also not clear whether his gibberish is to be regarded as a *reversion to a linguistic stage of childhood*." (p. 8, emphasis supplied)

This latter underscored comment is an indirect reference to what Maher (1966) has called "one of the commonest hypotheses to be advanced regarding schizophrenic thinking." (p. 407) Maher goes on to point out that this hypothesis (called the Regression Hypothesis) was formulated first by Gardner in 1931. The Regression Hypothesis regards schizophrenic thinking as representing regression to a previous, less mature level. "Schizophrenic thinking [and language], so this view holds, is essentially 'childish thinking' [and speech]." (Maher, additions by author.)

Lukianowicz (1962) has reported that some polyglot psychotics experience auditory hallucinations in more than one language: "They usually hear the friendly voices in their native language, the hostile voices in a foreign tongue." (p. 274) Exceptions to this generalization, as we shall see later, are explained by Lukianowicz on the basis of political circumstances in the home country that have a direct bearing on the patient as an individual.

The Lukianowicz report covers a broad span of time, geography, and culture. According to the author:

> Multilingual auditory hallucinations disregard all geographical, racial, religious and national boundaries: we met them among some Asiatic tribes' men who served in the Russian Army, as well as among the so called "European Voluntary Workers," whom German authorities brought from various European countries to work in the Third Reich during the war. After the war, we came across such hallucinations among the "D.P.'s" ("Displaced Persons") in Austria, Germany and Italy, and we observed this phenomenon among some soldiers of the Polish Armed Forces treated in this country between 1947 and 1951. Finally the same pattern of auditory polyglot hallucinations was found among some of the Hungarian Freedom Fighters, the most recent European refugees, who came under our care in the U. K. in 1957. (p. 274)[4]

Although the clinical picture varied considerably among this diverse patient population, some consistencies in symptomatology, etiological background, and cultural origin could be discerned. The non-European patients (mostly from Asiatic Russia, but including one Yoruba tribesman from Nigeria) presented a "uniform type of schizophrenia-like reaction," while the European group exhibited "the usual wide variety of clinical syndromes, ranging from an acute anxiety reaction through a neurotic depression to a typical schizo-affective picture." (pp. 274–75) Lukianowicz further classified the patients into three categories: (1) cultural group; (2) political group; and (3) genetic group. These groups are defined and illustrated as follows:

1. THE "CULTURAL" GROUP

It is postulated that the main causative factor in this group of cases was the sudden impact of an unfamiliar culture and a strange, restless, highly mechanized civilization upon subjects belonging to a more primitive civilization, often with a nomadic way of life. An important additional

---

[4] This and all following excerpts from N. Lukianowicz are reprinted by permission of *Psychiatria et Neurologia*, Basel, Switzerland.

precipitating factor was their home-sickness, exacerbated by the patients' loneliness due to their cultural, social and linguistic isolation. These traumatic conflicting forces were often frankly expressed in the contents of their auditory hallucinations. (p. 275)

Lukianowicz provides case histories of two Russian soldiers—both members of eastern Russian ethnic minorities—who reacted to the stresses of "culture shock" with symptoms resembling a typically catatonic pattern of initial excitement and subsequent extreme withdrawal. A similar reaction pattern is displayed by a twenty-two-year-old Nigerian of the Yoruba tribe who came to England as a student of economics:

> At first he settled down well, attended lectures and mixed freely with fellow-students. However after a few weeks he rapidly changed, went off food, lost sleep, became suspicious and withdrawn. He stayed in his lodgings, was restless, and kept passing the room, mumbling to himself in his native tongue. At night he continued to dash in his room and was shouting out. A doctor was called, but R. refused to see him. In the morning he left the house, and went to his friends in London. He was persuaded by them to see a psychiatrist, and later to enter a psychiatric hospital, where he manifested symptoms of schizophrenic excitement: he was restless, excited, his speech was disconnected, and he dashed about in an impulsive way, shouting out in English and in his native Yoruba. After two further days he became mute, immobile, incontinent, entirely withdrawn, and presented a typical picture of catatonic schizophrenia. —— This new syndrome disappeared after a few ETCs. The patient regained insight, and reported how he had heard "many voices" during his confusional episode. His English voices were stern and demanding "and they ordered me to stay here and to work hard; the Yoruba voices were sweet and soft. They promised to protect me from the White Man's Magic, and urged me to go home. All these voices kept quarreling in my head until I became muddled and didn't know what to do." —— R. soon made an uneventful and a complete recovery, and was able to continue with his studies at the university. (pp. 276–77)

2. THE "POLITICAL" GROUP

Lukianowicz further subdivides this category into (a) prisoners of war and DP's "in whom the psychotic reaction was precipitated by certain factors of political nature, causing an acute fear (of arrest, trial and death)" and (b) political refugees from various countries living in Britain.

An example of the first type of patient is provided in the case history of a young Russian soldier, W. I., who was captured by the Germans in 1942.

> A year later he joined the Free Russian Army, which was organized in Germany from the Russian ex-prisoners of war. As long as this new anti-communist force was trained inside Germany, W. I. was quite happy;

but when the time came for his brigade to move to the much feared Eastern Front, he deserted his unit. He obtained civilian clothes from his German girl-friend, and, pretending to be a Russian "East-European Voluntary Worker," made his way to Austria, where some of his friends were living in one of the many camps for "European Voluntary Workers" on the outskirts of Vienna. His fair knowledge of German helped him to reach the desired camp unmolested, but there he unexpectedly met with a traumatic experience. As on the night of his arrival several young inmates absconded from the camp, a detachment of Gestapo ("Geheime Staats-Polizei") was called in. The whole camp was placed under curfew and nobody was allowed to leave his hut before having been screened by the Gestapo and the camp commandant. W. I. became terrified, in case he might be recognized as a deserter, and court-martialled. But then, just when the Gestapo-men were entering his hut, the Allied bombers appeared overhead, dropping incendiary bombs, which started fires in several points at the same time. Hell broke out in the camp. People ignored the curfew and ran for their lives. W. I. luckily escaped unharmed and later, together with others, was admitted to a neighboring camp without anybody asking him for any documents. But there another shock was waiting for him. The commandant of the new camp was the former commandant of the camp where W. I. had been P.O.W. before he joined the collaborator General Vlasov. The patient was convinced that this man will inevitably recognize in him the former P.O.W. and will hand him over to the Gestapo. —— The same night he escaped from the new camp. Next day he was found in the near fields, confused, crying, and talking to himself. In the Observation Ward he remained restless and was conversing with his hallucinatory voices. (pp. 277–78)

The second group of patients, the political refugees, presents an interesting contrast to the POW and DP group. All of these patients suffer from homesickness, made more intense by letters from relatives behind the Iron Curtain, but they also are prey to intense fears of returning to their homelands. Says Lukianowicz: "The ensuing conflict is expressed in projected voices, heard in at least two languages, the native and one or more foreign tongues. However in such cases the originally 'foreign' language (i.e. English) takes over the part of the 'good' protective mother-language, while the original mother-tongue now represents the evil and threatening forces." (p. 279) This pattern is exemplified in the case of C. G., a twenty-five-year-old Hungarian university student who fled the country after taking part in the revolt of October, 1956. Two years later in England, while recovering from an appendectomy, C. G. became depressed and developed fears of insanity and severe physical illness.

At the same time he became home-sick, and insisted on returning to Hungary, in spite of the discouraging letters from his parents. Later he became suspicious and refused to see any of his Hungarian friends, suspecting them all to be "agents of the Hungarian Secret Police." After a few days of gloomy brooding he became "all mixed up" and began hearing voices. His English voices tried to dissuade him from returning to Hungary, in a firm but friendly manner. His native Hungarian voices were of two opposite kinds: some of them were friendly and warned him not to go back home, emphasising their advice with such expressive words as "you silly ass," or "you idiot." The other Hungarian voices obviously personified the Hungarian Secret Police. They threatened to shoot G. "like a mad dog," called him "a traitor, Judas, servant of the Imperialists, bastard," and many other rather uncomplimentary epithets. (pp. 280–81)

3. THE "GENETIC" GROUP

This last group of cases consists of subjects whose psychosis apparently was of a genetic origin, and was neither caused nor aggravated by any political factors. Yet, as these patients lived in a foreign country, their auditory hallucinations acquired a particular quasi-political colouring, and their "good voices" used mostly their native language, while the "bad voices" expressed themselves in the tongue of their new country. However, in some cases the opposite would take place. (pp. 281–82)

In illustration of the "genetic" type of patient, Lukianowicz presents the case summary of J. L., a forty-five-year-old Polish laborer who exhibited an acute schizophrenic reaction with religious content.

. . . He alleged that, "A miracle occurred in Bristol the other night. The whole sky became illuminated by bright stars. It all was in the papers on the following morning. Everybody knows about it." L. heard "voices of Angels singing Polish hymns. Sometimes they were interrupted by loud screams under my windows. Later a black dog began to follow me to work on building-sites. He talked to me in a human voice, but as he did so in English, I could not understand him. But I knew that it was The Evil One himself, disguised as a dog, and pretending that he could not speak Polish." —— In the ward the patient would spend hours reading his little prayer book and missal. He was cooperative and friendly, though for years he remained hallucinated. He heard "some English voices, calling out from Dundry Hill, and all over the fields. They are the voices of The Evil One." the "good" Polish voices were the voices of Angels, who encouraged the patient "to pray and to read the missal." (pp. 282–83)

Observations comparable to those of Lukianowicz were reported by Schaechter (1964). A group of non-British female migrant psychotic patients (N = 60) hospitalized in Australia was studied from the standpoint of bilingual auditory hallucinations. Patients with acute psychoses of recent origin tended to hallucinate in English, while patients with chronic psychoses of less recent origin and more gradual onset tended to hallucinate in their mother-tongue. It appeared that 23 of 37 patients with persecutory hallucinations heard the persecutory remarks in English. This occurred whether the patients could or could not speak English; they "knew" that the voices were speaking in English.

Those patients who hallucinated in their mother-tongue had regressed to an earlier form of language, since they were in an English-speaking environment. The fact that these patients were the ones with the most serious illness helps to make this finding agree with the Regression Hypothesis mentioned earlier in relation to the Robertson and Shamsie study. There may be another explanation, however, of the refusal of these patients to *live in the present*. Haley's (1959) article describes the language of schizophrenics as consisting largely of efforts to negate relationships and communication. One wonders whether Schaechter's findings might not indicate an action on the part of the chronic patients to negate their existence in a situation which must, for any migrant, be deemed uncomfortable. As Lukianowicz (1962) points out, "The hearing of aggressive voices in a foreign language occasionally may be advantageous to the patient, as he may pretend 'not to understand' their hostile contents. . . . This may be regarded as a psychological defense mechanism, which may be expressed thus: 'You' (i.e. the foreign voices) 'can't really frighten me, because I don't understand you.' " (pp. 292–93)

REFERENCES

Arsenian, S. Bilingualism in the post-war world. *Psychological Bulletin*, 1945, *42*, 65–86.

Brown, R. *Social psychology*. New York: The Free Press, 1965.

Dalrymple, A.E.C. Interlingual interference in a color-naming task. *Psychonomic Science*, 1967, *8*, 167–68.

Diebold, A. R. Incipient bilingualism. *Language*, 1961, *37*, 97–112.

Ervin, S. M. Semantic shift in bilingualism. *American Journal of Psychology*, 1961, *74*, 233–41. (a)

Ervin, S. M. Learning and recall in bilinguals. *American Journal of Psychology*, 1961, *74*, 446–51. (b)

Ervin, S. M. and Osgood, C. E. Second language learning and bilingualism. In C. E. Osgood and T. A. Sebeok (Eds), *Psycholinguistics* (*Journal of Abnormal and Social Psychology Supplement*, 1954), 139–46.

Haley, J. An interactional description of schizophrenia. *Psychiatry*, 1959, *22*, 321–32.

Kolers, P. A. Interlingual word associations. *Journal of Verbal Learning and Verbal Behavior*, 1963, *2*, 291–300.

Kolers, P. A. Specificity of a cognitive operation. *Journal of Verbal Learning and Verbal Behavior*, 1964, *3*, 244–48.

Kolers, P. A. Bilingualism and information processing. *Scientific American*, 1968, *218*, 78–89.

Lambert, W. E. Measurement of the linguistic dominance of bilinguals. *Journal of Abnormal and Social Psychology*, 1955, *50*, 197–200.

Lambert, W. E. and Fillenbaum, S. A pilot study of aphasia among bilinguals. *Canadian Journal of Psychology*, 1959, *13*, 28–34.

Lambert, W. E., Havelka, J., and Crosby, C. The influence of language-acquisition contexts on bilingualism. *Journal of Abnormal and Social Psychology*, 1958, *56*, 239–44.

Leischner, A. Über die Aphasie der Mehrsprachigen. *Archiv für Psychiatrie und Nervenkrankheiten*, 1948, *180*, 731–75.

Lukianowicz, N. Auditory hallucinations in polyglot subjects. *Psychiatria et Neurologia* (Basel), 1962, *143*, 274–94.

Maher, B. A. *Principles of psychopathology*. New York: McGraw-Hill, 1966.

Minkowski, M. Sur un cas d'aphasie chez un polyglotte. *Revue Neurologique*, 1928, *35*, 361–66.

Osgood, C. E. and Miron, M. (Eds.), *Approaches to the study of aphasia*. Urbana: University of Illinois Press, 1963.

Penfield, W. and Roberts, L. *Speech and brain-mechanisms*. Princeton, N. J.: Princeton University Press, 1959.

Robertson, J. P. S. and Shamsie, S. J. A systematic examination of gibberish in a multilingual schizophrenic patient. *Language and Speech*, 1959, *2*, 1–8.

Schaechter, F. The language of the voices. *The Medical Journal of Australia*, 1964, *2*, 870–71.

Spoerl, D. T. Bilinguality and emotional adjustment. *Journal of Abnormal and Social Psychology*, 1943, *38*, 37–57.

Weinreich, U. *Languages in contact*. New York: The Linguistic Circle, 1953.

Yamamoto, K. Bilingualism: A brief review, *Mental Hygiene*, 1964, *48*, 468–77.

CHAPTER 14

LANGUAGE BEHAVIOR
AND BLINDNESS

Communication systems contain at least four major structures, each of which is made up of several components or substructures. A communication must begin with a *source/encoder*. Within the context of human communication, we might identify as components such factors as communicative skills, knowledge of the subject, sociocultural systems of value and belief, subject matter, and attitudes toward the self. Second, the *message* must be intelligible in terms of its elements and structure, including the code, content, and treatment of the message. Third, the *channel* provides a means for conveying the message from the sender to the receiver; in the human instance, we would identify the channel with the various sensory modalities—seeing, hearing, touching, smelling, tasting. Finally, there is a *receiver/decoder,* whose substructural features are similar to those of the source/encoder.

Change or deficit in any of the components will alter the effectiveness of the communication system. The severity of the alteration is dependent upon the nature of the deficit. If the fault is major, its consequences for the entire communication system can be serious, even catastrophic. Blindness represents the topmost level of severity of deficit or change, and we shall attempt to assess some of its repercussions upon the functioning of language behavior in the communication system of the blind person.

ADJUSTMENT TO BLINDNESS

As noted previously, within the source/encoder is a component called attitude, which includes the attitude of the individual toward himself or

211

his self image. Herein lies the genesis for many of the communicative problems of the blind. Self image is part of a development process that begins quite early in life and can be greatly shaken at any point as a consequence of loss of sight. Whether the loss is congenital or adventitious in nature, the end results tend to be similar.

In the case of an adventitious loss of sight, the victim interprets his blindness as death to the way of life he has known and destruction of the relationships he has built up over the years. In addition, his sense of physical integrity is disrupted: his anomaly constitutes loss of wholeness of his body image. Carroll (1961) has ventured the interpretation that people raised in the English language as their mother-tongue have a particular difficulty in adjusting to their handicap. He suggests that they seem to make an unconscious association between the phonological similarities expressed in the loss of an "eye" as an attack on the "I" which it symbolizes. As a result, the blind react to their loss as a death of the self.

Contrary to popular belief, the blind do not, as a compensatory measure, automatically atune their remaining senses to superior levels. As a matter of fact, initially they lose faith in their remaining senses, withdraw, and become dependent upon others for sensory information. Only after they accept the fact of their blindness and begin to rebuild their self image do they attempt to sharpen the other senses by increasing the efficiency of these modalities.

This sudden withdrawal may be indicative of the central significance of sight in the communication channel. People rely more heavily upon sight than upon any other sense as a means of testing reality and checking to validate information received via the other sensory modalities. When sight has been lost, there is a tendency to question the validity of information from the other components of the communication channel. The doubting is not intellectual in nature, but rather, as Carroll (1961) puts it, "a sense of doubting due to disturbance of the pattern of the central sense. This disturbance assumes major proportions when it escapes the control of the intellect and the insecurity it arouses builds up a state of panic." (p. 42)

The effects of congenital blindness upon self image are even more profound. The sightless child is looked upon as helpless and unable to do anything for himself. As a result, little effort is made to stimulate him by means of the other sensory modalities; he becomes vegetablelike, and his resulting retarded and slovenly behavior is then accounted for in terms of his "obvious mental inferiority." Such a developmental pattern would have occurred in the presence or absence of sight, in all probability, as a consequence of lack of environmental stimulation. It is quite likely that such a lack of stimulation causes the congenitally sightless child to withdraw, sometimes to the point of not even attempting to initiate verbal contact with others.

AUTISTIC PATTERNS IN BLIND CHILDREN

The severity of such withdrawal can be noted from Keeler's (1958) description of a study done on five congenitally blind children. These children, all of whom had suffered blindness from the condition known as retrolental fibroplasia, showed a close resemblance in their behavior to the symptoms noted in autism.

The outstanding characteristic was the lack of language usage for communicative purposes. If they were spoken to, they would not respond, but they did show an understanding of the spoken word and seemed to have adequate memories. They would not initiate any activity of their own, but engaged in a continual rocking back and forth. They all showed a preoccupation with music and enjoyed playing with objects that made noise.

Their language did not develop normally. It was delayed in every instance, and exhibited echolalia, the repetitive use of apparently meaningless words or phrases, and a constant tendency to refer to the self in the third person. Sometimes words themselves were not repeated, but similar sounds were made by using the same tone and intonation pattern. Also, bizarre guttural vocalizations were frequent. By the time the children had reached two years, they were able to sing songs of a fairly complex nature but were unable to communicate verbally. They explored the properties of their physical environment by smelling and tapping things. One of the children, Cheryl, age six, showed a marked language delay. She spoke words at age three, and at age six could repeat words, phrases, and sentences but was still incapable of spontaneous conversation. At age six she was still unable to communicate her wants verbally. She had always liked music and had shown a talent for carrying a tune but never put words to the music. When examined by the speech pathologist, she did not respond, but would go with him when taken by the hand. Occasionally when asked, "Do you want to go home?" she would respond, "Do you want to go home?" (Keeler, p. 68) However, she did not respond at all when less meaningful things were said to her. In spite of her failure to respond, she did indicate that she had a full grasp of what was being said in her presence.

Betty, at four years of age, had not developed the proper use of language and she did not relate to adults or to children in an adequate fashion. She made sounds resembling phrases in songs, but no useful language had developed. She did not ask for anything that she wanted. In order to find out what she needed or wanted, it was necessary to ask her a multitude of questions. A positive reaction was registered by a "ugh, ugh, ugh, ugh. . . ." or not saying anything at all. A negative reaction was transmitted by shaking her head and making a face.

A study was also made, as a control, of children blinded from other causes. For the most part, the same language disorders were evident. These other children showed a delayed language development, a liking for music, and in general the same autistic patterns of behavior. Also, they explored their environment through smell.

Keeler's findings emphasize the crucial importance of the age factor in relation to the loss of sight. It seems apparent that the later in life an individual sustains a loss of sight, the less handicapped he is in acquiring the necessary language skills needed for efficient communication. Keeler states that blindness which occurs later in life results in less severe and pervasive autistic reactions, although some withdrawal is inevitable.

The aforementioned descriptions of the behavior of congenitally blind children are indicative of the necessity of visual cues for the establishment of a strong self image—a requirement for adequate communication. Although blindness in itself does not produce retardation, the fact that it is frequently coupled with emotional neglect and that it occurs so early in the individual's life is a powerful blow to the development of a self image of competence. As a result of a faulty self image, the individual fails to differentiate between himself and the outside world. The phenomenon of echolalia seems to be representative of the confusion of the "I and the not-I," between the activity of one's own body and that of other people's bodies. Also contingent on this failure to differentiate such activities is the tendency of the congenitally blind to refer to themselves in the third person. These observations all point to the fact that such an individual has failed to develop a strong ego, which is also a salient feature among autistic schizophrenic children.

PROBLEMS OF "VERBALISM" AMONG THE BLIND

It seems possible to trace a direct line from faulty ego development to a lack of confidence. And because of a lack of confidence and the inability to trust one's other senses, it is easy to adopt the visual cues utilized by the sighted world, or visually oriented blind teacher of the blind. Names of things are shared in common between the blind and sighted, as though they carried the same meaning for both. But the name of the thing seen, although it may be the same word, has a different meaning from the name of the thing felt or heard. Says Cutsforth (1951), "To a far greater extent than in sighted individuals, words become a source of self-stimulation, turning the individual towards himself and making him, as do his touch experiences, almost exclusively his own environment." (p. 64) Thus, the acquisition of speech serves both to objectify and to socialize the life of the blind child and at the same time to isolate him still further from the seeing world in which he lives. This is the beginning of verbal unreality.

A blind child may be quick to name things properly, and to associate visual descriptions to them in order to conform to the majority of sighted society, but this does not mean that he understands what he is talking about. He must be allowed to explore his environment through his other senses and thereafter form concepts grounded in his own experiences if he is to conceptualize and communicate with any degree of reality. Forcing a blind child to accept visual descriptions of an environment that he can never appreciate through vision, and preventing him from coming to terms with reality through his other senses, will only result in further communicative disorders such as *verbalism*. This phenomenon occurs where words are in opposition to reality.

Neither the seeing nor the blind fully realize the difference that exists between their respective worlds of experience and reality. Those with sight are not aware of the great extent to which they use their eyes in forming concepts of shape, size, color, texture and distance, brightness, and movement. Blind people are taught these concepts and how to use them from a visually oriented viewpoint. Thus a workable parity seems to exist between the blind and sighted, but in fact it does not.

The blind are forced to treat the world of unreality in some realistic fashion. As a result a great deal of "verbal mindedness" tends to develop in the blind. Word-mindedness or verbalism is not a social phenomenon found only in the blind. It can occur in any situation that requires the use of abstract concepts not verified by concrete experience. Words are symbols for objects, concepts, qualities, and feelings. They are of value if they represent the same experiences for all involved in the communication system.

Verbalism is not a social compensation made by the blind in an attempt to assert equality with their sighted associates. As mentioned before, it develops from an insistence by the sighted world to conform to the usage of visually oriented descriptions of their world. This meaningless use of such visually oriented words produces an injurious attitude toward the self. The blind feel that this sense called vision is by far superior to their remaining senses, and thus their experiences are inferior to those of sighted persons. In an effort to equate themselves with normal people, they adopt their visual superstructure. This effort satisfies the demands of society.

An example of the hypocrisy revealed in verbalism is illustrated in the following by Helen Keller (1903):

> On the third day after the beginning of the storm the snow ceased. The
> sun broke through the clouds and shone upon a vast, undulating white

plain. High mounds, pyramids heaped in fantastic shapes, and impenetrable drifts lay scattered in every direction.

Narrow paths were shoveled through the drifts. I put on my cloak and hood and went out. The air stung my cheeks like fire. Half walking in the paths, half working our way through the lesser drifts, we succeeded in reaching a pine grove just outside a broad pasture. The trees stood motionless and white like figures in a marble frieze. There was no odor of pine needles. The rays of the sun fell upon the trees, so that the twigs sparkled like diamonds and dropped in showers when we touched them. (p. 56)

Although the paragraph conveys the conventional meaning to the average reader, it is devoid of any reality based on her own experiences. A contrast may be cited from a literary sample by Kathryne Frick, who was both deaf and blind:

The grass in front of Wissinoming Hall was high, and there were daisies and clover blossoms there. My teacher let me walk about and pick the flowers. I discovered that there were no stones or fences over which I might fall, and therefore, decided it would be safe for me to run around alone. I loved to run, and did not like to be led. So I tried to get away from my teacher, but she was careful not to let me go far from her.

Then I made a plan to fool my teacher. I pointed away off, and pushed her a little, which told her that there were flowers over there which I wanted; then I patted the ground on which I stood to tell her that I would stay where I was while she picked the flowers for me. I thought that she would see that it would be better for one of us to go for the flowers instead of both, since less of the grass would be trampled down. One of my uncles was a farmer; I used to visit his place and had learned there that tall grass would not be trampled down, because it was wanted for hay. I tried to be very polite about it, for even at that early age I knew that nice manners are a power and can be used to deceive.

I could tell from the flash of sunlight reflected on the dress that my teacher was wearing that she had fallen into my trap and had moved away to get the flowers, and when I could no longer see the flash of light I felt sure she was at a distance. I knew that she was a good-sized woman, and, since she wore a pointed belt like my grandma's, I took it for granted that she was not young or overactive. My mother was slender and often ran after me when I slipped out of the back gate and ran away, but here, in front of this big, big house, where many gentlemen and ladies were, I thought that my teacher would not dare to run like a boy. So I darted away in the opposite direction.

I had not gone far before I felt her grasp my apron and try to hold me. Since the day was hot, I thought I could try to outrun her, so I jerked away, and ran faster. Oh what a good time I had! I thought I should find her puffing, with perspiration rolling down her face, and felt it would serve her right because she would not let me run around alone. (I did not know then that she taught physical culture in the evenings and that she enjoyed running almost as much as I did.) It was not long before she caught me and held me fast. She put my hand on her chin and shook her head vigorously, to tell me in a most emphatic way that I must not run away. I knew that already, but I tried to look as though I had not done anything wrong.

Then my teacher led me to the pond that is at the foot of the hill in front of Wissinoming Hall. She dipped my hand into the water and gave me a stick to hold in the water while I walked around the pond, to give me an idea of its size. Then by gestures she showed me how I should have fallen into the pond and how the water would have covered my head had I run much farther. I took warning then and there, and never again attempted to run away when we were anywhere near the pond." (*Atlantic Monthly,* 1930, pp. 440–41.)

Here is an example of an individual who utilized her remaining senses to conceptualize a realistic world for herself. She is a complete individual and does not need to abstract her ideas from a visual world. It is evident from this excerpt that the blind are capable of fully appreciating their own perceptual values. To ignore this fact results in undesirable consequences for the blind: uncritical habits of thought that lead to false values, warped concepts, and judgments which are lacking in validity.

Further examples of verbalism in the blind can be cited from an informal study that Cutsforth (1951) conducted with 26 congenitally blind children. Each child was asked to respond with the first quality he thought of when he heard the name of a given object. The children knew visual qualities only by hearsay, while they made constant use of touch, taste, smell, and hearing in their daily lives. Yet half of their responses were given in terms of visual qualities; only about one-third were qualities having to do with touch. Seven per cent referred to qualities of taste or smell, and 3 per cent to hearing. For example, in response to the word *Indian,* 1 child described it as "big," 13 answered "red," 3 "brown," 3 "dark," and 1 "copper." *Blood* was "red" 22 times and was only characterized 4 times by tactual qualities: "running," "wet," "sticky," "liquid." Even objects that are usually characterized by tactual qualities were described in visual terms. *Wool,* which is generally described with reference to its warmth and texture, was described as red, white, black, or gray. *Cotton,* which is usually "soft," "thick," or "hairy," was reported to be "white" by 4 children and "blue" by 1 other.

This high percentage of visual responses again supports the observation that the blind favor visual concepts over other sensory concepts that would be more meaningful to them. This seems indicative of the tendency to minimize the value of their own experience. Also, they lack discriminating terms for the attributes they know to exist for them. Birds are described with reference to singing, song, and sound; such characteristic sound differentiations as *twitter, chirp, warble,* etc. are unknown to them. The experience of touch reveals the same degree of undifferentiation: *harsh, gritty, pliant, sleek, glossy, slippery, ridged, bumpy,* and *gnarled* are equally unfamiliar terms. Finally, the large number of inappropriate visual responses suggests that the pupils prefer risking a dubious visual response to relying upon a familiar sensory attribute.

This tendency toward word-mindedness is symptomatic of a serious condition. According to Cutsforth an unwarranted use of meaningless visual terminology indicates a strong tendency toward unreality, in which valid relationships may be slighted. The child thus develops incoherent and loose thinking. He is organized without reference to either himself or his own experiential world.

Harley (1963) suggests two possible antidotes to verbalism: (1) to control the vocabulary employed in the educational materials for teaching the blind, and (2) to increase, through training, the ability of blind children to identify objects represented by words in their own vocabularies.

SPEECH DEFECTS IN THE BLIND

Young and Stinchfield-Hawk (1938) found speech defects in 49 per cent of the pupils in two institutions for the blind—a total of approximately 400 cases. The defects varied in type and etiology and included the following:

1. *Somatic defects,* among which were nasal, oral, and laryngeal malformations of a congenital nature.
2. *Faulty vocal expression,* attributed to a lack of environmental stimulation (which also contributes to lowered muscle tonus and general muscular ineptitude).
3. *Persistence of infantile speech,* as manifested in lisping, letter-sound omissions, and letter-sound transpositions.
4. *Imitation characteristics,* which lead to an adoption of voice qualities that are not suitable to the blind individual. He may copy the voice characteristics of his teacher, parents, or anyone whom he holds in high esteem.
5. *Faulty sound analysis* which is as prevalent among seeing children as it is in the blind. However, normal children are able to correct these mispronunciations when they begin to read. But among the blind, this phase of faulty auditory perception remains uncorrected and is a constant source of speech difficulty. The seeing

child is also able to see the lips, mouth, and jaw form the words, in addition to hearing the word. The blind are only recipients of auditory cues. The spoken language to the seeing child is a much larger stimulus pattern than it is to the blind, and accordingly the seeing child progresses in proportion to his perceptual advantage.

6. *Synaesthetic imagery,* which gives rise to a visual type of thinking process. Words are a superfluity and may hinder the thought process. The synaesthetic tends to proceed mentally in a wordless fashion, and when words become necessary for communication, he must laboriously select a verbal symbol that will express or describe as nearly as possible the subjective experience. This situation produces a slow, hesitating, halting speech with a low level of coherence. The laborious process of matching words with visual imagery can be circumvented in one way—by the rapid and uncritical selection of words. A facility of verbal speech may be acquired, but at the expense of accuracy and continuity.

7. A *negative-self feeling,* which is often the result of the many factors that influence the personality development of a blind individual. Speech is only one of the manifestations of these deficient self-regarding attitudes. They may be revealed in the form of stuttering, stammering, indistinct and hesitant speech in the timorous individual, or in the loud, brazen, forced speech of the one whose voice seeks to compensate for the lack of confidence he feels.

8. *Faulty localization of the receiver* as perceived by the speaker, which results in the "broadcasting voice." This is a voice without specific directional projection and is produced so that it will serve anywhere within a given space frame, which is usually judged larger than it really is. This defect is not too noticeable in close, direct conversation. It becomes quite obvious when the distance increases so that the localization of sounds becomes inaccurate, which occurs at about eight to twelve feet. At this point the definiteness of voice projection breaks down and the broadcasting voice appears.

Powers (1936) conducted a study of the verbal errors committed by a group of blind students. Among the most frequent errors noticed were: (1) mistakes in verb usage (incorrect tenses, double negatives, errors of inflection); (2) redundant prepositional usage ("from off," "where at"); (3) incorrect use of comparatives and superlatives; (4) faulty patterns of pronunciation; (5) omission of terminal consonants in words like *nothing;* (6) a broad category of defective grammatical usage ("drownded," "beated him downstairs," "I'm almost finish"). Powers attributed many of these errors to such factors as a lack of stimulation in the home, a bilingual background, or intellectual deficit. The remediable errors were alleviated after a few months of intensive speech training and therapy.

CONCLUDING OBSERVATIONS

So far, only the linguistic disorders that occur within the communication system of the blind have been analyzed in relation to the "seeing" substructure of the channel. The paralinguistic phase of such a disorder is also significant. The resulting loss of ease of spoken communication affects not only listening and speaking but also gestures, postures, mannerisms, and facial expressions. All of these constitute the unspoken elements of "spoken" language. Obviously, these sources of information are lost to the blind; therefore they must compensate for this loss through the other senses, especially hearing. It is accepted that the meaning of an utterance can be changed according to the facial expression which accompanies it. Since this information source is not available, the blind have utilized their audial cues as a way of assigning various inferences to an utterance.

Because the blind are not recipients of visual feedback, they are no longer reminded (or never were cognizant) of the various side activities that take place during the course of a conversation: facial expressions, hand gestures, change in posture, head movements, etc. are all integral parts of everyday communication. Yet when these paralinguistic features are omitted in a blind individual's repertoire, sighted individuals are quick to notice that "something is strange about him."

Also there are rather negative or careless forms of feedback noticeable in many sightless people. These mannerisms are known as *blindisms.* They are usually characterized by unnatural attitudes in standing or sitting—either too great rigidity or looseness. There is an unusual awkwardness as to position and motion of head and hands. Blindisms of gait include a protective kind of shuffle and a hesitant way of walking with the hands just held back from groping. The face is usually characterized by a bland, unchanging smile. These mannerisms can be avoided if the individual cares about conducting a normal conversation.

At first glance it may seem that for all his efforts, the blind can never be able to interpret the worst kind of communication: the silent conversation that is taking place in his presence. Yet, Carroll (1961) suggests that a blind person can learn to interpret the meaning of nonverbal auditory cues. For instance, he can learn to infer the meaning of various slips of tongue, rustles, fidgeting sounds, breathing symptoms of tension, certain types of coughs and sneezes, clearing the throat, and the sounds of a cigarette being lighted or snuffed out. As the blind individual becomes more proficient in the interpretation of such paralinguistic behavior, he becomes fairly accurate in his hearer's reaction to what he is saying.

REFERENCES

Carroll, T. J. *Blindness*. Boston: Little, Brown, 1961.

Cutsforth, T. D. *The blind in school and society*. New York: American Foundation for the Blind, 1951.

Frick, Kathryne.

Gesell, A., Ilg, F. L., and Bullis, G. E. *Vision—Its development in infant and child*. New York: Harper, 1949.

Harley, R. K. *Verbalism among blind children*. New York: American Foundation for the Blind, 1963.

Hathoway, W. P. *Education and health of the partially seeing child*. New York: Columbia University Press, 1943.

Hoffer, W. Development of the body ego. *Psychoanalytic Studies of the Child*, 1950, 5, 18–23.

Keller, Helen.

Keeler, W. R. Autistic patterns and defective communication in blind children with retrolental fibroplasia. In P. H. Hoch and J. Zubin (eds.), *Psychopathology of communication*. New York: Grune and Stratton, 1958.

Piaget, J. *The language and thought of the child*. New York: The Humanities Press, 1959.

Powers, P. V. Verbal errors in the Youngstown Braille pupils. M.A. thesis, University of Pennsylvania, 1936.

Ruesch, J. and Kees, W. *Nonverbal communication*. Berkeley: University of California Press, 1956.

Young, E. H. and Stinchfield-Hawk, S. M. *Children with delayed or defective speech*. Palo Alto, Calif.: Stanford University Press, 1938.

INDEX

Printed in U.S.A.